Living with Dying

Margaret McCartney

Living with Dying

finding care and compassion at the end of life

Living With Dying: finding care and compassion at the end of life

First published in the UK by Pinter & Martin Ltd 2014

ISBN 978-1-78066-150-6

Also available as an ebook

Edited by Debbie Kennett
Index by Helen Bilton

British Library Cataloguing-in-Publication Data
A catalogue record for this book is available from the British Library

Printed in Great Britain by TJ International Ltd, Padstow, Cornwall

This book has been printed on paper that is sourced and harvested from sustainable forests and is FSC accredited

Pinter & Martin Ltd
6 Effra Parade
London SW2 1PS

pinterandmartin.com

to my family

Acknowledgements

A special thank you to Tony Bonser, Deborah Bowman, Kate Granger, Elin Roddy, and Euan Paterson for your time, kindness and challenge in getting my thoughts straight. Thanks to Debbie Kennett for wise editing and Martin Wagner for steadfast support.

Contents

Introduction

Each day, almost 1,400 deaths occur in the UK.[1] Death is also happening, on average, later: we are living longer. A child born in 1900 had an average of about 50 years ahead of them; a child born today should expect around 80 years of life.[2] As a species, the increased lifespan humans have achieved in a relatively short period of existence is phenomenal. We are succeeding in becoming older. This is worth celebrating: a new generation of people who have the wisdom of a longer living memory can continue to inform and contribute to our society.

But this change has also created complex and unforeseen dilemmas with new difficulties around death. We humans are having to learn how to live longer and how to die of different things. War, famine and infectious disease still take an unforgivable toll, especially in the poorest countries. In the west, we are living longer but with more diseases. Over 40% of us have one long-term condition, and a quarter of us have two or more problems – like chronic bronchitis, diabetes, or high blood pressure.[3] So as we live longer lives, we accumulate more diagnoses, take more pills, and attend more doctors and nurses as we go. And in the end, we still must die.

So have the medical advances which have prolonged life also improved our deaths? In the last hundred years, science has discovered and created incredible things: the atom has been split; DNA has been unfurled and held open for examination. MRI scans have meant that searing anatomical detail can be exposed without a scalpel; vaccinations have enabled cohorts of children to grow up outwith the shadow of smallpox or measles. Keyhole and minimally invasive surgery has meant that many large operations are virtually day cases. Joint replacements have enabled millions to stay mobile and independent for longer. Endoscopies have meant that the bowel can be explored relatively easily and quickly. HIV can be a long-term illness rather than a death sentence; babies can be operated on within the womb. Medicine has reaped numerous harvests from science.

But medicine also harms. In my first book, *The Patient Paradox*, I explored how too much medicine can also damage us. Screening causes many people to be treated for disorders that would never have affected them, causing resources to be diverted from people who are sick and unwell to people who are healthy. At the end of life, medicine yields a similar power. It could give us a peaceful, painless death – but can also spoil and corrupt our humanity.

For when it comes to our still inevitable deaths, we have reached an awkward impasse. What kind of death do we want to have? We frequently use medicine awkwardly and badly. We perform cardiopulmonary resuscitation in patients in whom it virtually never works; meaning that the end of life becomes a violent struggle against death. People sue doctors who do not provide treatments at the end of life – even when these 'treatments' are extremely unlikely to help and come with draining side effects. We are living longer, we are dying later, and we struggle still against the end. Medicine has a new battleground in death, but death, in the end, can be the only winner.

But is death always the enemy?

The way we approach the end of life is troublesome. General practitioners are pushed and financially rewarded to diagnose and treat risk factors which would, in very many cases, never lead to death from the disease we were trying to prevent. We fund pharmacological treatments that make little difference to quality or quantity of life, while neglecting to fund proper, hands-on, humane care for people in their own home where they would often prefer to die. When it comes to the final illness, the desire to use more medicine to push death back can easily take precedence over the wellbeing and contentment of the dying person.

I want to explain how medicine can get in the way of good care, and suggest what we – citizens, families, carers, doctors, nurses, politicians and health service managers – should ask about what we want at the end of life and how we should work together to provide it.

Edward and Rosa: Take 1

What follows is one big anecdote; a story. I have constructed and edited it carefully to ensure that it does not reflect any particular patient or family I have served. However; the story is typical of the frustrations, dilemmas and failings commonplace in death care. This story represents the kinds of problems I have been part of, or have not dealt with well enough. It is here to illustrate the statistics and numbers I have presented, not to substitute them. It is here, not to excuse, but to explain.

Rosa has cancer. She is seventy two years of age. She wears her long, white hair in a knot, tucked into the nape of her neck. She is slender, her skin hanging loosely on the tendons of her arm and the bone of her jaw; she smiles, slowly, as she recognises me, and her eyes carefully follow me across the room. The flat is festooned with photographs, merrily cluttering the sideboards, bookshelves and television. The carpets are worn and the lights are weak. She is wearing loose clothing, whose drapes do not disguise the weight she has lost. Edward stands to her left, one hand – all knuckle and muscle – resting on her shoulder, and his other hand gestures for me to sit.

I sit on the chair, rest my medical case on the floor, and the brown folder of her medical notes on my knee. The coffee table is piled with books, magazines and, in the middle, a tray. This tray is stacked with packets of tablets and bottles of medicine, neatly lined up. Edward sits beside his wife and aligns his hand with hers; Rosa leans herself backward into a cushion, biting her lip against pain. The morphine is almost finished. I am here to discuss how to proceed.

'How are you, Rosa?'

'Well,' she says, 'the pain is still there. But the nausea is better.'

'Is the pain the same?' I ask. 'Same place?' She nods. 'And did the bigger dose of the sevredol do anything for it?'

'Not really. If I'm honest.'

I had hoped the bigger dose of morphine might have settled the pains in her shoulder and the front of her chest.

'The nights are bad, doctor. They're the worst. She can never get to sleep.'

'Ah, but he won't let me have my whisky, you see doctor... says it's bad for me.'

Edward and Rosa exchange a smile.

I've known them for almost fifteen years. When I joined the practice, Edward, who is the younger of the two, had retired from his job as an assistant in a school for children with behavioural problems. He lasted two weeks of having no job, complaining of boredom. He got himself a job working in a supermarket. Some of the time he spent collecting trollies from the car park, otherwise he was collecting prescriptions from local general practices to be dispensed by the supermarket pharmacy. We in the practice knew him from his daily visits, his brisk, long stride into the building, his contented smile and his whistling. Rosa hadn't been very pleased – I remember her asking me if it was really wise, working past the age of 65? But Edward would come in for checks of his blood pressure, wearing his lime green supermarket uniform, singing the praises of the 'young ones' he worked with. He didn't mind the rain, and he was pleased to be 'earning a wage'. I think Rosa had given up trying to stop him from working. The day after Rosa was diagnosed, she came to see me, and told me frankly; 'Eddie isn't taking it very well.' His needs went well before hers.

As we talk, the carer from the social work department arrives, knocking and letting herself in. She is wearing a grey tunic and slacks, her blonde hair piled up on her head.

'Morning,' she calls to us all – 'Here to help, my name is Jane', shines from her name badge. 'Kate's off today, so it's me today. Bathtime Mrs Anderson? Need the loo? Get you washed, shall we?' The beginnings of a blush appear on Rosa's cheeks. Edward and I share a glance and get up to move to the hall, waiting for their son. Jane is talking to Rosa, preparing to wash her.

Thomas arrives – tall, spectacles, short neat hair – apologising for being a few minutes late. His suit is pressed; he smells of aftershave. He greets us warmly, shakes my hand, shouts hello to his mother, who is being helped to the bathroom.

'Thanks for coming over,' I say. 'I know you're concerned about your mother.'

Thomas nods. But then Edward looks at his son – and me. 'I think maybe I should make you both a cup of tea.' He leads us into the kitchen. It's a galley, thin and long. We stand a little closer than we would have normally, and I feel slightly awkward. Edward dunks teabags into the mugs, with a slow tremor to his movements – he offers them to us, spills in some milk, bows his head, takes a crushed handkerchief from his pocket to mop his brow.

'I'm not sure I want – you know. I'm not sure Rosa really.... needs to know.'

'You mean, what to do next?'

'But Dad, Mum knows she has cancer. Hiding it isn't...'

'I know, son. But all this...' – he gestures, towards the commode, the bed tucked into the wall – Rosa has moved into the living room, getting up the stairs being too difficult. 'I don't know son, I don't know.'

He cries, silently. Thomas puts his arm round him. 'It's all right, dad.'

I am thinking about what to do next. Edward wants Rosa to stay at home. She is struggling to get to the toilet, and into bed, and is in pain despite opiate painkillers. Rosa is due to go to the cancer clinic tomorrow, where she has been receiving chemotherapy. At the moment, I am worried about how much effort it will take her to get there – even though the hospital is less than three miles away – and whether it will be worth it. I've spoken to Thomas once on the phone, when he told me that he was worried that his mother wasn't giving the chemotherapy a 'fighting chance'. 'She's only had one round' he told me 'and the consultant had recommended at least three, if not five.' That's part of the reason I'm here: Thomas thought his mum was 'giving up' and wanted me to try and persuade her to have more treatment.

'She says she doesn't know what to do. I've never seen her like this,' says Edward.

'I know, Dad.' Thomas puts his arm on his Dad's back. 'What do you think, doctor? Can you tell her to go back to the hospital? I think she's just giving up.'

When Julie is finished, we troop back through, and Rosa, now dressed, sits on the sofa. Edward delivers her tea to her hand, and she sips at it, tiny amounts, like a bird.

'Your husband and son are concerned about your chemotherapy. What are you planning to do?'

'I don't know. I really didn't manage it very well. They gave me sickness pills and injections but I felt horrible. And knocked out. I don't think I've recovered even yet.'

'But it's the best thing. That's just the cancer coming out of you. That means it's working, doesn't it?' Thomas is sitting down beside his mother. 'You need to get more chemo – they can give you better anti-sickness pills.' He reaches into his briefcase. 'I got these for you – vitamins, mineral supplements – to give you a boost. They said they'd help.' He puts the containers onto the table – Rosa smiles. 'Thanks, son,' she says. 'He looks after me, doesn't he?'

'Well, it's up to you, really, Rosa,' I start.

'We just want what's best for you,' says Thomas. 'It's only going to get worse without the chemo. We just need to build you up for it. The longer you wait the worse it'll be.'

Edward is nodding.

'What do you think, doctor?' 'Well,' I start, 'did they say how useful the chemo would be?'

'If it's best for her, doctor,' says Edward 'that's what we want too. We want her to have the best treatment possible, don't we son.'

Rosa looks doubtful. 'Do you think so?'

'Well,' I say, but I don't want to cause disagreement, and I have a clinic starting in ten minutes.

Rosa shrugs and says 'OK, if you really want me to, if it's for the best.' I find myself nodding too.

Everybody smiles.

* * *

Edward is on the phone. I am running late, in the middle of surgery. My last patient complained about being kept waiting.

'Her breathing's bad. She looks terrible, doctor.'

'When did she get out of hospital?'

'Yesterday. She was doing really well – she'd hardly been sick this time. But the last few hours she just looks awful, really grey.'

'OK. I'll be round as soon as I can. Is she complaining of pain or anything else?'

'Just the usual pain in her chest. That's all. I'll leave the door on the latch... She's in bed.'

I ask the receptionists to apologise to the folk in the waiting room. I am irritated by each red traffic light. When I finally arrive, it's obvious that Rosa is ill. She isn't fevered but her blood pressure is low, her pulse is fast, and she looks pale and frightened. Her thin arms, as crisp and friable as crepe paper, are marked with dark purple bruises from blood tests and intravenous drips. At her wrist, where I bend my fingers into her pulse, her bones feel prominent and unguarded. I crouch beside her.

'I'm worried about your blood pressure. You don't look very well.'

She agrees. 'I feel awful. Pains in my kidneys and when I breathe.' Her chest is noisy, crackles becoming louder the further down her chest I place the stethoscope. Edward is at the doorway, pacing. I tell her that I'm worried about sepsis – infection – that her immune system will be lower because of the chemo. She nods, Edward is frowning, and answers his phone to Thomas ('Yes, Tommy. The doctor's here. Not looking good. Best you come over. Wait a sec.') and covers the phone. 'What do you think, doctor?'

'I'm worried about infection,' I start, and Edward is beside us, nodding.

'She needs to go into hospital, doesn't she?'

I nod, and he goes back to the doorway – 'She's going back in. Yes. I'll phone in a minute' – and returns beside us.

'Are you in pain?' Rosa winces as I lay her back onto the pillow. 'A bit.' The bottle of morphine on the bedside table looks pristine, and I am wondering how much she's taken. She catches my glances. 'I've been a bit worried... in case it makes my breathing worse.'

'Is it?' I ask. 'Have you noticed your breathing being worse?'

'It said, on the packet... if it makes your breathing shallow to stop it. You know how Eddie worries.'

'OK', I say, but I am now distracted by phoning the hospital and explaining who Rosa is, and her chemotherapy, and her pulse rate: there is no bed, and she will have to go to the hospital on the other side of the city. I write a note, phone an ambulance; and ask her and Eddie to let me know when she is home.

* * *

'Just to let you know that's her out, doctor.'

'Glad to hear it. What happened in the hospital?'

'She had a terrible time. They had to put her on antibiotics,

in through the vein, then they had to put a line into her neck because the veins kept shutting down. And her heart wasn't managing it – she was in the ITU for a couple of days, I thought the worst to be honest. We got the priest in. But she picked up, they said she was amazing, but when she got out of there, back to the ordinary ward, she got a big infection.'

'Infection?'

'C. diff.' *My heart sinks;* Clostridium difficile *causes diarrhoea; it is a hazard with antibiotic treatment, and has a sizeable mortality rate. It can take weeks for people to get better, and they usually need to be nursed in a side ward to stop other patients getting infected.*

'It was awful, doctor. Thought she'd been lucky the first time to get through it. They said she might not make it, but she did.'

I tell him that I'll come round after surgery tomorrow, see if there's anything I can do.

* * *

The first thing is the smell; the flat is simmering with unaired heat and faeces. The curtains are closed; she's been trying to sleep. Rosa is pale, her cheeks are sunken, and her head solidly dents the pillows. Her nightgown is flapping open, exposing a breast – I have never seen her less than perfectly dressed before. When I take her hand to examine her pulse, I notice a trail of brown matter leaking from under her nails. Her breathing is harsh and her pulse fast and erratic. When she does speak, she is confused, thinking she is still in hospital, and alone. 'When will they come to get me?' she asks, hoarsely. 'I'm waiting and waiting...'

Edward says she has been like this since she came home; actually, she was like this in the hospital too. She is crying out at night, bewildered and disorientated. The night Rosa came home from the hospital, she woke at three in the morning, thinking that Carol was still alive. Carol, their daughter, died aged 11, in a road crash, over forty years ago. 'It was awful, doctor. I didn't know whether to tell her that she was dead, or not.' The cheerfulness I associate with Edward has been plucked away. 'What does that mean – it's affecting her in the head?' I can't lie, but there are other possibilities. I run through the possibilities – she may be simply dehydrated, in which case, she needs fluids, probably in through a drip. She may be septic, and need antibiotics quickly. Both those things would mean that she should improve reasonably quickly. Or, yes, it may be that the cancer has spread into her brain. The carers are coming round twice a day to bathe Rosa and help her to the loo 'but they're only here for a minute, they don't have a lot of time, they've got lots of visits to do'.

We agree that Rosa will be better in hospital. This time, there is a bed nearby. Edward is relieved – getting buses to visit her is much less complicated. This time, he says he'll phone Thomas from the hospital. 'He worries, he worries.' I try and tell Rosa what is happening. I think she recognises me, but her agreement is polite and, I think, superficial.

On the way home I wonder if I did the right thing.

* * *

Dr Kate Davies is the doctor on duty in the hospital. She has been graduated for two years, and she is having a busy shift. The nurses have been paging her constantly.

'Kate, can you see the lady in bed 2? She's dry and septic.'

'In a minute.'

When Kate gets to Rosa's bedside, Thomas and Edward are there too. Kate introduces herself and listens to Rosa's chest as Thomas narrates the story of the last few days. She is interrupted once by the nurses, who ask her to write a prescription for another patient, and once by her pager.

'It's really not like my mother,' Thomas is saying, 'she's usually sharp as a tack. I can't believe how confused she is.'

'We'll get tests done, give her some fluids, see how she is,'

says Kate, who brushes back the curtains beside the bed. A few minutes later a nurse puts up a drip. Rosa tries to pull it out, agitated. Another nurse wraps Rosa's arm in a bandage to keep it in place. Thomas takes his father for a cup of coffee. Shortly afterwards Rosa soils the bed, but it is a while until this is noticed, and she is distraught. The bed is changed but the drip has now been pulled out and needs to be replaced. Rosa, exhausted, disorientated, and in pain, sobs. Thomas and Edward come back to the ward, and sit with Rosa, trying to soothe her. Thomas tells the nurse that Rosa is distressed, and asks for her to be given 'something'. Dr Davies prescribes a sedative, and Rosa falls into a deep sleep.

* * *

Jane Black is Rosa's consultant.

'We just want her to get better, doctor.'

'Of course. Now there are a couple of problems. Her kidney tests are showing that there is impairment. So is her liver. And she's still confused. Then there's the C. diff.*'*

'What does that mean, doctor?'

'Basically – she isn't improving much and I think that's because her organs aren't working that well.'

'Oh...'

'So we've given her plenty of fluid, which should have sorted her out, but it's not being that effective now. So we need to get more tests done, see if there are any more problems we can treat.'

'What kind of tests?'

'A scan, more blood tests, urine tests. That OK?'

* * *

Two days later they have a further appointment with Dr Black.

'We've been concerned that she isn't passing much urine, and that is why her kidneys are failing. The scan we've done shows a blockage. If we don't do anything she could go into kidney failure.'

'That's serious, isn't it?'

'Yes, she could die of kidney failure.'

'So...'

'We need to put in a tube, inside the kidney, to drain the urine away.'

'Is that....'

'She'll be taken down to theatre tomorrow morning, and the tube will be inserted under a local anaesthetic. It should help.'

The following day Rosa comes back from theatre. She is not making any attempt to drink or feed herself. She is sipping from a cup when it is offered to her, but sometimes the water dribbles back out onto her chin. Although her hair has been combed, and tied back, it hangs asymmetrically and awkwardly. She is barely rousable. The bag at the side of the bed contains dark, amberish urine. The fluid has stopped dripping from the bag and is no longer making any progress into her arm. Her nightdress is sweatily stuck to the front of her chest.

Thomas and Edward are bewildered. Rosa has changed in a matter of days. She is no longer sitting up and talking; she is cowered in the bed, tubes protruding, and she looks skeletal. Her face is gaunt and chalky. Her eyes are dull, her eyelids yellowish, her lips cracked. Her nightdress – still – despite double knots – keeps flapping open. She kicks off the blanket so that one or two feet protrude. Her toenails are long and ragged, and it is that which shocks Edward, who knows his wife's liking for summer painted toenails. Her feet now look ordinary and very old. They don't look like Rosa's feet.

The nurses say that Dr Black will be around later. They catch the eye of Dr Davies, whose bleep goes off several times as they see her, pacing up and down the ward. She says she will come in a minute. It is 4 am before Rosa's drip is replaced, and this wakes her from fitful sleep. She tells the nurses that she wants to go home, and wants Edward. She continues to be agitated, and is given some more sedation.

* * *

The next day, the nurses say that they are planning to discharge Rosa at the end of the week. Charlotte is Rosa's named nurse. She explains how the district nurses will help to manage the tube going into Nancy's side to drain the urine.

'I thought it was coming out,' says Edward.

'Did you?' Charlotte says, puzzled.

'I thought it was just to unblock her kidney.'

'Yes, that's right. But she'll still need the tube in.'

'Is the blockage not gone?'

'No... what did Dr Black say to you?'

'That she needed the tube to drain the kidney. There was a blockage.'

'I'll get Dr Davies to talk you about that.'

When Dr Davies comes to Rosa's bedside, Edward detects a hesitancy about her. She closes the curtains round the bed and sits beside Edward on the other visitor's chair. Rosa is dozing.

'Did Dr Black not explain about the tube?'

'That it was to drain the kidneys because of the blockage. I didn't know it would have to stay in.'

'The problem is that the blockage is getting bigger, so that's why the tube needs to stay in.'

'Oh.'

'The blockage... the blockage is a tumour, you see. It might be spreading from the lung cancer, or from somewhere else.'

'Cancer?'

'Yes, the lung cancer – sometimes it spreads, and you get tumours in the abdomen, pressing on the liver or the kidneys. So the tube – that's going to need to stay in, unless the tumour gets smaller.'

Dr Davies and Edward are facing each other. She is careful with her words. She sees the upset in his frown lines.

'So some more chemotherapy, try and shrink it down. The oncologists are coming this afternoon. She could have her first dose tomorrow and then come back for the rest.'

'Do you... think she's... strong enough?' Edward whispers.

'See what the oncologists say,' says Dr Davies, who is holding her pen, her pager, and a notebook. The pager beeps again.

* * *

Thomas is at Rosa's bedside. Rosa is sitting up and sipping water. She has had some toast and she is wearing a jumper, not a nightdress, and she has arranged her own hair. She is still pale and has obviously lost weight, but she looks like Rosa.

Dr Jackson approaches them, carrying a set of notes. He has rimless glasses, and greying, balding hair.

'Ah, yes, yes, hello. I'm Dr Jackson, from oncology, cancer centre. Hello, you are? Ah, the son, yes, yes. So you had some chemo last month. I see, and the nephrostomy, yes? So the question is for more. More chemotherapy, to help.'

'Yes,' says Thomas, 'whatever would help. I understand about the kidney.'

'Yes, yes,' says Dr Jackson, smiling broadly. 'That will help the kidney. What I would say is, three, maybe six cycles, we can get started soon.'

'It'll help, will it doctor?' asks Thomas. 'With the kidney?'

'Expect so, hard to guarantee, but yes, should shrink it nicely. That OK with you both? Anything you want to ask, anything you're unhappy with?'

Thomas squeezes his mother's hand.

'Side effects – how did you find it the last time, then?'

Nancy's voice fails her and she has to try again. 'I was sick. And very tired.'

'We'll make sure that we give you plenty of medication to

help with the nausea. Not much we can do about the tiredness, though.'

'Do you think... it'll help, doctor?'

'It'll certainly improve things a bit.'

'I'm sure it's for the best, doctor,' says Thomas, meaningfully.

There is a box of chocolates and a bunch of lilies on the bedside table. Dr Jackson writes an order for chemotherapy. It's the first and last time he will meet Rosa.

* * *

Yesterday Rosa came back home. I have a discharge letter from the hospital. She is now on large, regular doses of morphine, laxatives, because of the constipating effect of the morphine, sleeping tablets, blood pressure pills, diuretic or water pills, and because this has made her blood salts low, tablets of potassium. She is also taking tablets to protect her bones from osteoporosis, a cholesterol pill, and anti-sickness tablets, which are of two types. There is a note from the district nurses to say that they are concerned about the site of the nephrostomy, where the tube goes under the skin. There is also a form from the palliative care nurse, who says that she has visited and will do so again. Edward has phoned to say that she can't manage to use the commode and is wondering what to do.

I don't know what to do either, but I go and visit, frustrated before I even knock on the door. Edward looks tired. Rosa is sleeping. She is sleeping more, but she wakes later in the day and is eating 'not bad'. We have a talk. The chemotherapy is exhausting, but they are giving her injections for the nausea and this is helping a bit.

'The problem is the commode,' she explains. 'I'm stumbling to get to it. I can't manage to let my legs get there. And I'm ashamed of asking him to help me. He shouldn't have to wipe me.'

'I know.'

'The carers are good about taking me but it's the morphine

– I'm bunged up, can't always manage to go when they're here.'

Her nephrostomy looks red and a little infected. I prescribe antibiotics. 'I'll see if I can get the carers to come in more often.'

'We already did. They're at the maximum. Four visits a day, ten minutes a time. I'm too much for Edward.'

Two days later there is a fax from the out of hours service. Rosa tried to get to the commode during the night. She tripped and fell, and was admitted to hospital with a suspected broken hip. The next day there is a fax from the palliative care nurses, who are concerned that they haven't yet made contact with her and want me to let them know when she will be going home.

* * *

Rosa died in hospital.

Edward phoned to tell me. They took her to theatre, to fix her fractured hip. She was in a great deal of pain. After the anaesthetic, they struggled to get her lungs working properly. She was in the high dependency unit. She was drowsy and then agitated, and was given sedation to stop her pulling out her tubes. She was most alert when she soiled herself, and was crying out for help. Edward stayed at her bedside. He thought she was getting better, as she seemed more settled, but later that day her heart stopped. They tried everything, he said. When they were resuscitating her, the doctors and nurses had pulled the curtains around the bed. But they were thin plastic, and he could hear everything.

He heard someone say, with what he thought was anger: 'But she has metastatic cancer? A nephrostomy? She's 72?' He told this to Thomas, who thought it might have been ageist; he is thinking about complaining. Edward is not so sure.

I express my sympathy.

Edward shakes my hand. 'Thank you for all you did.'

I feel crushed by guilt.

Chapter 1

The Modern Death

We are not dying the same. Here's the proof. Over the last three decades, our life expectancy is increasing. Women have historically lived longer than men: this gap still exists, but is narrowing.

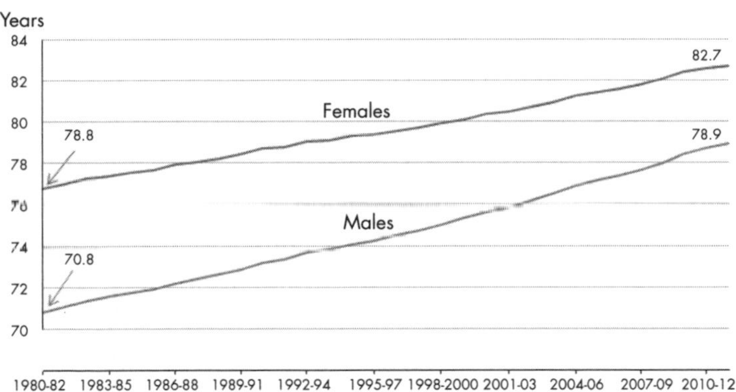

Figure 1: Life expectancy at birth, United Kingdom, 1980-1982 to 2010-2012 *(Source: Office for National Statistics)*

So when statisticians analyse the pattern of death rates, they find that our lives are lengthening by large margins. Over just ten years, between 2000 and 2010, the death rate fell by almost a quarter in men and a fifth in women.[4] This means more, older people, dying later. It is a remarkable, enormous and recent shift in the shape of our society. For every six people who die, one is aged over 90. Older people comprise a burgeoning societal group. At the start of the 1980s, there were 2.9 million people aged over 75 in England. By 2008, there were 4 million, and by 2033 it is expected there will be 7.2 million.[5] If success is measured in lifespan, we have surpassed ourselves. We have documented a near doubling of life expectancy over the last mere hundred years. Old age used to be the exception. Extreme old age had been rare. Now it is straightforwardly commonplace. Behind the front desk of the practice I work in, the walls are lined with shelves holding paper records. We arrange the storage of notes by the age of the patient. A couple of years ago we had to make new shelves to accommodate the new demographic of the people we look after – far more people aged over 70, 80, 90, 100.

This gear change in life length means that we die because of different things. The scourge of childhood illnesses which killed in early life can now be largely vaccinated against – smallpox, tuberculosis, measles. Cancers, heart disease and dementia are common causes of death, but it is old people who die of these diseases in the west. True, and terribly, there are still stand-out pockets of deprivation where lifespan is static or even falling in the UK.[6] But the trend, overall, is upwards, and this means that we die differently.

Around 20% of us die at home.[7, 8] Deaths in hospitals and care homes have replaced deaths at home over the last two decades.[9] Hospices – usually staffed by specialist nursing, pharmacist, physiotherapy and medical teams – have risen in many towns and cities, often funded by charitable donations rather than fully and centrally via the NHS. These institutions help patients and their families who are known to be terminally ill, and people are often admitted for short periods and discharged again once treatments are stabilised or optimised.

But the largest problem is that most deaths in hospices are 'expected', in the sense of arranging a bed in a hospice as one particular disease process, such as cancer, is predicted to cause death soon. The hospice movement, pleading for 'a good death', has rightly placed the relief of suffering as the priority at the end of life. Yet some palliative care facilities still avoid dealing with diagnoses other than cancer. Many are based outside of main hospital sites; many are run independently or partially funded from the NHS, and the chances of being allowed admission to a bed can be a lottery. Many nurses, some employed by charities, have become specialised in working with patients who know their life is immediately limited.

Undoubtedly many people and their families have been given exemplary care from hospices and specially trained doctors and nurses. But when the needs of people who are dying are dealt with by a specialist service, rather than by 'ordinary' general practice staff, there is no guarantee that the person will be able to access that service when they need to. And while cancer was the traditional remit of hospices, many other conditions, such as heart failure, stroke or dementia, need just as much palliative care – relief from pain, help to wash and dress, nursing care and support – as any death due to cancer does.

The idea that cancer is what can be expected to kill us in late middle age or old age is now outmoded. Clearly there are still thousands of deaths from cancer causing premature deaths, and we should not forget these people. The overarching trend is, though, not a straightforward sum of cancer and time. People are living longer after treatment for cancer. This has led to treatment doses for some cancers being adjusted downwards, to try and avoid side effects occurring many years later – because people are now expected to live long enough to experience them. For example, in breast cancer, the dose of radiation treatment has been reduced in certain cases – for even though the side effects of radiation damage to the lung becomes visible ten or twenty years later, the patient is now reasonably hoped to be full of life. Survival rates for many cancers, like Hodgkins lymphoma or bowel cancer, have been successively improving.

The new demographic is for people to die in old age, or extreme old age. The typical patient will have had multiple illnesses and diagnoses. The typical patient may also have been treated for cancer some years ago, and be now on reams of medication. This complexity is relatively recent. General practitioners like me are trying to balance the need for, or side effects of, medication along with the care needed for diabetes along with the other needs of co-existing chronic bronchitis and dementia, low mood or anxiety. Hospital specialists tend to work with one diagnosis at time – like asthma or kidney failure – and we need their expertise. Meantime, though, primary care has to deal with the interrelated problems across them all. And when it comes to palliative care specialists – who are not typically part of the GP practice team – we must know that death is nearing, so that we can ask for their help.

Predicting death

But is it possible to make that prediction? Is it so straightforward? In truth, there are many people living with conditions where I would not be surprised if they died with them at almost any time. Almost a million UK citizens have heart failure – where the heart does not pump blood efficiently around the body. Between 30-40% of people given the diagnosis in hospital will die in the following year,[10] with a death rate of around 9% per year after that.[11] This is a death rate worse than many cancers. I should not be terribly surprised if a person with this diagnosis dies. Yet most people with heart failure, especially if diagnosed more than a year ago, will not die in the next year. This means that thousands of people live with the uncertainty of their prognosis, as do their doctors.

This kind of risk from a distinct disease tends to be more obvious to patients and their doctors. Patients with symptoms of heart failure – breathlessness, fatigue, swelling of the ankles – are likely to be under regular review by their doctor or nurse, and their symptoms are likely to be noticeable. Most people will take daily medication, which, if missed, may cause noticeably worse fluid retention. But other diagnoses are less obviously a cause of death.

Type 2 diabetes, for example, affects over 2.5 million people in England alone.[12] At age 55, the life expectancy of men with diabetes type 2 is three to eleven years less than for the general population.[13] This represents a near doubling of the death rate for people with diabetes compared with people without.[14] So, again, as a GP, if I have a patient with type 2 diabetes, I know that their death risk is increased compared to my patients without diabetes. Yet most death certificates don't list diabetes type 2 as a cause of death, and only as the underlying cause in a minority, 6.4% of the time.[15] The same issues around certification are similar in dementia. Once the diagnosis of dementia has been made, the risk of death increases.[16] The graph below shows the difference – as the lines separate, the gap between them shows the number of years on average lost by the person with dementia. Again, death certificates don't always mention dementia as a cause, or contributory cause, of death.[17] Yet it is clear that having dementia increases the risk of dying. So this risk factor might make doctors less surprised if that person then dies. Yet, predicting the timing of death for an individual remains dangerously inexact.

We have seen this difficulty in predicting death publicly on many occasions. Abdelbaset Ali Mohmed al-Megrahi was convicted of 270 counts of murder when an aeroplane was blown up over Lockerbie in Scotland in 1988. He was sentenced to life imprisonment, but freed on compassionate grounds in 2009, following predictions from specialists that his death from prostate cancer was likely to follow in the next three months.[18] He died almost three years later in 2012.[19] Similarly, accounts of people who have been given a 'terminal' diagnosis which they easily outlive bubble up

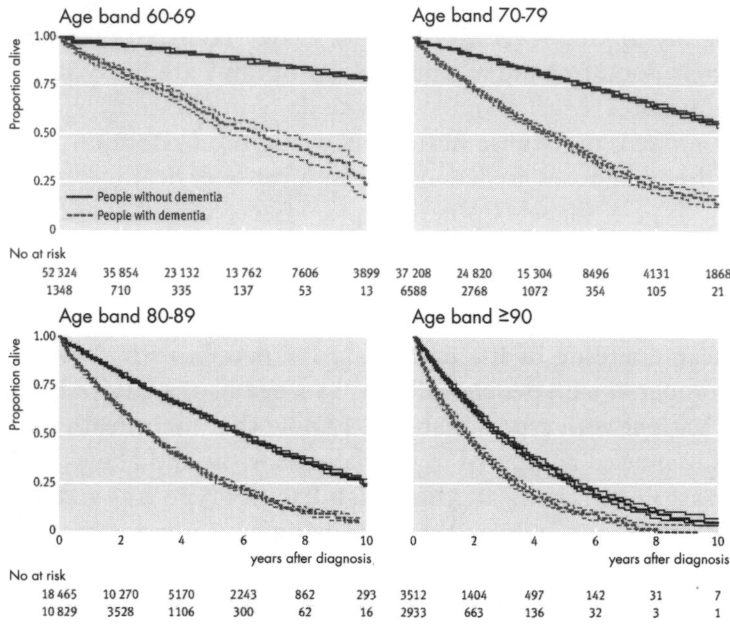

Figure 2: Kaplan-Meier survival curves for people with and without dementia

regularly in newspapers[20] with the message that the doctors have been 'defied' by patients who have outlived their life expectancy. Naturally, 'bad news' stories of when doctors have overestimated life length are less newsworthy. So how accurate can doctors be when predicting death?

Research suggests that doctors do find it difficult to gauge when death is likely to occur. There is a huge amount of data about what the average survival lengths are for groups of people with many types of cancers, heart and lung conditions. But this doesn't help much when trying to predict likely survival times in individual people.

For example, when doctors were asked to estimate the survival time of each patient referred to a hospice, they got it more or less correct (a third above or below the actual survival time) only 20% of the time. However 63% of the

> The Lockerbie bomber could live far longer than predicted by Scottish ministers when they decided to release him, a cancer expert has said...
>
> However, a range of specialists concluded in June and July this year that his condition had deteriorated over the intervening 10 months and the lower end of this scale was more likely.
>
> Megrahi's life expectancy was no longer deemed to be 'many months' but the report concluded: 'Whether or not prognosis is more or less than three months, no specialist would be "willing to say".'
>
> However, his personal physician said his condition 'declined significantly' between July 26 and August 3 and a life expectancy of three months was deemed a 'reasonable estimate'.
>
> Bill Aitken, Scottish Tory justice spokesman, said: 'In June and July, there was a consensus on prognosis of eight months. Where is that consensus now?'
>
> Johnson S, Porter J.
>
> **Lockerbie bomber Megrahi 'may live for many more months.'**
>
> *The Telegraph*, 25 August 2009: www.telegraph.co.uk/news/uknews/scotland/6089131/Lockerbie-bomber-Megrahi-may-live-for-many-more-months.html

prognoses given were over optimistic.[21] A systematic review published in 2003 makes the same point. The researchers looked at the time of death in terminally ill patients. The longer the lifespan left was, the less accurate the predictions were. Twenty-five per cent of the time, the doctors got the estimate right, down to the correct week of death. Twenty-seven per cent of the time, they overestimated survival by at least four weeks, and 12% of the time, they underestimated it by at least four weeks.[22] In other words, even for doctors whose daily work is dealing with people who are known to be terminally ill, working out how much lifetime remains is a hugely inaccurate business.

But as we have seen, it's not just cancers which cause death. Other conditions which we may not think of as typical causes of death but which increase the risk of it – such as diabetes or dementia, as discussed above – are more common as our lifespans lengthen. We know that 42% of people have one or more long-term conditions, and 23% have two or more; having a physical and a mental health problem in combination is common. At age 50, half of the population have one disorder; by age 65, a majority have two or more. Having more disorders is also more common with increasing social deprivation. The poorer the community which is studied, the more disease is found within it.[23] Yet the frail older person may live for a very long time.

What does this mean for our ability to predict death? There is a surprising paucity of evidence about how good general practitioners are at working out when death is imminent. One study looked at GPs' predictions of which patients were likely to die of heart failure. The doctors were asked 'would you be surprised if this patient died within the next 12 months?' Out of 231 patients, the GPs correctly identified 11 of the 14 that died, but only identified 133 of the 217 who did not die.[24] That's the unimpressive predictive power of a crystal ball.

So what about trying to predict death based on more hard-nosed science and less about doctors' thoughts and opinions? In fact, one of the best predictors of mortality used in research is simply 'frailty'.[25] This isn't dependent on a person being diagnosed with any particular disease. Instead, researchers, publishing in the *Journals of Gerontology*, have defined frailty as a syndrome where three or more of either unintentional weight loss of more than 10 lbs in the last year, self-reported exhaustion, weakness in grip strength, slow walking speed and low physical activity are present.[26] In a study of people over 70, 28% who died had been diagnosed with frailty in the last year of their life. Crucially, 'frailty' was a better predictor of death than cancer, organ failure or dementia.

What does this mean? For doctors trained to seek a diagnosis, which will naturally lead to treatment, diagnosing 'frailty' – seemingly, a subjective mishmash of symptoms – can seem counterintuitive. There is no blood test for it. We are trained to think of problems in a single gene, or a discrete fault in a biochemical pathway as the cause of disease – and the door to a cure. Yet frailty, with no clear single cause of its complaints, is a real pathology with what radiologists call an 'Aunt Minnie' quality (an auntie who is instantly recognisable, even if she is hard to describe) – 'subliminal or subconscious pattern recognition – a diagnosis or recognition mainly by gestalt'.[27] We know frailty when we see it. Crucially, for the majority of frail people – over 80% – it was not cancer that led to death, but the kinds of things that signify slow decline: advanced dementia, with significant disability; kidney, heart or liver failure; or chronic bronchitis. Because it is gradual and because there may be no one 'pathological' diagnosis, the diagnosis of 'dying' may be even harder than usual to make – and uncertain when it is made – and just as hard to share with the person. Hence the difficulty of asking palliative care specialists to become involved: we cannot be very sure that the person is dying, and we have no clear 'terminal' under-a-microscope diagnosis.

Similarly, when older people are discharged from accident and emergency departments in the US, researchers examined what gave the best prediction of who was most likely to need to come back into hospital, and who was at the biggest risk of death. The researchers found that counting things like difficulty shopping, bathing, bending down or concentrating was far better at predicting future ill health or death than singular pathology.[28]

So, crucially, if we rely on doctors to predict our death – either by informed guesswork or by using the singular diagnoses of disease given to us – we will usually be wrong.

Where we die

Remarkably, across continents, people are much the same when they say where they want to die. Given the choice, the large majority say that they would like to be at home given the opportunity.[29,30,31,32,33,34]

It's easy to see why. A hospital ward may be noisy or lack privacy; home is familiar and safe. Nurses or doctors known to a patient and her family may be a comfortingly familiar sight during a last illness. Being at home may confer a degree of control over death that may be feared lost in hospital; privacy is more likely; there are no rigid visiting hours; there is the luxury of one's own sheets on the bed, and a lock on the bathroom door.

But when carers are asked where they want the person they care for to die, the results differ. One Canadian study found that while fewer than 5% of patients wanted to die in an institution, such as a hospital or hospice, 14% of carers wanted the patient to die there. However, even though 30% of patients in the study did not die in their preferred location, in retrospect, 92% of their carers felt that the patient died in the most appropriate place.[35] People who are dying often wish to die at home; but when this does not happen, their carers usually feel that the place of dying was right.

In another study, UK hospital doctors and GPs were asked if they thought that individual cancer patients died in the right place. In the vast majority of cases, 92%, whether at home, nursing home, hospice or community hospital, the GPs felt the patient was in the right place. But the GPs also felt that hospital was the 'right' place for many people. In fact, 83% of the time, the doctors felt that death in hospital was the 'right' place.[36] However, there was a mismatch. For the same group of patients, GPs felt that 17% of deaths in hospital were in the wrong place whereas hospital doctors thought that 27% of the patients had died in the wrong place.

So there are disparities. Most people want to die at home, and frequently, this doesn't happen. When death does occur elsewhere, most of the time, carers and doctors feel this is all right. But when death occurs in hospital, about a quarter of hospital doctors think this was inappropriate and that death could have occurred elsewhere.

Another study asked people with terminal illnesses what their future plans were for their care. One said, strikingly: 'I have to stay here in hospital while on the antibiotics, then the doctor says I can go home – I'd rather stay here in hospital, but I'm afraid they'll need the bed.'[37] Some people want to die where there are qualified staff immediately available, for lots of different reasons; this is understandable and entirely valid.

For example, in a set of research interviews, one nurse said that 'I don't think people these days are used to caring for sick people, they rely very heavily on the health service and we can't be available very, very quickly, so people get very frightened and haven't got the skills that previous generations would have had.' Another said 'I think it is very difficult when people live alone or sometimes where you have maybe got a very small number of carers. Where you have got big families where there's much more resources in terms of care input from the family, people are more likely to remain at home I find.'[38]

At the moment, in the UK, around 20.8% of deaths occur at home; a rise from 18.3% in 2004.[39] Governmental policy has noted that 'many people do not die where they would choose to'[40] which has been used to support policies allowing more people to die at home.[41]

But does this push to home death help us to get the complex decisions at the end of life right? Compare it with decisions people make for their children at the start of life. We may wish for a birth which is natural, with no drugs, and at home or in a low-tech environment; we may want to breastfeed for six months or more. Yet unexpected hazards arise in pregnancy or in labour; breastfeeding can be difficult. We may end up making decisions which we would rather not have had to make. No wonder that many doctors have a frisson of concern when they see 'birthing plans' laid out by parents who aspire to a 'perfect birth': no one person, or doctor, has total control over anything. The sense of failure new parents can endure when births don't conform to their hopes can be pointed and sometimes calamitous. How we die may be more important than where we are when it happens.

In the same way, the last phase of life can produce dilemmas and unanticipated problems when we aim for a 'perfect death'. So, from the same series of interviews with nurses, one said 'His wife is determined to look after him at home and wants him to die at home, but every time he sees her a little bit stressed or whatever, he breaks down and he says "should I be going somewhere else, she can't do this"'.

The truth is, looking after a dying person can be hard and difficult work. Dealing with bathing and washing, toileting and personal hygiene, vomit and faecal matter can be unpleasant, and, though it can be hard to admit, sometimes stomach-turning, even for loved ones. Giving medication, monitoring symptoms, moving and turning a person, keeping up conversation and co-ordinating visits and appointments with healthcare professionals can be arduous, unrelenting, back-breaking work. Health professionals have training, practical knowledge, peer support and experience which insulates them at least partially from the rawness of the task. They also have time off. For family members these tasks can carry responsibilities which can be onerous – and from which it may not be possible to have any breaks at all.

Even planning for home care can be difficult given the inexactness of predicting death, as previously discussed. This can mean difficulties for family members to take time off work, with caring for other dependants, and care of the carer herself. As another nurse said from the study: 'Particularly towards the final weeks of life I would say, people often manage to a certain degree at home and particularly with carers with social services and continuing care, but when it reaches the final... weeks and days of life when people are very dependent, that is when often it is more difficult to keep people at home when they actually need 24h care.'

Who helps us die

Just as home births were commonplace in the early part of the twentieth century, so were home deaths. Our longer lives and easier access to hospitals and hospices have reduced our community knowledge of what the approach to death looks like and how to care for the dying person. While

> I spent alternate nights in a single bed three feet away from hers, the commode uncovered between us, the light left on because I never quite slept in any case. I watched the seasons change from her bedroom window, the evenings draw in and then out again.
>
> The home I had never really lived in for more than a few days at a time before this gradually became my home, our home.
>
> Our mother was almost never left alone, by day or night. My sister and I would sit with her, chat, do crosswords. Sometimes we talked about important matters, memories – setting the life story straight. But just as often we would chat about nothing. On one occasion she asked me what I would do when all this was over, if I would go back to Italy. Yes, I told her. It's where I live. She nodded, satisfied.
>
> She asked me if I was happy, and I told her that I was, and it was true. Despite my qualms about the practicalities of pushing to one side the business of my own life, qualms about work and bills, I was happy to be there with her and I knew it. And yet all of this simply happened: our only conscious decision was to keep our mother at home until she died.
>
> Looking back on that time, I see that what I often thought of as limbo was actually a state of grace. At the start, I'd ask myself when I'd be able to get back to my life. That feeling ended when I realised that what I was living was my life, in its purest, least distracted form. She died on 8 June 2011, almost a year to the day after our arrival.
>
> Lambert C. **What was it like to care for my dying mother**. *The Telegraph*, 8 August 2014. www.telegraph.co.uk/men/the-filter/another-mans-shoes/11000910/What-it-was-like-to-care-for-my-dying-mother.html

sudden deaths are common – a sudden collapse, a brisk loss of consciousness and a rapid descent towards death – the pattern of death in older people can be more prolonged. It often happens in the context of slower declines and a 'fading' into death. For family care givers, there are stark problems. How to give food and fluid when it is refused or only minimal amounts taken? How often to move or turn the person in bed to prevent skin damage? How to intimately wash and clean a parent or sibling when it is embarrassing to do so? Cleaning and disposing of urine or faeces can make even the most loving relatives feel nauseated. In hospital or hospices, there are professionals who will take on these roles and the responsibility with it. At home, however, there is not the same 24/7 wraparound care. The social work department can supply care assistants to visit a person at home, payment of which is usually subject to means testing. However, at maximum, this will give four short visits a day. The rest of the day is without someone on hand to help fetch water, assist to the toilet or commode, or to provide comfort and companionship. These gaps are commonly filled with family members; and in the UK, 11.9% of women and 9% of men provide some kind of free care to loved ones. That's approaching 5.5 million UK citizens. Incredibly, 1.0% of men and 1.2% of women are employed in delivering more than 50 hours of free home care a week – while also being in full time work themselves.[42]

This is an outstanding level of hands-on commitment. But it comes at a cost. Carers themselves are subject to higher than average levels of illness, and to mental illness in particular.[43] Some people have jobs which they might be able to put indefinitely to one side; but most people will have employment or employers who are far less flexible. Making decisions on behalf of parents – while already tired from ongoing caring – can be acutely painful, as described by Louise Smith in *The Guardian*.

I would never put my parents into a care home. Only selfish children did that. I knew that – until the night I dropped by the family home to find my father sitting on the floor. He had a vague expression, as if nothing unusual had happened. He was experiencing a massive stroke while my mother was asleep. Within three years they would both die in a local home. Of all my life's unimagineable scenarios, this was the most unlikely, but it happened to me and it could happen to anyone... From the moment of his stroke, it became clear that the thankless, isolating task of looking after my mother had played its part. Within a fortnight of taking over, I was ready to kill. My priority became the daily visit to the stroke rehab unit. My father was paralysed, unable to feed himself, and partially blind...

He never regained his short-term memory. Each morning, I ferried my mother to his ward, but at night she stayed at home, independent and resilient. I fell into a routine, exhausted, but running on adrenaline... On 28 December, one of the most wretched days of our lives, I drove my parents to the care home, dressed in their warm winter coats... I now believe I made a terrible mistake, putting my parents into a home, even if I felt I had no other option...

The day before my mother died, I was lucky. I had a brilliant visit. The call came at 7 am the following morning. She was alive, but unresponsive. We sat talking to her all day, holding her hands and using a baby brush on her wisps of white hair. I lurched between piercing fits of giggles (lifting the sheet to find enormous turquoise padded booties encasing her feet) and moments of incapacitating grief. Watching her die that night was, strangely, a wonderful experience, an enormous privilege for which I will always be grateful.

Smith L. **I never wanted my parents to go into a care home – then I had to face reality**. *The Guardian*, 18 May 2013. www.theguardian.com/lifeandstyle/2013/may/18/never-wanted-parents-in-care-home

Chapter 2

The Quality Problem

Does medicine help or hinder us to live well at the end of life?

Ageing is a success. It also brings the potential to accumulate diagnoses, risk factors, and a medication list. None of this is necessarily bad. Diagnoses may be useful. Treatments which enable us to live a better quality of life, and keep doing what we want to do are welcome. However, some medical interventions on standard offer will not produce much useful benefit in the quality of our day to day living. There is a tension between the medical interventions on offer and their ability to produce improvements in our quality of life.

What is this 'quality of life'? It's worth examining because many medical interventions are offered according to how much 'QOL' they give. It's another 'Aunt Minnie'. We know what quality of life means to us, and keenly feel its absence. Quality of life must be in the judgement of the individual; making assumptions about others is a dangerous sport. For example, when people with multiple sclerosis estimate their quality of life, physical disabilities don't have an impact on their description of how they view their quality of life – whereas doctors judge their quality of life differently, as if it does.[44] Having a good quality of life does not mean being able-bodied rather than disabled, having perfect health or being 'disease free'.

Medicine has been placed centre stage in the delivery of end of life care. But how much can medicine help to supply this 'quality'? For sure, medicine has some role to play in giving us a quality of life, but it is not the only – or even main – factor in producing it. When death becomes an immediate probability – rather than something unthinkably distant – we are likely frail, carrying more diagnoses, and taking more medication. Medicine is not enough on its own. Instead, it is the hands-on expression of human care which is key to living our last days and months well – but which is currently rationed to drips when we need a generous torrent of it. The irony is that we can offer cutting edge medicines of high cost but marginal or little value, or chemotherapy requiring hospital stays and nursing time, but the actual grit of care in day-to-day life that is essential for quality – simple washing, cleaning, dressing, and eating – is funded meanly yet is of fundamental humane value. We can have innovation and technology, but not humble, heartening, hands-on care.

Quality of life — whose values?

Measuring cost-effectiveness is key to how NICE, the National Institute for Clinical and Healthcare Excellence, works. They use the QALY as their measure of how interventions change the quality of life of the patient. 'Quality Adjusted Life Years' are described by NICE as a method of evaluating treatments 'to ensure our judgements are fair' on what they recommend funding.[45] A score of 1.0 is the 'best possible health', and 0 is the 'worst possible health', 'measured in terms of the person's ability to perform the activities of daily life, freedom from pain and mental disturbance'. In essence, the score of health multiplied by the years gained at this level results in a unit called the QALY, which can then be given a monetary cost. Trying to assess the worth of new or expensive treatments is not a modern idea; the ideas behind the QALY have been developed from 1956.[46] But the measurement has persistent flaws.

One published paper takes the fictional cases of Karen and Lisa. Karen is involved in a car crash and becomes paraplegic. Her QALY is 0.5 per year; half as good as a fully able person. If she lives for 40 years, she can attain 20 QALYs. A similar accident resulted in Lisa having a limp. Her QALY score is 0.95 per year – not far from perfect. She, too, has a life expectancy of 40 years, meaning that she can get 38 QALYs from her life. Suppose each then develops a serious heart condition which will cause death unless the patient gets a heart transplant. QALYs would mean that Lisa will be prioritised beyond Karen, because Karen is significantly disabled. Say the transplant costs £100,000. Karen can gain 20 QALYs, meaning that each QALY will cost £5,000. But Lisa can gain 38 QALYs for the same cost, meaning that a QALY for her will cost less, £2,632. Therefore, going on QALY scores alone, it is more cost-efficient to spend the money on Lisa.[47] Shouldn't we feel uncomfortable about this? Who is to judge what quality of life Karen enjoys? What's a 'perfect' life anyway? Shouldn't it be Karen, not an economic onlooker, who can tell us what value her life is to her?

When QALYs were first developed, they often contained basic near-guesswork by researchers as to what matters to patients in many instances. However, by the noughties, there was recognition that it was patients' and citizen's values that must count.[48,49] Asking patients and citizens what matters to them is implicit in any meaningful calculation of health interventions – we can't assume that the priorities of doctors or researchers are the same as a heterogeneous group of patients.

Similarly, the idea that a QALY of 1.0 is really 'perfect health' is slightly incredible; there are millions of people with long-term chronic illness with full lives. People with a 'major' disability may gain more pleasure (and contribute more) to and from their immediate and wider social spheres than many who are in 'perfect' health. Disability may only manifest when a rigid or unthinking society fails to accommodate and adapt to individual needs.

> Most parents-to-be still fear that their beloved newborn will turn out to be – oh, the horror – disabled. My personal fear is that my future child will turn out to be unhappy. I don't care what he or she can or can't do, how they talk or walk or how many fingers and toes they have. Because I don't think that is a good indicator of happiness.
>
> Martinez F. **Francesca Martinez: having the last laugh.** *The Guardian*, 17 May 2014. www.theguardian.com/culture/2014/may/17/francesca-martinez-having-the-last-laugh-interview

This leads us to a dilemma. NICE marks interventions as high or low value according to what QALYs they generate. But there is a conflict, because a QALY's values may not be a person's values. I have been buoyed by the diversity of what people tell me gives them 'quality of life': the want to get another crop of tomatoes from the allotment; helping with childcare for a next door neighbour; sketching, cooking, fishing, bowling, reading, sex, dancing, karaoke, going on a pilgrimage, keeping on walking the dog; the desire to get to a wedding – after the civil partnership – of their grandson and his partner. The choice of what brings meaning and pleasure to humans is bountiful and can never be captured by a simple economic score.

Indeed, there have been concerns that trying to assess the cost-effectiveness related to quality at the end of life is fundamentally difficult. Additionally, because life expectancy is short, there is not much time for QALY value to build up.[50,51]

As for the impact on family, carers or friends, take a device which improves continence. It may not make much difference to the quality of life of a person who has minimal awareness. However, it may be invaluable to the carers of that person, saving them energy and laundry. Health economists have developed other types of evaluation tools to try and overcome some of these problems[52] but none are perfect – or in as frequent use as the QALY.

Despite the problems, QALYs still have many uses. It isn't good enough to simply prove that a drug extends the length of a life. It should be demonstrated that these extra days are of value to the patient – there is little point in extending life by a few days if those days are spent unconscious or in a coma. At best, QALYs can help to minimise hyperbole from pharmaceutical companies who may try and use irrelevant laboratory data to support their claims for widespread prescribing of their latest product.

In 2009, NICE decided that cost per QALY for end of life treatments should be more flexible.[53] Reasonably, it was reckoned that when a person is terminally ill, treatments could still be valuable if they improved the quality of life, not just the quantity. Critics have noted that this will only be equitable if society as a whole (who fund these expensive treatments via taxes) places more value on the days when it is known that the end of life is near, compared to any other time. It is also clear that an intervention can be given approval and a high QALY if it results in a better quality of life, even at the cost of a few days' life.[54] In the meantime, 'value-based pricing' is set to further finesse NICE's use of QALYs.[55] This will attempt to give more weighting to the impact of treatments on society more broadly.[56]

So while agreeing that QALY measurements are frequently important in assessing new healthcare interventions, we need to keep in sight what isn't measured. This attitude is epitomised by the charts which professional carers have to fill in at the end of each visit to a patient to 'prove' that the task of dressing or washing is complete. The charts ignore the values of human care – the need for conversation, listening, and companionship.

Medicine and quality

With this need for balance in mind, how can we know whether the interventions offered to us through the NHS, having been appraised by NICE, will truly improve our quality of life? What interventions are available to us that will allow us to get to a wedding, to cook, to knit, to have sex, or to keep on bowling?

QALYs aren't capable of revealing this kind of information. If a blood pressure medication disturbs our sleep by the need to get up and pee in the night, or if a bone-strengthening medication makes us feel sick, it's easy to make the connection and see how it reduces our quality of life. Side effects affect each individual differently. Some people will find the same side effect a minimal problem; others, grindingly detrimental.

In 2012, the *BMJ* published a 'patient journey' describing how a man, aged 55, with known heart disease was started on a statin, as is standard practice.[57] His partner described his

> 'muscle cramps, especially at night, in his calves and thighs, usually after a long walk... he found it an effort to keep his arms aloft to wash his hair in the shower or to walk up even mild slopes. Sitting became uncomfortable, his neck and shoulders ached, and he experienced pain after mild exercise or even just standing for fairly short periods. He started to age visibly: his limbs lost muscle tone, his hair fell out, and he began to look permanently anxious as his confidence eroded.'

He became depressed about his permanent tiredness and weakness, and obsessed with finding out what was wrong with him, spending most days reading medical reference books. This fixation developed into a loss of trust with all but a few members of the medical profession with whom he came into contact during his illness. He felt that nobody was listening to him and that any discussion he wished to have about the documented side effects of statins and how they might be affecting him was met with a wall of silence. Two memorable remarks that contributed to his frustration were, "If you don't take the statins, you will die" (his GP) and "Ah, you're on statins, you will live forever" (a hepatologist).

Fisher C, Freris N. **Neuromuscular degeneration.**
BMJ 2012; 345: e6880 www.bmj.com/content/345/bmj.e6880

When he stopped the statins, his symptoms improved dramatically. His wife wrote that he regained his *joie de vivre*: '…it seemed that we could get our life back together again now that he was starting to have the energy to do the things he used to enjoy.' His GP recommended he restart them, but his symptoms later returned. He was later diagnosed with motor neurone disease. The last few years of his life were made much worse because of the side effects of statins.

How likely was the statin to reduce the risk of having a heart attack or stroke? The patient and his wife heard an impossibility; that he would not die for as long as he took them. Trial data suggests that the statin could cut his risk of death (from any cause) from 12% to 8% over 5 years. Another way to look at this statistic would be: for this gentleman, the benefit of feeling miserable, daily, due to the statins translates into a 4% chance, over five years that death can be avoided as a result of taking them.[58]

The motor neurone disease was not caused by the statins. We will never know if this man delayed his death because of them, but we certainly know that his life was substantively impaired because of them. Through their contract with the government, GPs, in situations like this, must justify why they haven't prescribed statins. It would be far better if GPs were judged on whether they helped people make a rational decision. The doctors in this man's case were following the statin guidelines. They would have been awarded Quality points in their contract and earned money for their compliance in following the guideline instructions.

Had the patient decided that the possible benefits were worth the definite side effects, it would have been his own informed decision. It is tempting to conclude that the value of taking statins was prized by the patients' doctors, but not by the patient himself. The patient is the only person who can truly make a judgement about where the balance of harm and possible benefit lies.

There are even more subtle changes after treatments that will go missed unless they are carefully searched for.

> The second I found out I had cancer I gave up drinking. I don't think I have any quality of life any more – well, it's not the type of life I want to lead. My life was extraordinary before; it was very different to the norm. Now it's all about 'being careful'. I take six tablets every morning. They make me feel sick and they've bloated me out. I only had a short burst of chemo. It's unpleasant – your mouth and tongue split, your taste buds go – I couldn't taste the difference between a jam sandwich and a pork pie. The doctors told me that it wasn't working so there was no point in having any more – there was 'nothing more they could do for me'. That sentence still goes round and round in my head.
>
> Shaitly S. **Living with death.** *The Guardian*, 19 June 2011. www.theguardian.com/lifeandstyle/2011/jun/19/living-death-terminal-illness-cancer

For example, one study found that there were numerous effects of treatment for early prostate cancer – not just the known incontinence and erection difficulties but complex psychological outcomes and men's uncertainties over 'their capabilities and themselves'.[59]

Illnesses and new diagnoses can make us vulnerable, and fracture our confidence to live well. As one correspondent told me, after a borderline PSA test: 'Every day, every ache or pain is now possible cancer. Life has become a daily threat.' We need to consider these unintended hazards when we offer medical interventions, otherwise we will continue to offer treatments using gross quality of life measures when we surely need delicacy. Quality is individual, composed of subtlety and graduation.

Less is more

We've looked at how medications may have both benefits and side effects, but it is debatable whether we are getting quality of life value, on our own individual terms. There is far less data for GPs like me about the value of stopping long-term tablets. As we get older, the chances of a medication reducing our risk of heart attack or stroke over ten years diminishes as does the likelihood of us being alive that long. This is one of the reasons why many medications end up as life-long prescriptions, with doctors contractually encouraged to continue prescribing them, and often patients are afraid of what might happen if they stop them. Doctors, too, may be afraid to strike a drug off a list. Will they be blamed if a heart attack or stroke occurs without the patient being on preventative medication? Will the patient sue – despite what the statistics might say about the drug being unlikely to be responsible?

Despite the uncertainties about how much value for quality of life we get out of many of these kinds of preventative medications, the funding for them is easily had and unquestioned by the Department of Health. But in terms of our quality of life, should we keep taking medication until the end 'just in case'? We can never be sure about the future, except that we will at some time die. We have to decide what interventions make it worth our while until then. What do we spend our shared taxes on that gives us the best chances for good quality of life – on our terms?

Medical interventions are far from the only, or even best, solution to give people the ability to do what they want to do for longer, or to have a comfortable death.

Non-medical interventions can help improve people's lives just as much – or more – than pills or operations might. So, for example, in Uganda, people with HIV or AIDS who do not know where the next meal is coming from have worse physical and mental health.[60] It may seem obvious; but it is clear that it is not just effective medication which improves the outlook of people with AIDS, but the basic needs of life. People who have cancer often complain of tiredness, which can be due to the cancer itself, or the treatments used like chemo or radiotherapy. However few tablets have been found to be effective for it – beyond things like iron to correct anaemia, for example. Instead, it is not medication but exercise – like walking or cycling – which has decent trial evidence showing a useful improvement.[61]

Breathlessness caused by cancer, severe bronchitis or motor neurone disease can be a nasty, anxiety-inducing symptom for the person and their family to live with, and can be usefully helped by breathing training and walking aids.[62] Occupational therapy can increase independence and make deterioration less likely in people who have had a stroke.[63]

Certainly, there are numerous non-drug treatments that have no useful effect beyond placebo – like acupuncture – and we have to be equally critical and demanding of evidence of all interventions whether they come in the form of biochemicals or not. Pharmaceutical companies have the funds to run trials of new, profitable drugs; drugs which are out of patent or cheap are of far less interest. This means that investigating simple interventions – like exercise, or providing regular meals – will usually attract less money for research or, indeed, publicity of the findings.

So if we become frail and unable to dress without assistance, or unable to get to the shower, fixing these things may give us more quality of life than any statin or blood pressure medication can offer. In the research literature, there are few trials comparing medication and social care. We are left with a paradox; medications showing tiny potential gains will be approved and funded by NICE, but social care may be just as capable of giving us a better quality of life. But it comes with no guarantee of funding in the same way that highly rated QALY medicines are, meaning a fragmented mismatch of needs and funding.

Human needs with memory loss

As we age, gaining risk factors or drug prescriptions, we should therefore consider what will enhance or detract from our wants for our quality of life. And here it becomes impossible, and unhelpful, to distinguish health and social care needs.

People living in nursing homes are likely to be there because they cannot get enough care from social services visiting at home; because of their physical health – often including frailty – and, commonly, through dementia. Many people with dementia can clearly express what they want to prioritise in life – dementia is not necessarily 'all or nothing'. Some people have mild intermittent symptoms; some will find that by limiting their tasks and physical space they can remain orientated and able to gain much pleasure from their days. Other people, as the disease progresses, will be disorientated, hostile, will wander, will – entirely uncharacteristically – expose themselves, swear, or say abusive things to loved ones.

Nursing homes should bridge the gap between social and medical needs. However, if a person needs nursing home care, this may end up being self-funded, partially or fully, by the patient, through savings or equity in their home. Social care is funded in Scotland but not in England. But what's a medical need and what's 'social'? Losing the ability to eat and drink regularly; to wash and wear clean clothes, to take care of kitchen hygiene and remember to take medication; it's easy to see how these supposedly 'social' needs, if left unmet, deteriorate quickly into malnutrition, gastroenteritis, uncontrolled diabetes, falls and broken bones, skin and chest infections, all of which would then need NHS resources. Families and patients don't divide up their needs into social and medical. The two are in symbiosis. However trying to get access to required care and appliances can turn into a frustrating game of a funding pass the parcel.

An example of how social and medical care are interrelated is in the use of antipsychotic medication. This so called 'chemical cosh' has been commonly used to reduce aggressive or challenging behaviour in people with dementia, either as an 'as needed' or regular prescription. However, there is a clear association between the use of the drugs and increased death rates.[64] Consequently, the percentage of dementia patients being prescribed these drugs is now rapidly falling.[65]

Given the risks, why are these drugs still in use? One paper described doctors who faced 'genuine dilemmas about how to respond to distressed patients, relatives and carers, often in

And then the picking apart of my dads care needs started according to the domains we were looking at. It felt like a process, we were just an inconvenient number causing extra work in paperwork that would always have the same outcome – no funding. So lets look at my dads care needs in more depth at the time of the assessment. He was totally bed bound, could not obey commands and needed turning regularly on an air mattress. The only way to get him out of bed was to use a hoist which was extremely difficult as he was frail and unable to understand direction. In the chair he needed pillows to support him otherwise he would lean to one side.

He wore pads as he was unaware of the need to pass urine and was unable to feed himself. His swallow was impaired and [he] had to have thickener in his drinks and pureed diet which were given to him by my mother. His appetite was low and he was loosing weight something we were keen to emphasis at this meeting and common with advanced dementia. His medication needed to be crushed and given to him and much of the time he would spit it back out. He could not be left unsupervised as [he] was unable to do anything for himself and we felt as a family his care needs were high, he was at risk of malnutrition, dehydration and pressure sores and prone to recurrent infections. He was also on Warfarin for Atrial Fibrillation and a previous heart attack and in recent years had been treated for bladder cancer.

However none of this seemed to be defined as a health need, sadly because he was bed bound he was a low falls risk so scored low.

Marciano S-A. **No one should have to pay for End of Life Care...**
Extract from a blog post by Sally-Anne Marciano, 22 June 2013.
rayissunshine.blogspot.co.uk/2013/06/no-one-should-have-to-pay-for-end-of.html

ethically complex situations that involve a variety of risks'.[66] Essentially, these drugs may be used to help keep people at home where family members are trying to care for them, and where there is little other support to allow them to do so. Indeed in nursing homes, training and support for staff, for example in other ways to de-escalate difficult behaviour, can reduce antipsychotic use – often dramatically.[67] Social support can therefore have a profound effect on how much medicine people are given. Better social support can mean fewer medical needs.

The obvious and far more ethical answer would be for doctors to be able to prescribe more time and contact with skilled carers first, rather than medication. In the meantime, there is a struggle. Carers and doctors work with a constant

> Dad was a big, imposing man, who walked constantly, displayed agitation, confusion and some aggression, and an all-consuming desire to get out of the secure confines he found himself in. For the staff on that over-stretched, demanding ward, the simplest answer was to put him on medication so that he wasn't a 'problem' to them anymore. Our 'problem' with this, however, was considerable. Visiting someone who was suddenly struggling to walk and talk, was sleepy, incoherent and frankly even more confused, was alarming to say the least.
>
> Even with our then fledgling knowledge of dementia, we were convinced there was a better way, and challenged the ward staff. Our success was very limited however; they had their policies, and clearly had been allocated a staffing budget that did not allow for the one-to-one care needed to replace the easy-to-administer 'chemical cosh', with the more time-consuming and specialised therapeutic care that we were advocating.
>
> Moving dad to his first nursing home brought a refreshing change in attitudes. The staff were keen to remove the medication, and supported by the GP this was successfully achieved. For us it was exactly what we wanted, we had dad back. No matter what his symptoms, we found ways to manage them, and the care home staff were, for the first time, able to get to know the real man behind the dementia, and what a blessing that was.
>
> Britton B. **Ending the 'chemical cosh'**
> D4Dementia blog, 18 July 2012.
> d4dementia.blogspot.co.uk/2012/07/ending-chemical-cosh.html

dilemma; do these drugs, with their significant side effects, allow a person their preference to stay at home? Or are these drugs actually 'treating' a deficit in hands-on care?

I don't think it is ever possible to avoid all antipsychotic drugs in people with dementia – but it is much easier to cut them back when there is skilled nursing and social care to call on instead.

Quality of life is no less of an issue for people with dementia. But carers may not view quality in the same way as patients. About half the time, people with dementia can rate their own quality of life. One study in England measured how well the scores from patients matched with the estimates given by staff in residential homes. Essentially caregivers ascribed a lower quality of life score to the judgements people made for themselves. Caregivers also suggested that there was a lower quality of life when the person had behaviour problems. But residents, meantime, scored their quality of life lower if they were anxious or depressed. Overall, it was the person's mood which was the best predictor of quality of life – not the level of dementia.[68] When it comes to how to improve quality of life for people with dementia, research points firmly towards what happens person to person – talking, reminiscing, making things, exercise, and a feeling of making a 'meaningful contribution'.[69] For people in nursing homes, these kind of activities can reduce the risk of depression and behavioural problems.[70] We cannot divorce our social circumstances from our health.

Loneliness and health

The impact of loneliness on health is another illustration of how social and healthcare cannot be rationally separated. A review published in 2008 documented the ways in which isolation and the lack of close personal relationships related to health.[71] Between 5 and 16% of people aged over 65 in the UK describe themselves as lonely. Loneliness was found to be a risk factor for depression as well as a risk factor

According to a recent survey by Age UK, 10 per cent of adults aged over 65 feel lonely often or all of the time. With our growing older population this means that over 1 million older people are feeling chronically lonely today. This survey mirrors older research into the levels of loneliness in the United Kingdom and, worryingly, it seems to be getting worse.

This survey also found that:

- Just over one in ten older people said they felt cut off from society
- Almost a third of respondents said they would like to go out more often
- Two in five (41%) older people surveyed said that their TV or pet is now "their main form of company"

Neill-Hall J. **Latest statistics: over a million lonely older people in the United Kingdom**. Campaign to End Loneliness blog, 6 May 2014. www.campaigntoendloneliness.org/blog/latest-statistics-over-a-million-lonely-older-people-in-the-united-kingdom/

for poor physical health. Is this cause or effect? It may be more difficult for people with disabilities (bad bronchitis or arthritis for example) to get out to church or clubs easily. But it may also be that people who are unhappily alone miss the support of friends and family who would assist them with health problems – obtaining medication or accompanying them for appointments – to prompt seeing a doctor for new or worsening symptoms. The bottom line is that old people who describe themselves as lonely are more likely to die sooner compared to people who do not feel lonely.[72,73] Some researchers have even concluded, after systematically reviewing the evidence, that loneliness is as big a risk factor to health as being inactive or obese.[74] Furthermore, people who are lonely come into contact with health services more often, and see their GP twice as often as people who rarely or never feel lonely.[75] At its most potent, loneliness can masquerade as a deficit in healthcare. But medicine isn't what's needed – patients are at risk of having loneliness treated by medications like antidepressants when instead the need is for routine, regular human contact. This is too big a problem to be fixed by individuals; it's a problem concerning how society chooses to conduct its affairs.

People who describe themselves as lonely describe more pain, more fatigue, and more depression.[76] Older people who have less social interaction have a higher risk of depression.[77] Social isolation and chronic illness or disability in older people increase the risk of suicide attempts.[78] There are all sorts of crossover effects; in the US, a study found that people who felt a purpose in life had a lower risk of stroke.[79] In Australia, older people reporting a higher number of depressive symptoms had more falls compared to people

> When she was living 200 miles away I spent all my time imagining her unconscious in the stream at the end of her garden, developing hypothermia because she had forgotten how to put the heating on, or starving to death because she was forgetting to eat.
>
> Mum had also become terribly lonely. She had given up going out because she felt vulnerable. Her friends had melted away, and her family all lived busy lives and were too far away to see her regularly.
>
> So when she first came to me the change in her was delightful. Her face lost the haunted look it had started to acquire, she touchingly exclaimed every five minutes or so that she loved living with me, and she became her usual sociable and animated self.
>
> But it didn't last. First her ability to entertain herself deserted her. Reading was no use; she couldn't remember the plot. She started to hate her embroidery, unpicking it every time she did it and bemoaning her own 'stupidity'. After one particularly trying evening I hid the embroidery in the attic. It was never referred to again.
>
> Talbot M. **The sound of dementia.**
> Alzheimer's Research UK Defeating Dementia blog,
> 23 October 2013. www.dementiablog.org/sound-dementia

with lower symptom scores – and antidepressant medication increases the risk of falls.[80] Our physical, mental and social needs are intertwined, and we may as well embrace the fact.

A US study from 2007 took 823 older people who did not have dementia. Over the next four years, 76 developed Alzheimer's disease. The researchers asked people at the beginning of the study about how lonely they were and found that the risk of developing dementia was doubled in people who were lonely. Could loneliness increase the risk of dementia, or does dementia cause loneliness?[81]

The same study made over a hundred pathological examinations of the brains of the people who died during follow up. Brain tissue was examined for the typical pattern of cell and connection loss which indicates dementia. And while loneliness had doubled the risk of developing the symptoms of dementia – the loneliness was not related to having brain changes seen under the microscope. So loneliness increased the risk of developing the memory loss symptoms – but not the cellular changes in the brain which indicate Alzheimer's disease.

The symptoms we experience of memory loss may, therefore, not just be down to what is happening in the cells of our brain, but the interactions we have with the people around us. And, similarly, the use of antipsychotic medication for many people with dementia may depend on how much hands-on care we have, and not on how bad the dementia is. Again, and again, our social and health needs are dependent on each other.

Chapter 3

Too Many Tablets

Medical multiplication at the end of life

As we get older, we don't just gather more diagnoses, but more pre-conditions – risk factors, rather than diseases. That's another slew of medication – for high cholesterol or blood pressure, or to try and prevent thinning of the bones.

The grand plan is that this diagnosis of risk factors will prevent disease and keep our quality of life higher for longer. Doctors are now trained and computers equipped to search medical notes for these and our daily work is organised around their measuring and reduction. General practitioners have a contract with the government, where to be paid, they have to demonstrate that they are recording and treating risk factors. It is generally thought of as good practice; indeed, the points which GPs are awarded for doing this work are called 'quality and outcomes measurements'. And, indeed, preventing disease rather than treating its consequences would be the logical preference to prevent a potentially serious condition.

The outcome of the multimorbidity plus preventative medicine combination means drugs; lots of them. It means that in the UK, half the population over 60 years of age receive five or more medications annually. The rate of prescribing is going up, meaning that year on year, more people take more drugs.[82] People in nursing homes take an average of between six and eight medications daily.[83]

So what's the problem? These are medications that treat mental health problems, or high blood pressure. They are for people who are in pain, or are designed to help stop bone loss in people who are at risk of, or have, osteoporosis. Aren't these pharmaceuticals good for us? Isn't this progress – less suffering of anxiety or depression, less risk of heart attack or stroke, more ability to get up and down the stairs without knees that hurt, less risk of a fall leading to a hip fracture?

Perhaps. But, as we have seen, our social circumstances can cause people to go to the doctor when the problem is really loneliness, or a lack of social care. While there have been some moves towards 'social prescribing',[84] – like gardening clubs – the commonly offered ten- or twelve-minute appointment when the doctor's tools are prescriptions and referrals may hardly meet the person's needs. Even though doctors say they would like to use social prescribing, and people say they would like to have it, it is still a minority activity.[85]

In 2004 the *BMJ* published a study of 18,820 patients who had been admitted to hospital in Merseyside, England, in a six-month period.[86] The researchers wanted to know how often medication, through side effects, was responsible for the admission into hospital. They found that for 6.5% of patients – 1,225 admissions – the reason for the need for a hospital stay was related to an 'adverse drug reaction', leading to a median stay of eight days in hospital. The drugs that were implicated were the bread-and-butter drugs of modern medicine – aspirin, water pills like frusemide, warfarin (the blood thinner), antidepressants, betablockers (which are used in heart disease and for high blood pressure) and codeine-based painkillers, like co-codamol. These are the kinds of drugs that I, and GPs up and down the country, prescribe daily and, for me at least, with the comfortable cloak of familiarity. Sure, all drugs carry risk; but these are not the kinds of drugs which cause me to check my prescribing guide out of fear. Some of them can be bought over the counter in pharmacies; some can be bought with the milk and bread in a supermarket aisle.

But I am wrong – my comfort is misplaced. *The House of God* explains it well. Roy, the junior doctor, is asked by a nurse to prescribe aspirin to a patient, Sophie:

> …as I started to sign my name, I realised that I was responsible for any complications, and I stopped. Had I asked Sophie if she was allergic to aspirin? Nope. I did. She was not. I started to sign the order, and stopped. Aspirin causes ulcers. Did I want to have this poor LOL [little old lady] in NAD [no apparent distress] bleed out and die from an ulcer? I would wait for the Fat Man and ask him if it was all right. He returned.
>
> 'I've got a question for you, Fats.'
>
> 'I've got an answer. I've always got an answer.'
>
> 'Is it all right for me to give Sophie two aspirin for her headache?'
>
> Looking at me as if I were from another planet, Fats said 'Did you hear what you just asked me?"
>
> 'Yes.'
>
> 'Roy, listen. Mothers give aspirin to their babies. You give aspirin to yourself...' [87]

The book was written in 1978. In 1986, the use of aspirin in under 12s was banned in the UK due to the risk of developing Reye's syndrome, which can cause brain damage and organ failure; around half of children with the syndrome will die from it.[88] Since the change in advice, cases of Reye's syndrome have fallen from nine per year to one per year. [89] There is no question that the ease with which parents gave aspirin to their children in the 1970s was misplaced.

As for adults, Roy was also right to wonder whether aspirin was safe. Aspirin is an anti-inflammatory with blood-thinning qualities which is capable of treating heart attacks and muscular pain. But it comes with a risk of causing bleeding, especially in the stomach and, to a lesser extent, in the brain. In 1997, doctors in England analysed the case notes of 620 people who had been admitted to hospital with stomach problems. They matched them with a group of patients admitted to hospital but without stomach symptoms. They found that 31% of the people with gastric symptoms were using anti-inflammatories compared with 16% of comparable people not using them: and the more ill these patients were, the more likely they were to have been using anti-inflammatories.[90] A review of evidence of harm of anti-inflammatories published in 2000 showed that the risk of bleeding from the stomach or oesophagus because of taking them was increased by two to five times when taking anti-inflammatories regularly. There is a greater chance when risk factors accumulate – for example, age. This meant that, taking the baseline risk of a stomach bleed to be 1 in 1000 for a 75-year-old not taking anti-inflammatories, but a risk of 20 in 1,000 when they were taken regularly.[91] While, overall, the risk of gastric bleeding is more likely not to be down to anti-inflammatories, the drugs are likely to have caused 3,500 out of 8,500 hospital admissions due to bleeding from ulcers which occur annually in the UK, and 400 deaths.[92]

Roy was right to hesitate. If a drug works, it also has side effects. If it has side effects, it can do us harm. So when we prescribe it, are we doing the right thing? Where is the balance and how do we know when we have achieved it?

Preventative medicine

Older people are offered many types of screening to identify risk factors for diseases. There is more detail on what screening is and why it comes with attached problems in *The Patient Paradox* but, briefly, screening is done to people who do not have symptoms of a disease, in the hope that earlier knowledge of a disease process can lead to reduced problems later.

But diagnosing and treating more risk factors in older people comes with specific problems. Take osteoporosis, or thinning of the bones. As we get older, our bones lose some of their density. When we are between 25 and 30 years old, our bone mass is as its maximum, and after that, our bones are in a state of slow decline. This is the same for men and women, except in the years immediately after menopause, when women lose their bone mass more rapidly.[93] The cells in our bones are in constant flux, as bone is repaired and new cells laid down. Osteopenia means that the bones are of below average bone density – osteoporosis is more severe. The idea is that by identifying people at high risk of osteoporosis and osteopenia, treatments – usually via regular medication – can be given in order to prevent a fracture occurring by strengthening the bones and thus reducing the risk of a later fracture.

The problem is not just determining what is 'normal' when it comes to bone density, but also what benefit there is of screening and then treating it before there is a fracture. The tablets commonly used to try and treat bone density – calcium tablets and a daily or weekly tablet of bisphosphonates – are common prescriptions in older people. When we consider that 35% of Europeans aged over 50 are estimated to have a fracture caused by osteoporosis[94] the amount of people who would subsequently be treated with medication would enter the many millions – and between 23 and 46% of the female population who are thought to be higher risk for bone mass testing, are also eligible for preventative treatment.[95]

Over a million people in the UK take the most common kind of bone-strengthening medication – bisphosphonates – making them one of the most commonly prescribed drugs in the UK.[96] There is no doubt that a hip fracture, particularly in an already unwell person, can be a serious problem. Sometimes it is so serious that it leads, often through complications such as pneumonia, to death – analysis of NHS statistics suggests that 14% of people admitted to hospital aged over 65 and with a hip fracture will die.[97] So it would seem rational and humane to try and prevent fractures, especially if they lead to death. So how useful are the prophylactic treatments offered?

> I don't have Monday morning blues – I get them on Tuesdays instead. That's when I have to take my 'bone pill': alendronate, a commonly prescribed drug for osteoporosis. I religiously follow the packaging instructions: to swallow the tablet with a large glass of tap water, stay fully upright afterwards and neither eat nor drink for at least 30 minutes. So, no early morning cup of tea, no breakfast and no going back to bed, either.
>
> It may sound feeble but I've come to dread this early-morning ritual. I tell myself I'm lucky – a few years back, before the advent of the weekly pill, women on alendronate had to take it every day. I tell myself that I'm lucky in a deeper sense: thanks to sophisticated scanning techniques, my osteoporosis was diagnosed early (at 55), while the development of drugs such as alendronate (called biphosphonates) means, so the specialists tell me, that my weakened bones can be rebuilt and the future risk of painful and disabling fractures reduced.
>
> But two years after starting this treatment, I'm still ambivalent about it. Every week, I wonder whether or not to take my tablet. And, judging by the agonised discussions on internet forums, there are thousands of women in my position who feel the same.
>
> Hicks C. **Osteoporosis: is it being over-diagnosed and over-treated?** *The Telegraph*, 30 August 2010. www.telegraph.co.uk/women/womens-health/7967602/Osteoporosis-is-it-being-over-diagnosed-and-over-treated.html

For women who have already had osteoporosis diagnosed, a Cochrane review examined the effect of alendronate, one of the bisphosphonate group of drugs, which increases bone mass. Taking 100 women who already had a fracture or who were known to have osteoporosis, the drug could reduce the number of spinal fractures from 12 to 6. For 100 woman, hip or wrist fractures could be reduced from 2 to 1 per 100. Hip or wrist fractures could be reduced from 2 to 1 per 100 women. However, for women who had a normal bone density, or who did not have a fracture in their spine, they concluded that alendronate 'probably prevents fractures in the spine' and 'probably leads to no difference in fractures of the hip, wrist or bones other than the spine'.[98]

A Cochrane review from 2014 found that people at the highest risk of a fracture were most likely to benefit from taking vitamin D and calcium tablets – for example, for people living in a nursing home, there are around 54 fractures per 1000 adults, which can be reduced by 9 via taking the tablets regularly. However, for low risk people, the chances of benefit are much smaller. For older people living at home, the background risk of a hip fracture in a year is 8 per 1000, and this can be cut to 7 through the vitamin D and calcium tablets.[99]

How useful is the diagnosis of osteoporosis to direct preventative treatment to people most likely to benefit? One study looked at hip fractures occurring in a group of just over 8,000 women over five years. By the end, 243 of the women had a fracture – and 54% of those women had a normal bone density at the start of the study.[100] Bone density is not very useful for picking out women most likely to have a fracture.

So who has a disease, and who doesn't? Who should take preventative medicine, and when is it useless?

In 1992 a small group of researchers met in Rome as the 'World Health Organisation Study Group on Assessment of Fracture Risk and its application to screening for postmenopausal osteoporosis'. While they recognised that there is no true 'fracture threshold' they noted that the recommendation of when to start preventative treatment was 'somewhat arbitrary'.[101] So how did they decide what was normal? As reported on US National Public Radio, Dr Anna Tosteson recalled that 'Ultimately, it was just a matter of, well, it has to be drawn somewhere. And as I recall, it was very hot in the meeting room... and people were kind of in shirtsleeves, and it was time to move on, if you will. And I can't quite frankly remember who it was that stood up and drew the picture and said, well, let's do this.' The result was millions of people defined as having 'osteopenia'. However,

> The National Osteoporosis Foundation and American College of Obstetrics-Gynecology have expanded osteoporosis therapy recommendations by changing the treatment threshold. We determined the impact of this recommendation using nationally representative U.S. data. The new threshold changes the number of women for whom treatment is recommended from 6.4 million to 10.8 million among women age sixty-five and older (at a net cost of at least $28 billion) and from 1.6 million to 4.0 million among women ages 50-64 (at a net cost of at least $18 billion). Whether or not offering treatment to these additional women will reduce the number of hip fractures is unknown.... Broadening disease definitions can have major implications. Some patients may benefit from treatment that they would not otherwise have received. But broadening disease definitions also means that more people become patients. Simply labeling people as diseased leads to worry and has been shown to make people feel and act sick.2 Also, as more patients are diagnosed, more are treated, thus exposing them to the potential harms of treatment.
>
> Herndon MB, Schwartz LM, Woloshin S et al.
> **Implications of expanding disease definitions: the case of osteoporosis.**
> Health Affairs 2007; 26 (6): 1702-1711.
> content.healthaffairs.org/content/26/6/1702.full

Tosteson was clear that the category of osteopenia was created mainly to help researchers, not patients. They 'never imagined... that people would come to think of osteopenia as a condition to be treated'.[102]

This is important, because it can add to the medication list older people are asked to swallow down. Osteopenia is regularly hunted for in the UK, with private health companies offering screening for osteopenia. These scans often offer a smaller version of standard NHS equipment, which measures bone density in the wrist or heel. It's so portable I've even come across it being used in a booth in a shopping centre with an invitation to passers by to walk in and get tested.

The division between 'normal' and 'abnormal' bone density is thus unclear. While the NHS is clear that screening everyone isn't shown to be useful[103] women who have had a bone fracture or are at high risk of having one – like using long-term steroid tablets – are usually referred for scanning as part of normal NHS service. Doctors are encouraged to assess the risk of all women over the age of 65 using one of two risk calculators, either QFracture or FRAX.[104]

FRAX doesn't publish the details of how it's worked out – which is unusual.[105] Most of the other kinds of risk-calculating tools used in the NHS are freely available, with their foibles open, debated on and discussed. Not this one.

Frax was developed by the World Health Organisation in 2008 in an attempt to promote preventative treatments for osteoporosis.[106] However the meeting was sponsored by various foundations with links to pharma.[107, 108]

One of the organisations involved noted that they accept financial support from industry: 'it is a principle of the ISCD that collaborating with and accepting financial support from industry does not necessarily reflect a conflict of interest'.[109] Another noted: 'corporate support enables the Society to leverage its resources and increase its scientific offerings and impact'.[110]

> Not infrequently you see younger women who have been scanned for one reason or another and have been told they have osteopenia. These women have a low risk of fracture and don't have anything to gain from being on anti-osteoporosis treatments.
>
> Quote from Professor Stuart Ralson. In: McCartney M. **Clinical trial company tempts patients with free health screening.** The BMJ blogs, 21 May 2013. blogs.bmj.com/bmj/2013/05/21/margaret-mccartney-clinical-trial-company-tempts-patients-with-free-health-screening

It's impossible to know for sure how much influence pharma have pressed into the Frax calculators: all we can know is that the process cannot be guaranteed independent of industry. This, together with the veil over the calculations, means that informed consumer choice lacks in clarity in terms of influence.

In 1995, Fosamax, alendronate, was approved in the US as a drug which could be used prophylactically to reduce the risk of later fracture. The same year, Merck, the manufacturers, set up the Bone Measurement Institute. This organisation was a non-profit, with its own factory producing small, transportable Dexa scanners. The results were colour coded: a green test meant normal; red meant osteoporosis; amber meant osteopenia. A clinical professor on the board of the Institute said in a press release that 'only a small percentage of the 38 million women over 50 in the United States have had tests for measuring their bone mass, even though this group is considered at increased risk for osteoporosis'. There were 'promising treatments'.[111] As the numbers of these small bone scanners sold increased, so did the sales of Fosamax – from 281.3 million in 1996 to over 3 billion in 2004.[112] This drug was a blockbuster, aided and abetted by the portable scanners and new category of 'osteopenia'.

But thinking about an older person being offered a drug to prevent fracture, how much does it help? It's clear from the Cochrane reviews that most people taking them don't benefit. Alendronate has to be taken on an empty stomach, with one tablet taken with an 8oz glass of water. The person must not lie down or eat anything for 30 minutes after ingestion, side effects include inflammation in the gullet, mouth ulcers, flu-like symptoms, stomach pain, vomiting, dizziness, headache, hair loss, joint swelling and rashes.[113] There is also the question of what Merck calls 'jaw bone problems... infection and delayed healing after teeth are pulled'. This is osteonecrosis of the jaw, where the bone in the jaw fails to heal; the risk, in 2007, was thought to be between 1 in 10,000 and 1 in 100,000 per patient years on the drug.[114]

However, there was a high degree of uncertainty, and it was clear that in the first trials of alendronate, looking for dental or jaw problems specifically had not been done.[115] In 2010, a postal survey dedicated to looking just for mouth and jaw problems with people on long-term alendronate found that 1 in 952 people reported osteonecrosis of the jaw – a far higher risk than had been estimated.[116] As is often the pattern in medicine, if side effects are not specifically looked for, they aren't found.

Overall, jaw necrosis is still an uncommon side effect. But supposing you are being asked to take these tablets 'for the good of your bones' but feel unwell on them – what then? Where does the balance of risks lie? What's the chance of the drug stopping a fracture compared to the risk of the side effects?

There are no easy answers in taking or stopping medication. The Cochrane Collaboration has calculated the risks and benefits of taking alendronate for women who have been diagnosed with low bone density or have already had a fracture in their spine, and also for women whose bone density is closer to normal (see box on following page).

The vast majority of women will get no benefit from taking alendronate. Some women will want to take the drugs because they have no or tolerable side effects, and are content with the possibility of a small chance of benefit. Other women will be troubled with indigestion or be concerned about rarer side effects, and, balanced with the chance of preventing a fracture, will decide not to take the medication.

But do we get a chance to decide? Most bone scan reports make recommendations for treatment rather than the chances of risk and benefit from it. General practices have been incentivised through their contract to find and treat women who could benefit from treatment and have to justify why patients aren't on treatment – rather than why they are.[118] This bias risks treating people with medication which, given the information, they'd rather not have.

The best estimate of what happens to women who have already been diagnosed with low bone density or have already had a fracture in the bones of their spine:

Fracture of the spine
- 12 out of 100 women had a fracture when taking a placebo
- 6 out of 100 women had a fracture when taking alendronate

Fracture in the hip or wrist
- 2 out of 100 women had a fracture when taking a placebo
- 1 out of 100 women had a fracture when taking alendronate

Fractures in bones other than the spine
- 9 out of 100 women had a fracture when taking a placebo
- 7 out of 100 women had a fracture when taking alendronate

The best estimate of what happens to women whose bone density is closer to normal or who may not yet have had a fracture in the bones of their spine:

Fracture of the spine
- 3 out of 100 women had a fracture when taking a placebo
- 1 out of 100 women had a fracture when taking alendronate

Fractures in bones other than the spine
- 1 out of 100 women had a hip fracture when taking a placebo
- 1 out of 100 women had a hip fracture when taking alendronate

- 3 out of 100 women had a wrist fracture when taking a placebo
- 4 out of 100 women had a wrist fracture when taking alendronate

- 13 out of 100 women had a fracture somewhere other than the spine when taking a placebo
- 12 out of 100 women had a fracture somewhere other than the spine when taking alendronate

Wells GA, Cranney A, Peterson J et al.
Alendronate for preventing fractures caused by osteoporosis in postmenopausal women.
Cochrane Summaries, 7 September 2011.
summaries.cochrane.org/CD001155/MUSKEL_alendronate-for-preventing-fractures-caused-by-osteoporosis-in-postmenopausal-women

Searching for depression

The purpose of the contract general practitioners work to is to standardise treatments – and also to diagnose more conditions – which generally means more medication.

So, for example, if a person has a heart condition, they are also asked about symptoms of depression. This increases the chances of a person being prescribed antidepressants – around 80% of people who are coded in their doctors' records with depression are prescribed medication for it; and prescriptions for antidepressants in the UK now costs £364 million per year with 7.3 million prescriptions issued every 3 months.[118]

In practical terms, this means that many older people are diagnosed with depression along with their angina or chronic bronchitis. Antidepressant tablets are instantly prescribable, with no waiting list to join or appointment to arrange. But antidepressants come with side effects; for example, nausea, dizziness and sedation, even falls and confusion.[119] In patients who have been diagnosed with Alzheimer's disease, there is a concern that the medications don't work and simply produce side effects.[120] It is also clear that antidepressants don't have a useful effect in mild depression.[121] Additionally, it is common for antidepressants to be continued long term after someone has had several episodes of depression; but for older people, it is unclear whether taking the pills will help or not.[122] But the main alternative, cognitive therapy, will have a waiting list of months before starting – in my area, a typical wait is of 12-16 weeks. Even referring people for therapy opens a labyrinthine system – patients often have to be 'triaged' over the phone (uncomfortable for many), then repeatedly contact the clinic to say that they still want to be seen. Falling through the cracks is easy – depression can erode the self-confidence it needs to talk to a stranger about intimate feelings. This combination puts pressure on doctors to prescribe and results in millions of pills being given to older people – and many won't get anything but side effects.

Depression is a serious condition which is often very

disabling and distressing. There is evidence that medication is more likely to work the more depressed someone is.[123] If antidepressants were of clear benefit and little harm; fair enough – but they're often not.

Finding memory faults

The Department of Health decided, in 2012, that all patients aged over 75 admitted to hospital should be asked if they had noticed being more forgetful recently. To incentivise staff to do this, payments were made to hospitals who reached a 90% target of asking the question within 72 hours of admission; people answering 'yes' were to be given further assessments.[124] In the same year, part of the funding for the GP contract was given over to fund the screening of patients 'at-risk' of dementia.[125] The impetus for this policy came out of the political desire to increase the diagnosis rates of dementia; the health secretary, Jeremy Hunt was quoted on a press release as saying that 'NHS England is to tackle "shockingly low" dementia diagnosis rates with plans that could see 160,000 people who are unknowingly living with the condition identified and treated' within a year.[126]

In normal medical practice, when doctors, patients, family members or carers notice or disclose possible memory problems, it will be investigated and diagnosed as appropriate. Family members may accompany a relative to their GP, having noted a change in their behaviour, or short-term recall, looking for advice, reassurance, or a diagnosis. This is usually followed by further careful assessment, and diagnosis and treatment, as needed.

Screening people who are not otherwise complaining of memory problems is a very different matter. When teaching, I ask my young students whether they ever think their memory isn't good; on each of a dozen occasions, more than half have said yes. A healthy memory is imperfect; clearly, an imperfect memory does not mean dementia.

Government policy suggests that there are people who will benefit from a diagnosis who do not already have one or who will not be diagnosed through symptoms being noticed by the person, the doctor or family or friends.

This means screening; trying to detect a condition before it has been noticed by the patient. 'Mild cognitive impairment' (MCI) is frequently detected when older people fill out the memory questionnaires, like those used in the NHS.[127] When older people are asked, door-to-door, about their memory, around 5% turn out to have the criteria for diagnosing MCI. Yet this MCI will lead to dementia in only a minority of cases – less than 10% a year – with the majority of people not progressing to dementia over ten years of follow up after MCI was detected.[128] This means that screening which is intended to pick up dementia actually finds MCI, which will most likely not result in dementia. Furthermore, between 40-70% of people diagnosed with MCI will go on to have no worsening, or even an improvement – not a decline – in their memory.[129] Is MCI even a useful diagnosis?

Additionally, screening for dementia gives inaccurate results. A meta-analysis found that if 6 in 100 patients had dementia, a doctor would correctly identify 4 out of the 6, missing 2 people. However the doctor would also identify 23 people as having dementia – when they did not.[130] This is an enormous false positive rate – almost a quarter of people tested were in the 'dementia' category when they didn't have it.

Are there advantages to having a diagnosis made of MCI or dementia sooner than would have naturally happened when people or families seek help for noticeable memory problems? It may mean changes to driving, travel insurance costs, and anxieties for the future. Making a will and appointing a legal guardian are good things for all human creatures, with our limited life expectancies, to do. But being told we have a disorder for which there is little effective treatment and an expected decline may, where life is already at a good quality, have the potential to impede life rather than enrich it.

Nor does memory loss equal dementia – stroke, depression,

vitamin deficiencies, thyroid problems, the effects of excess alcohol, some prescription medications – can give similar symptoms. People with memory symptoms, especially if impacting on the ability to do things – can benefit from careful diagnosis, especially if there is a reversible or treatable cause of memory loss. For people who are living full lives and who have mild cognitive impairment, medication, in the form of cholinesterase inhibitor drugs (donepezil), has little to offer apart from side effects.[131] The chances of benefit from these drugs is higher in people who have been formally diagnosed with dementia – but is not revelatory. A Cochrane review has found that people taking them had an average increase by almost 3 points in a 70-point cognitive testing scale over a year, and a small improvement in the clinicians' 'global' impression of how the patient was doing, as well as the activities the person was able to do. However the people themselves did not rate their quality of life higher with the drugs; and there was no reduction in the time the carers spent helping people with tasks like getting washed and dressed.[132] The drugs are not curative: side effects include nausea, vomiting and diarrhoea, mainly 'mild' but severe in a few.

It's important to set the political drive for more diagnoses of dementia into context. There is no question that people who are having difficulties with memory, or their families and carers, should be able to get appropriate help and support as well as diagnosis and treatment. The hazard of driving up diagnosis rates through crude targets is of allowing many people to 'catch' a diagnosis of memory impairment when they won't benefit from the diagnosis – and can only be harmed from it.

And just to place this into wider context again: way back when donepezil was launched, in 1996, it was described as increasing the proportion of 'treatment successes' by 245%, with other professionals describing it as able to halve the incidence of Alzheimer's disease. The drug companies involved offered doctors promotional material including incomplete unpublished studies and ballpoint pens marked with the brand name.[133] The National Institute for Health and Care Excellence was lobbied strongly by charities to approve the drug. But the publicity may have misled some doctors and politicians about the effectiveness of drugs – even Jeremy Hunt wrote that 'drugs can help stave off the condition for several years'[134] when there is sadly no evidence that this is true. Some doctors did urge caution, way back in 1996 when the drugs were being appraised by NICE. Professor Raymond McAllister told the press that 'The problem with these drugs is that they have a very small effect in patients with advanced dementia which is of uncertain value. I would rather see resources allocated to the provision of better services for patients with dementia.'[135] Money and time is in danger of being directed at people with the least symptoms and ignoring people with the most and 'there is a risk it will result in reallocating resources that are badly needed for the care of people with advanced dementia.'[136]

Treating pain

Recognising when medicine is not useful or even harmful is crucial. The relief of suffering is a core value of medicine, and the identification and control of pain has become a pressing concern of healthcare over the last couple of decades, with the uprising of 'pain clinics' where patients who have hard-to-treat pain can be seen by specialists. Margo McCafferty, a nurse who has written extensively about the need for good pain management, famously said that pain is 'whatever the experiencing person says it is, existing whenever and wherever the person say it does.'[137] This view has much to commend it, as pain is subjective, personal, and varies according to what we are doing – being distracted from pain, for example, reduces our experience of it.[138] The standard healthcare response to pain is, usually, the prescription of painkillers. However the balancing of benefit and harm with medication can be extremely difficult.

This is especially the case with the trend to use dosette

boxes for older people who are taking multiple medications. Instead of a person taking individual tablets out of separate bottles or strips, the medication is placed inside a card where the tablets can be pressed out as a group at intervals during the day. These are designed to increase the amount of tablets taken and to reduce the risk of error. However when a person does not need the tablets – in particular, pain relief – but they are in the dosette box, they may be taken anyway. This means that medication is taken with no prospect of benefit – but with the risk of side effects.[139]

So what should we use to treat pain? Paracetamol is the standard first line for aches and pains, as it is relatively low in side effects. It certainly has a role and has been shown to be better than placebo in many situations such as for headaches.[140] However, it isn't that useful in other situations – for example, in the short term treatment of back pain paracetamol is only as good as placebo.[141] If the patient is keen on medication for pain – rather than tolerating it or trying to distract oneself from it – to be better than placebo, it needs to be of a different kind.

The next step is to use either anti-inflammatories or opioid-based drugs. The group of opioid-based painkillers includes codeine, tramadol, morphine, oxycodone and buprenorphine. They are stronger than paracetamol or aspirin and are usually prescribed for 'moderate' to 'severe' pain. They typically cause constipation, which often necessitates the addition of a laxative. Laxatives themselves can cause nausea, wind and cramp. Treating side effects results in even more drugs being prescribed – an endless catch-22.

Other drugs which are used to treat nerve pain such as gabapentin and pregabalin can cause nausea and sedation, and, like opiates, have also been reported as addictive.[142]

How hazardous are our pain medications? For many years, co-proxamol was a standard issue medication for people still in pain despite the paracetamol. Co-proxamol was paracetamol plus dextropropoxyphene, but concerns about its safety resulted in it being withdrawn by 2008. It was particularly toxic in overdose, whether intentional or not. After it was withdrawn there was a reduction in deaths due to poisoning from it: however, there were also increases in other pain medications being prescribed, and especially codeine-based medications.[143]

Tramadol prescribing has also increased in recent years. It acts on several brain receptors – it has opioid effects as well as serotonin and noradrenaline effects.[144] In 2005 there were 5.9 million 'daily defined doses' prescribed in the UK. Seven years later, it was 11.1 million.[145] That's an enormous upswing. Side effects include hallucinations, agitation, and nausea. A similar increase in prescribing is seen for fentanyl, which is mainly used via a patch delivery system which is absorbed through the skin and lasts for 72 hours. The number of prescriptions for it more than doubled between 2005 and 2009 alone. Buprenorphine, similarly, has increased its use year on year with a tenfold increase since 2005.[146]

So do they work? Certainly, opioids have been used for centuries internationally for precisely this reason; but opioids also bring a parallel accumulation of harm. Addiction and use for pleasure rather than for pain is well documented, from opium dens onwards, and people addicted to heroin are now offered medically prescribed substitutes. The truth is that it is easy for doctors to prescribe pain medication in the long term and it is easy for patients to take them, particularly in dosette boxes, for prolonged periods of time, even when they aren't working very well, accumulating side effects.

Twenty or thirty years ago, opioid painkillers were used primarily for cancer pain when death was expected to be weeks or months away. Now opioids are used for non-cancer pain, and for years at a time. As the British Pain Society said in 2010, 'the safety and efficacy of opioids in the long term is uncertain as is the propensity for these drugs to cause problems of tolerance, dependence and addiction. The benefits of opioid treatment for the patient must be balanced against burdens of long-term use as therapy for persistent pain must be continued for months or years.'[147]

What's going on? Pain may be better recognised and better treated. But maybe these drugs are being prescribed too often – to the extent where they become harmful. Tramadol, for example, causes dizziness and constipation, and many people complain of feeling unpleasantly 'woozy'. An analysis in the *BMJ* in 2011 expressed concern that in the US, the increase in prescribing opiods for non-cancer pain had been accompanied by an increase in deaths involving them.[148] There are signs that opioids are not useful for many of the things they have been prescribed for – arthritis of the knee or hip, for example. A Cochrane systematic review concluded 'the small to moderate beneficial effects are outweighed by large increases in the risk of adverse effects. Non tramadol opioids should therefore not be routinely used, even if osteoarthritic pain is severe'.[149] Often opioid-based drugs are used to try and avoid the hazard of gastric bleeding due to anti-inflammatory use. However a US study which examined over 36,000 patients with arthritis found that opioids presented safety risks similar to the rates of side effects with some anti-inflammatories, meaning that we should not presume that they are safer or better for us.[150] Finally, the disparities between rates of prescription of opioids between one part of the UK and another raise the question of whether it is the patients who are different – or the doctors prescribing them.[151]

Concurrently, awareness campaigns and websites created by drug companies such as Pfizer seek to get people to talk about their pain.[152] They have also sent GPs prompt cards to supposedly help patients to 'talk about pain'. The push to prescribe new pain drugs doesn't necessarily come directly from drug companies – but indirectly via patients who have (often unknowingly) been targeted by drug companies.

Sometimes it's more overt. In the US, the manufacturer of oxycodone – another opioid – used sales reps to target the doctors with the highest prescriptions of opioids – and thus the highest amounts of patients in chronic pain. They set sales targets, and issued coupons to give patients a free

30-day supply of medication. Prescriptions for this drug in non-cancer pain in the US rose from 670,000 in 1997 to 6.2 million in 2002. The sales reps were told to tell doctors that the risk of addiction was less than 1%, yet other studies pointed to a far higher rate of up to 50%.[153] While there is no suggestion that similar targeting by drug reps has occurred in the UK, we are in new territory. Sure, many people will take pain medication in limited amounts and with good effect. Many people won't get much in the way of side effects. But as we increase the numbers of people taking pain medication in the long term, we can expect new hazards of side effects and long-term use.

What about anti-inflammatories like ibuprofen or diclofenac? Side effects are more common in older people.[154] These drugs can interfere with kidney function, and there is a risk of stomach irritation and inflammation, risking bleeding. For older people in particular, this usually means adding a drug like omeprazole, which decreases acid secretion within the stomach. This is fair enough: there is evidence to suggest that it will reduce the gastric side effects caused by the anti-inflammatory.[155] But the side effects of drugs like omeprazole can include nausea, headache, abdominal pain, wind and even, rarely, vomiting. Less commonly they can produce a dry mouth, swelling of the fingers and feet, dizziness and fatigue. Certainly there are many patients who can use these drugs intermittently without too much trouble and who will find their pain abated and their lives improved. The downside is that some will not.

Clearly, no patient should be in unnecessary pain. But the proliferation of available, strong opiod-based drug prescriptions in long-term use has brought an uncertain mixture of hazard and benefit which deserves scrutiny – and consideration before swallowing.

Sleep and sedation

We have thankfully moved on from the routine overprescribing of hypnotics like Valium (diazepam) and temazepam which occurred in the 1960s and 1970s with little concern about their addictive potential. The number of prescriptions for temazepam, which is a longer acting drug, is in gradual decline, but the overall numbers of these benzodiazepine drugs prescribed is now more or less constant.[156]

When a junior doctor, it was drummed into me that benzodiazepines could be useful for a few days to help disrupted sleep – after a bereavement, say – but were a bad idea in the long term. It's estimated that around 80% of all hypnotic drugs are prescribed for people aged 65 and over[157] and about 20% of prescriptions are for long term use.[158] Why the concern? The side effects of benzodiazepines include problems with memory and attention, as well as increasing the risk of accidents, including road traffic accidents – which although small overall, must be considered when the tablets are in widespread use.[159] Crucially, they cause dependence, which means that stopping them suddenly can make many people feel anxious, agitated, low in mood – and occasionally, can result in hallucinations. Even a single dose of diazepam given as a test to otherwise well older people resulted in small but detrimental effects on memory, and the ability to grip strongly.[160]

Many people feel not simply physically but psychologically addicted to these types of drugs – the modern versions include zopiclone and zolpidem – and don't want to stop them. For doctors, it can feel easier to continue the prescription rather than challenge the need to try a gradual reduction in doses. No surprise, then, that reviewing the evidence, and finding multiple harms and a lack of benefit of long term prescribing for patients, the *Drugs and Therapeutics Bulletin* decreed that 'The current and long-standing high level of prescribing of hypnotic drugs, mostly in older people, represents a risk to individual and public health and cannot be justified.'[161] Another study from 2000 examined the reasons for prescribing hypnotics in people aged over 65 when they were admitted to hospital and found that almost two thirds were essentially inappropriate – not benefiting patients and risking harm.[162] In other words, older people are taking benzodiazepines outwith guidelines and with side effects. And let's not forget that these are not miracle drugs to begin with. People taking them for insomnia get less than an extra hour's sleep beyond placebo – a difference, but not an enormous one.[163]

Most worrying, these drugs have been implicated in raising the risk of dementia. A study in France examined over a thousand people, with an average age of 78.2, over 15 years. In the people who had never used benzodiazepines, the risk of dementia was 23%. In people who started to use them, the risk was 30%.[164] This was not a forward-looking, randomised controlled trial, and it's not possible to conclude that the drugs caused dementia. It may have been, for example, that people with dementia also had more disturbance in their sleep and sought help resulting in these drugs being prescribed. However a similar association in the diagnosis of dementia was found in Caerphilly in Wales, in a study of over a thousand men, over 22 years, published in 2011. This study tried to reduce the risk of bias by adjusting the results for psychological distress – because it could be that sleep problems cause the dementia rather than the benzodiazepines – but still found an increased risk of dementia after using the drugs.[165]

While still not absolutely conclusive, the uncertainty over whether benzodiazepines are implicated in causing dementia should at least mean caution. Why do we still use them in the long term? Frankly, and in the main, because they are addictive. A small sample of older people were asked in 1996 why they started taking them; the reasons given included stress and being overworked. But the reason as to why they still took them included habit, to control irritability, and 'doctor's orders'.[166]

> A case study in the *Journal of the American Medical Association* described how an 87-year-old woman, who had taken benzodiazepines for 15 years, started on them because 'I had nobody to talk to for advice or anything. I saw a doctor and he suggested Xanax (alprazolam) [a benzodiazepine]. It just took my mind off what was going on for a while. So I got hooked on this. I know it's an addiction, but I had to clear my mind to keep living. So many times, I felt like jumping into the pit of a subway station to get it over with. I was so tired and downcast. I felt very low, and maybe depressed. Nobody seemed to be able to help. But a certain doctor gave me Xanax. So that was a bit of relief.'
>
> Salzman C. **An 87-year-old woman taking a benzodiazepine.** *JAMA* 1999; 281 (12): 1121-1125. jama.jamanetwork.com/article.aspx?articleid=189206

Was it useful and humane to prescribe this medication for her, when she was in such distress? Or was it inviting addiction while not addressing her underlying problems? Psychological services are in short supply and with long waiting lists – one in five people wait over a year for treatment.[167] Many people find it difficult to engage with talking therapy, for a variety of reasons. For some, it is difficulties with time, or transport – others will feel discomfort in such an intimate relationship, and have pain not just of disclosure, but vulnerability. Clearly it would be wrong to force people into psychological treatment, and it's easy to see how some may feel worse if pushed into a treatment they don't have confidence in or feel raw or exposed in. Short-term prescribing is far less of an issue – but every long-term prescription began with a shorter term one. The reason for starting the prescription may not be the reason why it is continued; dependency and addiction, acknowledged or not, is likely to be a contributing factor in many cases. And the long-term, slow reduction in doses recommended can be difficult to achieve, needing much patience and time.[168]

It might be more useful to examine how much sleep we need anyway. Older adults frequently need less sleep as they age, or sleep but with a period of wakefulness during the night.[169] There is a wide variation in 'normal' and a broad range of sleep patterns which can still give the person enough rest. If a lack of sleep is causing tiredness non-drug treatments can be useful, such as talking treatments.[170] But the waiting list for psychological treatment is usually weeks or months; the cost of temazepam is pence and can be immediately prescribed. And while these should not be the most important factors in the prescribing equation, in reality, sadly, they often are.

Gathering medicines, like storms

These examples show how the risk of being prescribed multiple regular medications – polypharmacy – is promoted by a lack of rapid access to psychological services, pressures to prescribe from the GP contract, pushes from the pharmaceutical industry, and often a desire for treatment from patients and their families. I do not wish to be nihilistic. Even if the chance of benefit, from, say, preventing a fracture through taking alendronate is only 1 in 100, this would still stop thousands of fractures if millions of women took it. The question for each person is of balancing benefits and risks.

Generally, when drugs are tested, they are done in trials of people who tend to be healthier than average. Older people are less likely to be included in trials examining treatments for heart failure, angina, dementia and depression.[171] This is ironic, given that people over the age of 65 are on an average of two daily drugs, and 10% are on more than five drugs. So, while people over the age of 65 make up 20% of the UK population, they take almost half of all drugs prescribed nationally.[172] Some multiple prescriptions are standard. A patient who has had a heart attack will be put on aspirin, a beta blocker like atenolol, an ACE inhibitor like ramipril, two blood thinners – one being aspirin, a cholesterol-lowering statin, and a GTN spray to use in case of further chest pain; these are recommendations borne out of high-quality research demonstrating reduced risks of later heart attack.[173] These will all be anticipated life-long treatments (with the exception of one of the blood thinners, usually prescribed for a year only.). For a patient with chronic bronchitis, at least one, if not two or three inhalers will be routinely prescribed.[174] A patient with high blood pressure may be treated with multiple medications to get it under 'control';[175] a patient with back pain or arthritis can be expected to be treated with paracetamol or anti-inflammatories, codeine or amitriptyline, which is an antidepressant in large doses and a painkiller in smaller aliquots. But what about taking multiple drugs together, and the side effects?

Predicting who will get what side effects is very difficult. Ironically it can also be difficult to sort out side effects from the condition one was trying to treat in the first place. Prescribing often has a 'chain reaction' effect: one prescription leads to side effects, which leads to another drug to quell the side effects, and a ballooning of symptoms and prescriptions, such that distinguishing the symptoms of illness from the

> One of my colleagues told me a salutary story. He went to visit a patient of his the day she died, and the lady's daughter said: 'Would you please get rid of these when you leave, doctor?' She handed over two black bin-bags.... full of bottles of simple linctus, courses of tetracycline, throat sprays, topical NSAIDs, antihistamines, clotrimazole cream, vitamin tablets, evening primrose oil, all those prescriptions we issue when time is short and there's nothing wrong with the patient. He was confronted with a decade's worth of untouched useless medication, and the hard evidence of hundreds of consultations where the hidden agenda had been well and truly ignored. He told me he had never been so embarrassed.
>
> Peverley P. **Strontium limited.** *Pulse,* 6 September 2014 www.pulsetoday.co.uk/strontium-limited/10917772.article#.U6bzHxYdU20

side effects caused by medication is bewildering – escalating rapidly and almost unstoppably.

This is one side of medication overload – some people opt out of taking any. Other people don't take all their prescribed medication all the time, either because they forget, they have intolerable side effects, or because they simply don't want to. This can include people who don't want to take the medication and don't want to tell their doctor or nurse of their decision.

The World Health Organisation calculates that about 50% of people don't take their medication as prescribed.[176] Over the course of a year, medicines taken for mental illness are stopped over three quarters of the time. Little wonder, when the side effects include sexual problems in over 60% of men and almost 40% in women; in one study, 25% of patients were unhappy with their medication and over 80% had said they missed or skipped doses.[177]

Patients have a right to autonomy over what they do with their tablets. The more telling question is why people don't take prescribed medicines which should have been decided upon with discussion and agreement.

One US study performed by a pharmaceutical company found that while cost was a reason for stopping medication, the next most common reason was side effects.[178] The same pharmaceutical company, Merck, also found that the more side effects a woman experienced on alendronate for osteoporosis, the less likely she was to take it.[179] Another study found that treatments for overactive bladder were stopped because they either didn't work – or because of side effects.[180] In the meantime, in another study, people taking regular medications for pain were concerned by the potential for addiction, side effects on withdrawal, and whether or not they needed the medication.[181]

Looking past the promotion of medications, many patients have mixed feelings about taking regular medication. Side effects may seem medically insignificant on paper and to doctors – 'nausea', 'fatigue' and 'constipation' are often classed as 'minor' symptoms – but in real terms may be absolutely horrible and unacceptable to patients.

Much research has focused on trying to find ways to increase the numbers of patients taking their prescribed medications.[182,183] This may be reasonable, since other research has found that patients who don't take certain prescribed medications regularly, such as beta blockers after a heart attack, are at increased risk of death.[184]

This is complicated by research showing what's called the 'healthy adherer' effect. A large meta-analysis – which pulled together multiple studies – examined almost 50,000 people taking medicine in different scenarios. The examiners looked at the relationship to death and how well people stuck to taking the prescriptions the doctors ordered. The death rate was lower in people taking their regular, beneficial, medication. But, crucially, the researchers also examined people who were taking placebos, biologically inactive substances; dummy pills. The death rate was also lower in people who took the placebos regularly. In other words, people who take the tablets they are prescribed die less frequently – but this isn't necessarily because of what's in the tablets.[185] It may be because these people – the 'healthy adherers' – also happen to have other healthy lifestyle factors – such as eating better or exercising more. The tablets themselves may sometimes be a partial red herring.

This gap between what some patients feel about taking medication – concerns about side effects and addiction – and what doctors are meant to be doing – following guidelines – can create a conflict. We have thankfully shifted from 'compliance' – patients expected to follow doctors' orders – to 'concordance' – an agreement between patients and healthcare staff as to what medication or treatments to take. This should mean dialogue, discussion and free choice rather than paternalistic instruction.

But how often does this kind of informed discussion happen? The pressure on primary care is enormous; despite appointment times now being almost 12 minutes long in the UK.[186] On average, 2.5 problems are discussed per appointment – and 40% of the time, more than three separate issues.[187] The computer prompts the GP to do or record certain things – a flu vaccination, a question about smoking; if a patient is not prescribed the instructed medication, in order to claim contract points the patient must be 'exception reported' rather than simply left alone. Every day I am ashamed of how much all this background is distracting me from what the patient wants to talk about.

How far have we come in helping patients make good choices about medication – and thinking about side effects? The language used by the British Medical Association to describe the circumstances in which a patient may be 'exception coded' as not taking a medication is insightful. ('Exception coding' is the means whereby patients are taken off the standard treatment protocol, as recommended in the GP contract.) For example:

> '...patients who have been recorded as refusing to attend review who have been invited on at least three occasions... patients for whom prescribing a medication is not clinically appropriate eg those who have an allergy, contraindication or have experienced an adverse reaction... where a patient does not agree to investigation or treatment (informed dissent) and this has been recorded in the medical notes following a discussion with the patient...' [188]

The language is of polarisation; the doctor is assumed to intend to prescribe, and the patient either 'refuses' to attend for a review, or 'does not agree' to take medication. The patient is on the defensive against medical interference, and the doctor is on the prescribing offensive. There is no mention, in the exception coding, for the kind of evidence-based, shared decision making which allows people to weigh up their priorities and preferences against the uncertainties which guidelines may not make obvious. The BMA say that 'practices may be called on to justify why they have "excepted" patients from an indicator during verification and this should be identifiable in the clinical record'. In real terms, this means that, every year, patients have to be re-exception coded. Doctors have to regularly justify why they are not prescribing, rather than why they are. The words of Charlotte Williamson, the first chair of the patient liaison group of the Royal College of General Practitioners, had it right. 'Patient autonomy requires that the patient be free of coercion, whether overt or covert. The doctor, too, must be free of coercion, free to explore values, perspectives, anxieties and clinical evidence, free to discuss all possible courses of action with the patient.'[189]

There are scarce research studies examining the interactions of so many medicines. Older people are at greater risk of side effects from many medications, but the intonation from research papers encouraging doctors to 'be aware of the risks and fully evaluate all medications at each patient visit to prevent polypharmacy from occurring' is, with the current pressures on the NHS, easier said than done.[190]

This is important because as we reach the age when death is to be expected, our lives are not simply about the number of days we have left to live, but how we intend to live them. If we cannot get out to visit friends or to tend the garden – or whatever it is that is important to us – because of the side effects of medication, we should question it. We may have started a medication in good faith and because it seemed, initially at least, to help us; but it is just as important to know when to stop it. In many ways we have a perfect storm; more medications for more risk factors or for diagnoses which we didn't need – but the accumulation of side effects. For older people in particular, talking about the risks and benefits of medication and making choices to take or stop should have a high priority. This isn't primarily about saving costs – it's about quality of life.

Chapter 4

Caring Not Curing

When the best treatment is palliative

In practice, palliative care is usually basic and unglamorous. It is talking about which cancer treatments to take, and what to stop. Thinking about where it would be best to die. Ongoing, personal conversations about where the pain is, or how the bowels are working. Care of the partner, the children; making sure that enough sleep still comes, and that the pleasures of life – a book, a bath, the garden – are prioritised.

'Palliation' is often taken to mean an emollient when we 'fail' to 'cure' symptoms, a shoulder-shrug to 'hope', and a dose of pessimism where patients 'give in' and doctors 'give up'. Many people who hear the 'palliative' word will imagine that treatment is now over and death is imminent.

It should mean nothing of the sort. Palliative care means diligent attention to symptoms – nausea, pain, frailty, constipation, mobility, nutrition. It is about time and effort attending to distress, whether physical, mental or spiritual. The aim is not necessarily to live longer, but to live better.

The NHS often fails to provide enough palliative care. Many hospices, whose speciality is in the delivering of palliative care, are not fully funded by the NHS but by charity efforts, meaning that funding can be erratic, and bed numbers are based on the ability of the community to fundraise and not simply on the needs of the people living there. In practice, most palliative care is provided by general practitioners and district nurses.

Palliative care should not be patchy. It should be centre stage, one of this century's block-busting medical interventions – for it can give quality and quantity of life that healthcare without it can't provide.

It seems illogical. Indeed, there had been concerns that perhaps people who opted for palliative care rather than active treatment of some disease might die sooner. In the *Journal of Pain Symptom Management* in 2007, researchers reported on a sample of 4,493 Medicare patients being treated for certain cancers and congestive heart failure (which can have a prognosis similar to some cancers). They looked at the time terminally ill patients lived for and whether or not they used hospices. The results: hospice care did not shorten lives. In fact, patients who had hospice care lived longer, by an average of one month.[191]

Living longer is all very well; what about quality of life – the aim of palliative care? That study wasn't designed to answer that question. However, another study published in the *New England Journal of Medicine* in 2010 was. Patients with a particular type of lung cancer were randomised to two groups. One group were given palliative care early on, the others got standard care. There were differences. One third of the group given palliative care had aggressive care – such as cardiopulmonary resuscitation – at the end of life, versus 54% in the usual care group. But here's the thing; the palliative care group reported a higher quality of life and better mood in their last months, but also lived longer. Thirty months into the study, 30% of the palliative care group were alive compared with just over 10% of the control group.[192] Were palliative care a drug, one could imagine campaigns, slogans and incentives to push doctors into prescribing it. But such a simple, patient-focused and technologically modest intervention is not the stuff of dramatic advertising.

Why should attention to the basics make such a difference? One profound reason is postulated by the researchers saying 'patients who are already in a very weakened condition avoid the risks of overtreatment when they make the decision to enter hospice. This factor may be particularly relevant to terminally ill oncology patients who forego aggressive cure-directed therapies. Intensive medical interventions such as high dose chemotherapy or bone marrow transplantation always carry a significant risk of mortality.' The treatments designed to lengthen life may paradoxically reduce it – along with the patient's quality of life.[193]

Still, one survey of doctors looking after people with lung

Health, social, and palliative care services are continuing to fail many people with progressive chronic illnesses in whom death may be approaching, reflecting a failure to think proactively and holistically about their care... Prognostic paralysis has been described, whereby clinicians of patients with uncertain illness trajectories prevaricate when considering end of life issues... one general practitioner graphically summarised the feelings many experience in caring for people with terminal heart failure: 'You're paddling down-stream to Niagara.' Another felt reduced to clinical tasks: 'I feel impotent, merely a blood leech and monitor.'... Estimating prognosis is an inexact science, but prognostic uncertainty should not prevent us talking with our patients about this issue, as a noteworthy number will die suddenly. We must not inadvertently fall into the trap of prognostic paralysis. So when we are next monitoring prognostic indicators and observe an irreversible decline, why not simply ask ourselves: 'Would I be surprised if my patient were to die in the next 12 months?' And if the answer is no, we need to give the patient and his or her family an opportunity to plan for a good death, instead of just monitoring a downward set of physical variables until death.

Murray SA, Boyd K, Sheikh A. **Palliative care in chronic illness.**
BMJ 2005; 330 (7492): 611-612.
www.ncbi.nlm.nih.gov/pmc/articles/PMC554893/

cancer in the US found that only a quarter referred their patients to palliative care colleagues; many said it could alarm patients or their families, or that patients wanted to focus on 'cures'.[194] Certainly, talking about death and *appearing* to suggest a 'less hopeful' route of palliative care can be uncomfortable. If a doctor knows she is running late, under pressure to get to the next patient, it can be easier to let the chance for an emotionally difficult discussion melt away. Families, too, have reported that it can be hard to hear and accept bad news.[195] Bearing in mind the difficulty in predicting when death will occur, it can feel more comfortable for doctors and patients to leave the subject alone. This would, though, be a mistake, meaning that people did not get a chance to decide on whether palliative care would be more likely to improve the quality of living.

In 2010, the *Journal of the American Medical Association* published a study of 332 patients with advanced cancer.[196] A third of patients reported having a discussion with their doctor about care at the end of their life. The patients were then followed up. The patients who had talked through and planned their end of life care had less chemotherapy, less intensive care, less mechanical ventilation, less resuscitation, and more hospice care compared to the other group. And, crucially, the patients who did talk it through with their doctors had a higher quality of life in their last days compared to the other patients. This study wasn't able to compare the difference in survival rates between the two groups of patients. But the researchers were able to find out what effect these choices had on the bereaved families. The families of people who had more aggressive care had a higher risk of mental health difficulties later on. In other words, the evidence of harm in this study was in not having a conversation about the end of life, rather than having it. Additionally, families reported more feelings of regret, and unpreparedness for the death, when that conversation hadn't been had.

The patients who had these end-of-life conversations

> The failure of doctors to talk to their patients about end of life decisions perplexes me. This gap in vital communication results in poor care, uncontrolled pain, futile treatment and death in hospital or nursing home, where no patient wants to be... I have generally taught my students that this failure results from a 'culture of cure'. Doctors and patients focus so hard on treatment, whether it's fighting cancer, heart disease or even Alzheimer's, that they ignore the reality that all life eventually ends. Lost is the opportunity to plan for end-of-life needs, which can deny the patient and family a gentle passing. Doctors falsely see death as the great enemy, instead of suffering and disease. Often the illogical emphasis on cure at any cost is key to poor end-of-life communication.
>
> Salwitz J. **Man: the demi-god dies.**
> Sunrise Rounds blog, 29 January 2013.
> sunriserounds.com/man-the-demi-god-dies

would have been talking about what treatments they would, and wouldn't, want to have. They would have discussed their symptoms and their fears. More of these patients had accepted the terminal nature of their disease, and more wanted interventions to help with pain, and improve quality, rather than extend their life. Most asked not to be resuscitated if in cardiac arrest. Indeed, as more time was devoted to the fair discussion of pros and cons, the less medical treatment people wanted – but the more medical care they got.

Iatrogenic (doctor-caused) harm is often not obvious except in harsh, sceptical retrospect. Many patients who have had difficult or unpleasant treatments – blood tests, scans, biopsies, operations – will want to believe that they endured the side effects to live longer. We have to confront the truth. Basic nursing and doctoring can, in many situations, improve quality of life better than aggressive medical treatments. Looking after peoples' symptoms well, and using hospice care, makes people live, on average, longer and higher quality lives. Families of bereaved people do better when the death was planned for, and when less aggressive treatment is given. The death is more peaceful, and the patients who had these discussions were no more likely to be depressed than those who didn't.

If only this knowledge was shared with patients and families who are more afraid of palliative care than of chemotherapy or radiotherapy. In fact palliative care may still involve both of these – radiotherapy can, for example, reduce the size of tumours to relieve pressure on nerve endings – but the aim is symptom relief, not 'cure'.

Simple, crucial, humane care

Such low-tech, human care pays dividends. This does not just hold true in formal palliative care, but for frail people living in nursing homes. Small studies have shown that people with mild or moderate dementia can become less agitated if paracetamol is given on the presumption that distress is a sign of pain;[197,198] treating it can improve the quality of life of the patients.[199] And paracetamol is cheap, simple and relatively safe.

Another straightforward intervention is a 'psychosocial' programme, often run by a psychologist, occupational therapist or nurse, for staff in nursing homes for people with dementia, which as we have seen, can reduce antipsychotic medications used; indeed, it is the culture within organisations which appears to predict most closely the rate of prescriptions of antipsychotic drugs.[200]

But what is this 'organisational culture'? It's easy for media commentators to distill this kind of study into the quick conclusion that, obviously, the staff are insensitive, workshy and uncaring, and that the universal fix of 'more training' or 'more awareness' for staff is needed. If this kind of pronouncement could fix the faults in caring, it would be sorted by now.

Instead, if we want sustainably better care for people, we have to understand why the interactions patients have within health services go wrong, and how they could be helped to go better. We have to examine where the vast majority of healthcare comes from in order to support it. Not from technological black boxes, but from the hands of healthcare professionals, family and friends, and patients themselves – and how we can do it better together.

Care and pathways

The Liverpool Care Pathway came about through good intentions. There were not enough beds in hospices. So the end of life decision-making common to palliative care was encouraged in general hospital wards and general practices. The actual pathway made clear that 'Uncertainty is an integral part of dying. There are occasions when a patient who is thought to be dying lives longer than expected and vice versa.' Comprehensive and clear communication about what treatments were recommended to be used and to stop was 'pivotal'. It was also clear that the LCP 'does not preclude the use of clinically assisted nutrition or hydration or antibiotics... A blanket policy of clinically assisted (artificial) nutrition or hydration or of no clinically assisted (artificial) hydration is ethically indefensible'.[201]

The LCP was developed in the 1990s, applauded widely and noted as 'best practice' in the NHS Beacon Programme in 2001. Hospices generally get good press. The Liverpool Care Pathway got anything but.

In late 2012, newspapers started to run features and news articles claiming that the LCP was a 'death pathway'. One columnist opined that it was 'a backdoor form of euthanasia' and claimed that 'Terminally ill patients have been heavily sedated and deprived of essential nutrients and fluids in order to make them die more quickly.'[203]

One professor of neuroscience was reported as saying 'The lack of evidence for initiating the Liverpool Care Pathway makes it an assisted death pathway rather than a care pathway. Very likely, many elderly patients who could live substantially longer are being killed by the LCP.'[203] He gave an example of a 71-year-old patient who bled into his brain. This resulted in seizures. He already had dementia and required assistance to walk. After the brain injury, he developed pneumonia and, agitated, continued to have seizures. The doctor and nurse on the ward had placed the patient on the LCP and started a syringe driver containing morphine. His relatives said they did not agree to this, and the neuroscientist described 'significant resistance' as he removed him from the pathway. He was discharged four weeks later. He needed a wheelchair, ramps to be put into the home to allow him to get in and out, a commode, a hoist to lift him in and out of bed, and community nursing. He had a PEG (percutaneous endoscopic gastrostomy) tube inserted for feeding and died 14 months later of pneumonia.[204]

We do not know what the patient himself felt; whether his life was tolerable or pleasurable, or whether he was in pain or discomfort; only he would know. Clearly, doctors and nurses should not be the judge or jury when it comes down to making decisions about quality of life. The idea of a healthcare professional deciding that our life is no longer of sufficient quality to merit treatment, thus leaving us to die, should strike us as abhorrent.

Not informing patients as to what is happening is poor practice and should not be defended. Going against relatives' wishes is deeply problematic, although there are times when this is the most ethical thing to do – for example, if a patient has previously expressed contrary wishes to those of the relatives. (The opposite is also true – a relative wanting no treatment when the patient desires it.)

High technology medicine can be used to prolong life without taking into consideration whether this is a wise, or kind, action to take. Compelling doctors to deliver medical treatments when there is no chance of benefit – as CPR (cardiopulmonary resuscitation) or renal dialysis would be in many circumstances – would serve to standardise medical cruelty. No death would be allowed until every last possible intervention had been tried – chemotherapy, operations, toxic drugs, or ventilation machines. We know that most people want to die at home; it is also clear that many people do better with palliative care and would prefer not to have aggressive interventions with little benefit. A precedent that insisted that all treatments must always be offered would not allow for peaceful, gentle deaths at home. Every death would become a battle against the odds and always a failure of medicine.

So if the compulsion always to treat cannot be enforced, how should we find our way? Certainly, we can no longer look to the LCP. The media campaigning resulted in a review, published in 2013, titled *More Care, Less Pathway*. It concluded that 'when the LCP is operated by well trained, well resourced, and sensitive clinical teams, it works well'.[205] However, it was clear that communication from hospital staff was often described as poor by relatives, and, crucially, there were stories of dying patients being refused a drink – which is painful to read, and in absolute contradiction to the statements within the pathway itself.

What is the evidence for use of the LCP in practice? One study of 255 patients found that the use of the LCP was associated with fewer symptoms when compared to it not being used,[206] while previous reviews had found insufficient evidence of benefit.[207] When the LCP was withdrawn, palliative care experts voiced concerns that dying patients or their relatives were afraid to come into hospital, lest they too were subjected to the LCP.[208] It's also worth noting that doctors had been criticised for not placing patients who were dying onto the LCP, citing 'limited training' and 'level of knowledge' about it.[209]

It may simply have been that doctors were afraid to use the LCP because they did not want to give the impression that it was being done as a tickbox exercise – and no wonder, given that junior doctors reported their hospital training revolved around how to fill in the forms rather than how to deliver good palliative care.[210]

I'm no fan of guidelines in general or the targets they can lead to. They are capable of summarising evidence without capturing or explaining the caveats or uncertainties underlying them. They are capable of providing a recipe for adherence rather than a springboard for thoughtful decision making.

While the LCP was not inherently problematic its implementation was. When guidelines are simply applied, rather than carefully considered, well meaning health professionals can do active harm. Replacing guidelines with more guidelines overlooks the heart of the problem; the real world where people use them.

When professionals go bad

Prospective medical students are judged at entry to medical school as to whether they have demonstrated 'acts of altruism and voluntary work'[211] or 'evidence of experience and reflection in a caring environment'.[212] I remember my own interview, when I stumbled over my words, trying to explain my sense of vocation without sounding trite, rehearsed, or naive.

The fact that these vocational attributes are requested and required of embryonic healthcare professionals is a powerful demonstration of their importance. It is not just academic prowess, intelligence, and the ability to assimilate and repeat facts that is desirable – it is to be able to care. My pleasure at teaching medical students is in part because I enjoy admiring their fresh, deep wish to do well for patients. Watching young students carefully ask a patient if he is in pain before examining his abdomen, assisting another person to get up from sitting – small human gestures, simple, polite transactions. But take some of the comments from *Patient Opinion*, a website that tries to improve healthcare by bringing patients online with hospital staff. So 'patients were ignored when needing toileting, leading to incontinence, screaming with pain'[213] or another story where a relative complained that 'I have never witnessed such detachment to patients from staff whilst we have been visiting this week. We have witnessed no interaction, just a sense that patients are little more than an inconvenience to the daily duties. This just ridicules the profession that people have spent years studying and training to become.'[214]

Why does this happen? Why do people who begin their career with a sense of vocation and purpose, anxious to help, end up displaying such uncaring hostility to the needs of patients? Why do we end up placing more importance on the need to concentrate on the computer or the tickboxes of a 'pathway' than the patient complaining of thirst?

It's easier to be kind and helpful when one is not needed in four different places. While our government pays lip service to the concept of evidence-based practice, the reality is that there is a strong evidence base for mandatory better staffing levels, and it has essentially been ignored. Worse, as happened in the Mid-Staffordshire NHS Trust, staffing levels were reduced in a hospital that was already struggling. In the UK, hospitals are fined for failing to meet targets, such as the four-hour wait targets in A&E.[215] The obvious answer for pressed trusts is to reduce staff hours or decrease the skill level to appoint people to posts.

- What does this mean in practice? Our population is trending towards older people with more chronic diseases – yet we are hardly accounting for their needs. Staff feeling constantly under pressure. Rushing, trying to be quick. Not having time to feed someone slowly and chat while doing it. Being interrupted from giving out medication as someone else, out of the corner of your eye, risks slipping. Remembering about the water jug you promised to fill half an hour ago. The phone ringing, but knowing you will not get to it in time, and being late to record a person's fluid intake or urine output. Avoiding conversations that you know will be long and difficult because half a dozen patients are needing help with routine tasks, and you are behind with them all. It means more of your stressed colleagues phoning in sick. It means feeling that you are not doing the job that you entered the profession

> to do. The classic 1973 paper 'From Jerusalem to Jericho', describes theology students, on their way to give a talk, coming across a distressed, disheveled person. Some of the students were giving a talk about the Good Samaritan, a story where the protagonist stops to help a person in need. The rest of the students were talking on a more bland topic. The other variable was that the students were told to be in a hurry, or not. The topic of the talk made no difference to whether the student stopped and helped. Being in a hurry, though, made the students less likely to stop and ignore the person in need.[216]

Empathy from government for the position that understaffed professionals find themselves in is absent. The former health secretary, Andrew Lansley, said that understaffing should not be used an excuse for mistakes:

> There is no excuse. We're talking about the incorrect administration of insulin, putting someone in a boiling hot bath or failing to identify a patient using their name identifier. That isn't because you're understaffed, that is because you are doing it wrong and because there is no process by which that is properly checked.[217]

Yet there is clear evidence that understaffing is associated with mistakes and near-misses.[218,219] It's no surprise that poor staffing doesn't just risk poor care, but chronic stress and burnout. The psychological impact of professional workload is kept hidden from full view in the NHS.

I've spoken to many psychologists who have been bemused and surprised at the lack of peer support for most healthcare professionals. Most psychologists have 'supervision' – a weekly or fortnightly timetabled slot to reflect on and discuss the care of their patients, and related issues, with a colleague. The time is usually protected from interruptions, and the emotional toll of the work is acknowledged and respected. As a trainee, I had a minimum of an hour a week with my trainer, a vastly experienced GP, to discuss patients and decisions that I'd made. I could discuss my handling of the uncertainty of diagnosis or plans to follow up patients. I had space to articulate the thoughts that I could have done more, better, or differently.

But in work, now fully qualified, it's different. My time to seek advice, solace or reassurance from colleagues has to be done in the blink of a coffee time, which itself is done while printing prescriptions, checking queries from patients, and dealing with letters from hospitals, x-rays and laboratories. The pace, volume and insistence of the routine demands displaces to the margins the time to gather thoughts, to offer support to colleagues, to discuss difficult problems, or to check I am doing clinically much the same as my friends and colleagues.

Indeed, mental health nurses have been found to have less emotional exhaustion and depersonalisation if they had more clinical supervision sessions[220] – and showed fewer 'cold negative attitudes' towards patients.

Caring for healthcare professionals – ensuring there are enough of them, that they have time to reflect on what they are doing, to support and listen to them – should be seen as an essential part of ensuring good care for patients. If the staff are recruited for their ability and wish to act well for sick and ill people, and fail to do so in practice, the environment they work in should be examined for flaws preventing compassion to shine through.

After nurses in Stafford Hospital were accused of leaving patients 'lying in their own faeces for days, forced to drink water from vases or given the wrong medication';[221] the Francis Enquiry was set up to investigate the high death rates from the hospital. The report, published in 2010, described 'many stories of shocking care... Morale at the Trust was low, and while many staff did their best in difficult circumstances, others showed a disturbing lack of compassion towards their patients. Staff who spoke out felt ignored and there is strong evidence that many were deterred from doing so through fear and bullying.'[222] Many departments were understaffed, with 'intolerable' pressures; the bullying culture in some wards was not just between staff and staff, but staff and patients. The report depicts misery. One telling passage is of a patient waiting, in some distress, for a commode. The nurses said 'we will be here in a minute, we are just finishing these notes. He said; no, my Mum needs one now. And he stood up and he waited, and then it was a tut and one of them got up and went with him.'

Most people, given that description, will feel anger, dismay, or shame at the treatment of one human by another. Who could feel sorry for this nurse, who prioritised her paperwork beyond the urgent intimate needs of a patient? Not many; certainly the media as they reported the events. Interviews for places at nursing college and medical school set high store on the need for students to have a vocation and desire to care; most apprentices have spent time in a caring role – such as auxiliary nursing or volunteering in a care home – to demonstrate their suitability for this kind of career before they can be offered a place to study.

What goes wrong? In the Francis report, there is an email from a nurse who told a consultant that nursing staff numbers had dropped by a third. A third. She stated plainly that 'patient safety is being put at risk'. The financial problems at the Trust had been going on for several years; staffing levels were cut because of a 'perceived need to save money'. Nurses regularly left meetings where they were set targets to move patients quickly out of A+E, in tears. One nurse said 'I felt that I would have to be in about ten places at once… There was not enough staff to deal with the type of patient that you needed to deal with, to provide everything that a patient would need. You were doing – you were just skimming the surface and that is not how I was trained.'

Let's consider this. High numbers of patients who need to be washed, dressed and fed. Patients who are incontinent of urine or faeces, who have been sick, who are in pain, who are disorientated, frightened, or scared. Medication, meals, baths, toilets, rehabilitation, injections, information, ward rounds, recordings of blood pressure, fluid intake, urine output. Their relatives, who are also afraid, and who may be upset, demanding of time or attention (rightly), or who may be angered by the adverse conditions on the wards. Add to this mix the depleted staff numbers, and a culture where complaints by healthcare workers to management about their unsafe working practices have been ignored.

How should workers respond to this? With enthusiasm at the challenge? How long could that be maintained, or would there be increasing despair at the lack of effect that raising concerns had? Is it good for patients to be looked after by staff who feel constantly harassed or overwhelmed with tasks? What happens to one's pride and pleasure in work when the pressure to do the same job with less manpower is unrelenting?

All this directly affects patients. If safe levels of staffing were a drug or the product of a checklist, we would be instructed to immediately do it. One would expect acknowledgement from the policy makers of the importance of the need for time for healthcare staff to respond immediately and directly to the needs of the sick people in their care.

When I talk to healthcare staff, many express frustrations at the obstacles between them and their patients. The paperwork required for each patient has burgeoned without any concomitant resource to allow the time to do so. I have admissions papers from hospitals containing thirty or forty pages of complex forms for documentation of everything from risks of pressure sores to religion, risk of blood clots to disclaimer forms for patients' belongings and valuables. Nurses have told me these take almost an hour to fill in completely; if some paperwork – for example, a dementia 'screening' questionnaire, mandatory for patients aged over 75 – is not completed within a set time frame, the hospital is fined. Any diversions from the key purposes of directly caring for patients should surely be fully justified in terms of both the cost of professional time, and value to the patient. It is easy for managers to count the numbers of forms that have been correctly filled in, or the targets for throughput which have been fulfilled. It is far harder for managers who exist remote from hospital wards to appreciate whether or not form filling was prioritised before patient care. Think about that nurse, intent on completing her notes while a patient needed her. What produced this skewed set of priorities? It is easy to blame just her. It is more important to try and find out why the system she worked in made her attend to the paperwork first.

So what were the prevailing conditions for these front-line workers? While there was never any direct evidence about patients 'drinking out of vases', the distressing image was fixed by a media who continued to reference it years after the report was published. Morale amongst the healthcare professionals deemed responsible was clearly low. In 2011 the Royal College of Nursing reported that 23,000 clinical posts were either cut or lost due to 'efficiency savings';[223] small wonder that in 2013 the college published a survey of 10,000 nurses, which found 62% had thought about leaving in the last year because of intolerable stress in their job.[224]

It should be no surprise that being treated well at work impacts on how workers behave. In the Netherlands, managers were asked about their style of leadership. Managers who described themselves as prioritising tasks as opposed to relationships led nurses with a higher rate of sickness absence.[225] Staff sick time is commonly held as being a proxy measure for stress and distress amongst staff working on the ward. England's NHS staff had an average of 9.5 working days off sick in 2012/13, an increase from 9.3% the year before.[226] This is almost double the rate of the UK average, of 4.5 days per year.[227]

And then there is the association between staffing levels and sickness absence. A 2007 study of medical records and nursing numbers found that nurses working in better staffed wards reported more satisfaction with their work and less burnout; as the staffing levels worsened, so did their morale. Most importantly, as staffing levels increased, patients were less likely to die.[228] There is so much lip service paid to the need for a 'healthy workforce'; but if the workforce is expected to absorb the strains of chronic understaffing without complaint, this should be seen as a dereliction of duty. Too few staff means an increased patient death rate, as well as low morale and burnout, both of which are known risk factors for sick leave, which compounds the problem.[229] More staff costs money; but it would also reduce death rates and allow for people to be cared for properly, by nurses who could pay enough attention to their patients. And the improvement in re-admission rates, postoperative complications, and a reduction in sick leave might balance the books. When talking about care at the end of life, we must factor in the need for enough staff time to serve patients properly – and ensure the staff are themselves treated well enough to allow them to care for others.

The unpaid carers

The same respect needs to be given to unpaid carers. What is it like to look after your husband, wife, sister or child in their last few days? A literature review from 2005 found opposing views from carers describing the death of a loved one, from 'it was a beautiful experience, and one that I will value and cherish always' to 'it is an experience I wouldn't wish on my worst enemy'.[230] This reminds me very much of stories about giving birth, which sometimes are narrated with nostalgic pleasure, and sometimes with painful horror. The review found evidence that caregiving was, for many, a 'burden', which could produce adverse effects in the family. It has been calculated that unpaid carers would cost around £57 billion in the UK to replace, around the same annual spending on the NHS.[231] The review went on to report that

> ...tiredness, difficulty getting enough sleep, and feelings of resentment and isolation were the most commonly reported disruptions... Caregivers suffered from lack of control over everyday life, lack of self-confidence, changes in paid employment, reduction in leisure time, deterioration in their

own health... and feelings of distress.

Like birth, we cannot hope or wish to be unaltered by the experience of death. It would be impossible, and undesirable, to go unchanged by the knowledge that a loved one is dying. Nor is it possible for life to continue identically when someone close to us is terminally ill. But just as in birth we have nurses, doctors and assistants to prepare, explain, soothe, encourage and intervene as needed, we also need a kind of 'midwifery' through the passage of death.

The reality for many families is of not having the kind of care that is needed. When I started in general practice, the preference for death at home was in gestation. We were encouraged to raise the possibility of staying at home rather than going into hospital for care at the very end of life. This made sense; who wanted to be lifted from their home in order to die with staff you had only just met and in a stiff, rubber-mattressed bed with metal cotsides? We could surely try and do better in keeping people comfortable at home. But dealing with dying is often hard, psychologically and physically, and even after years of training and decades of experience, there are still times when I don't know what it is best to do. For a son or daughter, a wife or husband, dealing with unfamiliar distress, changing or rattling breathing, pain, distress and new medications can be bewildering and frightening. And there is also the unspoken problem of relatives or friends being asked to care for a person when the relationship with them has been fraught, fractured or even abusive in the past. An assumed 'love' might be complex or non-existent; a sense of duty might overwhelm a sense of fairness.

This is the background doctors and nurses are up against when trying to organise professional care for people dying at home. It is a fragmented patchwork, with pieces missing. I was dismayed, as a newly qualified GP, when I realised that there was no possibility of 24-hour home care from the NHS – I had presumed that the person dying at home could have the same level of hands-on care at home compared with hospital. Instead, there could be visits from district nurses – but who were already hard pressed across the city. There was also the tantalising possibility of a nurse to stay with the person, but who was employed not by the NHS but by a charity. Trying to arrange for one of these nurses to visit was like chasing the end of a rainbow. There were only a few of them, and they were 'already booked'. They might be able to attend the next day, or the next. But they, of course, were already looking after patients – and they were unsure when those patients would die and they would be able to take on another patient. It was impossible to plan. The gaps in care were stuffed with uncertainty and anxiety.

In the meantime, and as social care budgets are cut, it is family and friends who offer themselves as helpers. Just as professionals need care for themselves, there is a pressing need to care for this task force – which census data tells us is composed of 5.8 million people. A quarter of these people care for more than ten years; 1.25 million carers work for more than 50 hours a week.[232]

Caring for carers

One study from England interviewed a random selection of people closest to a recently deceased person. They were asked about the last year of caring and their own feelings and health. When their loved one had died at home, there was an increased risk of distress compared with when their loved one had died elsewhere, with 50% of people whose loved one died at home saying that they had come to terms with the death, compared with 59% when the loved one had died elsewhere.[233]

It's possible that carers taking on the responsibility of home death have personality traits which make them at increased risk of distress later on. But the point remains that, whatever the cause, when carers assist with loved ones dying at home, we also must have a duty to them.

Other studies point to the risk of death in a carer after the death of the patient. An American study compared the use of hospice care compared to home care on the mortality rates of carers. Eighteen months after a death, 13.7% of husbands had died when their spouses did not use hospices, compared to 13.2% who did use hospices.[234] This is a small difference, but could represent an unanticipated harm.

Another US study compared the families of people who had entered into hospices up to three days before death, compared with people who had been in hospice care for longer. The families of the ill people who had short hospice stays were far more likely to report major depressive symptoms – 21% – months after the death, compared with caregivers whose family members had more hospice care, at 9%.[235] Many carers will report the pleasure at assisting a loved one, a sense of purpose and fulfilment. But continual pressure, lack of time off and support can leave carers open to the increased risk of depression, especially if they share a home with the person they support.[236] It is no wonder that carers report more depression and stress.[237] Again, it may be that there are other factors which contribute to these effects; but the bottom line is the carers who provide more hands-on care do so with a bigger risk to their own health. Crucially, a Cochrane review has shown that when families are given home palliative care – staff visiting regularly at home – people die more comfortably, with fewer symptoms. Additionally, it is cost-effective – and does not lead to any more grief in families and carers. Direct, personal, caring support works.[238]

Looking after someone with chronic illness can be exhausting both physically and mentally. Relatives and spouses who care do so out of love, duty, concern and responsibility. Many people try hard to avoid all external sources of help, feeling that it is their job to do everything for a loved one. Often the cared-for person does not want outside help either, feeling that they are already a burden and are undeserving. A relative may feel especially awkward in assisting with washing, intimate hygiene, urination or

Mrs Green and her husband, David

Mrs Green has been caring for her husband for the past 10 years. Her husband, David, has had a stroke. She is needed day and night to provide physical care. She also needs to provide emotional support as David's confidence has been badly affected by his illness. She feels that she cannot leave David alone without arranging for someone else to be there. Physically, she often suffers from pain aggravated by her caring role. This pain is made worse by often being tense and stressed. She also feels her emotional wellbeing is affected; often feeling tired, stressed and depressed.

Social Policy Research Unit.
Hearts and minds: the health effects of caring.
Carers UK, 2004. Available from: www.york.ac.uk/inst/spru
www.york.ac.uk/inst/spru/pubs/pdf/Hearts&Minds.pdf

defaecation. The need for constant reassurance from a confused adult can be wearing; trying to steal out of the house to collect groceries can feel like subterfuge; it is easy for the carer to slip out of their own circles of friends, given the high demands on their time at home and the need to rest when they can.

There is little more heartbreaking than to see a carer driven to guilt and despair through the overwhelming and unstopping needs of another. Even asking for help can feel profoundly upsetting to someone who wants so badly to 'cope'.

Research studies have examined cognitive approaches to caring – giving people thinking skills such that they are better equipped to deal with the demands on their time. What is striking from the literature is the lack of trials looking at the effects on carers when they are given more help from social workers or care assistants to do practical tasks and to give them a break from caring duties. Perhaps this is because it is too obviously a useful thing to do. However, the absence of

> You feel guilty about everything. Guilt for noticing they're declining, for worrying about them, for feeling like you're not doing enough, for feeling lonely and isolated, for saying 'no' all the time, for not having money, for wondering what the future will bring, for resenting them getting ill, for resenting this illness, and guilt for allowing yourself to wallow in self pity from time to time. You feel guilty when leaving them with professional carers; you don't think they can do it as well as you can – they don't know them, not really. You feel guilty when you get irritated at dementia, at their behaviour and repetitions. You know it's part of dementia and not them, and you think that knowing that, means you should be able to rise above it.
>
> **Dealing with guilt: thoughts of a guilty carer.**
> Dementia Challengers
> www.dementiachallengers.com/dealing-with-guilt.html

trials of social support is dangerous because it may lead to the assumption that only interventions that are designed to maintain the caring status quo are worth having. Yet more practical help and more social care may be more effective than any cognitive therapy approach which we offer to carers. Just as the provision of more staff is a potent answer to lowering hospital mortality rates, giving more practical help to care for people at home is not simply a compassionate response to overburdened families, but will also help to sustain the health of carer and cared for people.

It's clear from survey evidence that people who report their role as unpaid carer are more likely to report ill health.[239] Indeed, a study in the *Journal of the American Medical Association* in 1999 compared older healthy caregivers to a control group of matched adults who were not caring for relatives. Over the next 4.5 years, carers who reported no strain in giving care to their spouse had a death rate of 3.6%. But if their partners described strain, their death rate was 7.4%.[240]

Given the sleep disturbance, the lack of time off, and the

constant need to put someone else's wellbeing before one's own, it is no wonder that GPs now mark the records of all carers so that they are on special alert if they consult. Sadly, it is common to find carers who, despite suffering from, say, gallstones, delay surgery which could have made them feel better out of concern for being unable to care for their relative. It is not uncommon to find people who are 65 or 70, and with health problems of their own, being the primary carer for their parent in their 90s. Local charities can provide support through a 'listening ear' or counselling sessions, but the invitations sometimes aren't taken up out of a fear of leaving the person on their own.

So if emotional or mental strain is linked to an increase in the death rate in carers, what can we do about it? Befriending schemes for carers, where the carer is offered emotional support through a volunteer listener, have been shown not to be popular with carers, or to improve their anxiety and depression scores.[241] It is hardly a surprise that carers find it hard to make time for themselves. And it may not be listening that they need most, but rest breaks and some one else to lend a hand.

The grand-sounding 'National Carers' Strategy Demonstrator Sites Programme' evaluated the effects of offering breaks to carers; of offering 'health checks' and better NHS support. The study was not run as a trial and it is difficult to draw any firm conclusions from it, except that carers appreciated the ability to have breaks, and that at the 'health checks', carers had physical symptoms or illness that they had not previously made time to have addressed.[242] Tellingly, they said 'we know that unless replacement support is reliable and of high quality, carers will not take or benefit from breaks'. Yet in many areas, carer support is patchy or non-existent. One option from a local authority is of volunteers rather than paid staff who 'do not undertake personal care, although they will escort service users to and from the toilet. They are not able to do any lifting or housework, but will make snacks and drinks.'[243] Other councils offer a one-off payment of £250 per year to use 'for anything that carers feel will provide them with a break from their caring role, such as paying for activities, a short break or holiday or a regular therapy'. [244] However, payments are limited and depend on 'eligibility and volume of applicants'.

This is meagre funding. Compare it to the way that cancer treatments are campaigned for, approved, and obtained. The allowance paid to carers in the UK is £61.35 per week, which is only allowed if spending more than 35 hours a week to do it; it makes the minimum wage look outstandingly generous.[245]

The carers I meet are not doing it for money, recognition or reward, but out of duty, compassion, loyalty and love. Carers may have cut hours in their own paid work – or given up – and still have other dependants themselves. And we repay this badly. The bureaucracy and time-consuming form filling required to claim hardly invites people to request carer's allowance. We offer little in the way of regular release from duties, and fill gaps with volunteers unable to provide the same wraparound care. Looking after carers should not be about fluffy, hand-holding, meaningless 'support' but hands-on, human help in the bathroom, the shower, the housework, the cooking, the feeding, the laundry, and making up for sleep deprivation. So why do we not supply it?

Chapter 5

The Politics Of Death

A humane society would ensure that each citizen had a basic standard of living, especially when disability or illness prevents a person from taking care of their own modest needs. I am a devotee of the need for evidence in healthcare: but there should be no need to prove that giving people dignity is the right thing to do. It is a brave politician who does not openly profess love for the values of the NHS, and wishes to uphold its service as 'free at the point of use' to all citizens.

We are failing to do this. Prescription charges were introduced in 1952, abolished in 1965, but restarted in 1968. Although many people are exempt from paying the charges (because of unemployment or certain long-term conditions), millions are not. The charges have varied over the years; at some point concerns were expressed that the rise was over and above inflation. The devolved Scotland and Wales got rid of prescription charges in 2011 and 2007 respectively, out of concerns that people were not taking up all of their medicines because of cost and were increasing the risk of illness or disability because of it. A survey from the Prescription Charges Coalition in 2013 found that over a third of people who were not exempt from prescription charges did not cash in all their prescriptions because of the cost. As a result, 10% thought that they had ended up in hospital; and while this would need to be validated against the person's medical records, it highlights the dilemma of patients with chronic illness and who are at risk of hospital admission.[246]

In 2001 the Citizens Advice Bureau found that half their surveyed clients had difficulty affording prescription medicines, and again, almost a third missed some of their prescriptions because of cost.[247] This finding is in keeping with research, published in 1986, which tracked the relationship between prescription prices and how many prescriptions were cashed in by patients. This demonstrated that when the costs of prescription drugs go up, there is a decrease in the amount of medicines dispensed.[248] A study analysing what happened to patients before and after the charge was dropped in Wales showed that it led to a small rise in the amount of medicines prescribed – and more people obtaining them.[249]

Similar barriers are created when giving people social support. In England, a 'needs assessment' is carried out to determine how much help a person requires; funding is usually only available when this is at 'critical' or 'substantial' levels.[250] Lower levels of assessed need do not get funding, meaning that the person has to pay for it themselves. For many people, this is an expense beyond what can be afforded. In Scotland, personal care, but not home care (like shopping or cleaning) is provided by the state. The division which has been placed between social care and medical care by a choice to freely fund one but not the other is curious. Loneliness, low rates of social interaction, a lack of fresh food or difficulties with maintaining personal hygiene can all contribute to ill health. Not funding a basic level of social care is likely to contribute to a poorer quality of life.

Social care and healthcare are two sides of the same coin. The functional, low-tech nature of assisting with people's day to day needs – washing, dressing, eating, toileting, occupation – rarely attract much media attention (except on the occasions when it goes badly wrong.)

The chronic lack of adequate funding for decent stocks

of equipment highlights the artificial health/social care interface. Take a Welsh study looking at the difficulties healthcare staff faced when trying to get basic 'social care' equipment, such as commodes, or a hoist to get in and out of the bath. The state was slow and bureaucratic; a patchwork of charity and self-funding was used to allow people to get home. Staff bent rules in order to have even basic equipment like a commode ready on the ward to offer people who were able to get home without a long wait to obtain it.[251]

> Dad could not be left unsupervised as he was unable to do anything for himself and we felt as a family his care needs were high; he was at risk of malnutrition, dehydration and pressure sores and prone to recurrent infections. None of these needs seemed to be defined as a health need and it took five weeks to reach a decision on whether he was entitled to continuing health care – five weeks of his life that we can never get back while health and social care fight over who pays for his care, where is the person in all of this, where is what is best for them?
>
> Then began our next battle, it turned out that dad's care package had to be arranged through the hospital's social services team which meant that dad could no longer have the care agency he had been using for the previous two years. Dad had had the same carer every morning for five days a week for the past two years. She had become like part of the family and although you are supposed to keep a professional distance it's very hard not to become friends with the carer that you rely on so much, who comes to be part of your life, is the first person you might see after a sleepless night and is the one always there for you day in day out. For my mum this was a huge blow; they were taking away the only familiarity and support they both so needed at this time.
>
> Marciano S-A. **Ray's story**.
> Personal story included in the Commission on the Future of Health and Social Care call for evidence. The King's Fund, 2014. www.kingsfund.org.uk/projects/commission-future-health-and-social-care-england/patient-stories

Unnecessary stays in hospital expose the patient to an unneeded risk of hospital-acquired infection, as well as using a bed that isn't required, meaning it is not available to others (through no fault of the patient). This increases stress within the hospital and outside it (it has become a routine, every winter, for GPs to be told that hospital beds are under extreme pressure and to only admit patients if there is a dire emergency). To call a commode or a hoist a 'social' need makes only partial sense if one is discussing the person purely in a financial framework. People are more complex than binary paper ticks of 'need'; the effects of failing to care for someone adequately causes distress to them and their family, and reverberates in the way people then need the NHS.

The division between health and social care, for patients, as well as healthcare professionals, is artificial when it comes to considering quality of life and death. A study of 399 people who died from COPD (chronic obstructive pulmonary disease) published in 2005 showed that the majority had pain, low mood, fatigue and weakness, as well as the typical breathlessness of the disease. Over two thirds had no assistance from social care services in the last year of their life.[252] Despite people with COPD often having equally severe or worse symptoms compared to people with lung cancer, 40% felt that financial support – which can be used to pay for social care – was delayed after they became eligible for it compared with 10% of people with cancer. A third of patients with lung cancer had help from specialist palliative care nurses or hospices; 'almost none' of the people with COPD were offered equivalent services. Patients with COPD felt their quality of life was poor – in one study, only a respiratory nurse – working 'outside her remit' helped them get the support they lacked.[253] Cancer might sound 'worse' than COPD, but in reality, either may have mild or life-threatening symptoms. It is the individual person's symptoms and needs, not necessarily their diagnosis, which should dictate the care that people get. The problem for the people with severe COPD in this study wasn't a lack of medicine. It was a lack of human care. There was a lack of support, of explaining, helping, understanding, of enabling people to try and live within their capabilities.

This kind of work is familiar to most NHS staff who work directly for patients. It's possible to make a correct diagnosis, issue a correct prescription, and dispense a good information leaflet and not give the patient what she needs. The needs of people who are suffering from unpleasant, frightening symptoms and who cannot dress easily, who, if they run out of milk or bread, cannot manage to get to the shop at the end of the road, and who fear for the future, cannot be easily drawn into a to do list. It's also well established that anxiety is associated with both accident and emergency and GP visits[254] and GP attendances.[255]

Again the division into social and healthcare is obvious nonsense. Is the need for reassurance, explanation and human support social care or healthcare? Better social support systems are associated with a decreased need for people with anxiety or depression to see their GP.[256] The knowledge of these intertwined effects should be embraced, understood, and used to the advantage of patients – not ignored in a political fight about whose job it is, who will fund it, and how many forms must be filled in to obtain it.

Professional carers

So what care is available to people and their families? Every patient should have a general practitioner who can visit at home if necessary. GPs can help with assessment of symptoms and planning medication or other treatments to relieve distress. District nurses are employed by the local primary care trust to work in the community in attendance to housebound patients. They will assist with medication, catheters to the bladder, injections, setting up syringe drivers – which are often used to deliver medication at the end of life. Then, carers, who may be privately contracted via the local council, can be assigned to people who need help with bathing, washing, dressing, feeding and toileting. It is the humane administration of these basic tasks which provides dignity, safety and often companionship.

Because of the reasons why many older people need home care – due to the 'frailty' and multimorbidity already described – it is likely that many of the people who home carers visit are at high risk of dying. We have already seen the difficulties in accurately predicting when death will occur. For this reason, it can be useful to think of home care as part of the care at the end of life – even if that terminal care takes place over weeks, months and years, rather than days. It therefore make sense for end-of-life care to be a matter for generalists – GPs, district nurses, carers – rather than a specialist pursuit. But do we value this care?

What are we are willing to pay for?

The tragedy is that while NICE will argue over what drugs are cost-effective, and medical charities will criticise whenever something massively expensive is not funded, there is little of the same publicity over the dilemmas in social care funding. While NICE is prepared to pay around £30,000 a year for a single QALY,[257] the benefits of hands-on, continuous care for washing, dressing, eating and other basic activities goes almost unseen. NICE do make 'social value judgements'[258] but do not decree, for example, that the benefit of professional overnight care would be more than the comparatively little benefit of an expensive cancer drug.

NICE makes judgements about the effectiveness of treatments, many of which, legally, local health authorities have to fund.[259] NICE had a big opportunity in 2014 to demonstrate the necessity of adequate hands-on care for patients. The Department of Health had chosen, in 2013, not to insist on minimum staffing levels for hospitals.[260] But in 2014, NICE, in draft guidance, had said that there should be at least one nurse per eight patients.[261]

This is evidence based: it is clear that nurse staffing levels in hospitals directly affect patient care. As discussed, in 2007, an analysis of nurse staffing and discharge records in the NHS found that one nurse could be looking after between seven and 14 patients. There was a corresponding stepwise increase in death rates, with the patients who were cared for by the nurses with the most patients to look after having a 25% increased death rate (the average death rate being 2.3%).[262]

A systematic review and meta-analysis published in 2007 found that on intensive care, medical and surgical wards, fewer nurses meant more patient deaths. The researchers found a 'dose response' – as the 'dose' of nurses increased, the number of deaths fell.[263] Another study found a higher death rate on stroke units with a smaller proportion of nurses, with one extra death per 25 admissions in the least well staffed wards.[264]

In 2013, the Royal College of Nursing asked 2,000 nurses about the staffing levels where they worked. Over a third reported unsafe staffing levels on a weekly basis. Eighty-six per cent of community nurses – the community where care is delivered to those infirm or vulnerable people with multiple illnesses and fragile health – said they were understaffed as a result of vacancy freezes and posts being cut; half of ward sisters said they were not allowed to authorise extra staff shifts when necessary. Many others said that in any event their requests were ultimately turned down.[265] Yet the recommendation for evidence-based, minimum staffing was withdrawn by NICE when the guidance was finally published.[266]

The policy may have had strong support from nurses[267]but not politicians or some policy commentators. On the 15 October 2013, the editor of the *Health Service Journal* tweeted, in response to a BBC programme about the need for more midwives: 'Is there any clinical prof(essional) that doesn't think answer to NHS's prob(lems) is to hire more of their profession?' Neither did the Berwick report, published in 2013, titled *A promise to learn – a commitment to act: improving the safety of patients in England*, recommend minimum staffing levels.[268] Jeremy Hunt, health secretary, specifically rejected minimum staffing, saying 'I don't believe that I, at the centre, should tell every hospital that "you should recruit this many doctors or this many nurses"'.[269] Yet there is no stopping politicians who make mass policy decisions without an evidence base elsewhere in the NHS.

Given the evidence on staffing, the dichotomy between what we can guarantee for patients is striking; shiny new drugs and technology, but not professional human hands.

Understaffing leads to untenable staff pressure which ultimately harms patients. An undercover television programme found in 2009 that home carers could be trained with four 20-minute DVDs and a 90-minute tutorial. One 89-year-old woman, with dementia and doubly incontinent, had 'dropped off' the system and went unattended for a day, leaving her sitting in her own waste, having had nothing to eat or drink for a day before she was found. The undercover worker found that on some occasions, overbooked and unsure what she was meant to do, visits to patients' homes were very short, and on occasion, just three minutes.[270] An investigation for the consumer organisation *Which?* found that while there were some excellent visits to patients by home carers, there were also cancelled and rushed visits, including delayed administration of essential medications like insulin.[271]

Care workers used to be employed directly by local councils. While this remains true for some carers, others are now employed by a private company contracted to the council. One manager explained to *Which?*: 'We're under a huge amount of pressure to find savings and it's increasingly difficult not to have a negative impact on service delivery. Our margins are so tight that we have no spare capacity to provide support to carers if things go wrong on call.' Are we really offering quality of life to people now assessed as needing home care? As people stay at home for longer, and are frailer, the relative risks get higher. A carer described to *Which?* the changes in her workload: '15 minute calls used

> On shift, Hayley finds tight schedules causing havoc for staff. While visiting a 77-year-old terminally ill man, her colleague's phone rings. As the elderly client asks for oxygen, his carer is talking on the phone about work throughout...
>
> 'You had back to back appointments and you weren't factored in travel time. So it meant that if I had to drive 20 minutes outside of York, I would be late before I even started. And on top of that, if any service user needed a little extra bit of care, no matter how small like just extra time to get to bed or they needed a little longer on the toilet that day, that time wasn't factored in,' says Hayley.
>
> **Britain's home care scandal.** BBC Panorama website. 9 April 2009. news.bbc.co.uk/panorama/hi/front_page/newsid_7990000/7990682.stm

to be 'check' calls, or to give medication. Now, we've got to microwave a meal, empty a commode, and get to the next person in that time as well. It's an impossible ask.'

Where does this pressure come from? Who is responsible? A brief search on the internet finds jobs as a carer for the payment of around £7 an hour; this is in the lowest 10% of wage earnings.[272] While some carers are paid more than this, this is hard work, dealing daily with human distress, relieving loneliness, working with people who may need to be cleaned of vomit, sweat, urine and faeces. If this is all we are prepared to pay it looks as though we hardly value it.

The same search for cheapness, rather than for quality, is exemplified by the NHS. 'E-auctions' have been used in the NHS to get low bids for stationary and other office supplies. Instead of bids going up, they go down, and the lowest bidder wins. In 2009, NHS London held 30 such auctions for £195 million worth of palliative and dementia care for patients being discharged from hospital. One director of adult social care services said 'If you put providers into an auction, pushing them to a lower and lower price, somebody is going to lose out, and the losers in this case are vulnerable elderly people and their carers.'[273]

Indeed, the budget for social care in the UK was cut by 6% in the UK in 2011 – a drop of £900 million in one year. Yet the numbers of elderly and disabled people are rising by 3% a year.[274] Is it even possible to create 'efficiency savings' of the magnitude to fill the budget gaps but which do not affect patient care? If the same funding cuts were performed in cancer care, there would be an outcry.

There is good reason to suspect that we are failing even more than the figures suggest. Many people do not ask for the care they need – being embarrassed, ashamed, stoical or determined to manage on their own. Nine per cent of people aged over 65 need help with dressing and bathing; just over 80% of these people do not receive any state assistance to do so.[275] Some of these people will not wish any carers to visit. Many will manage, more or less, until something else happens – something as seemingly minor as a urine infection or a trip may cause an older person to become suddenly bedbound and unable to get through the day reasonably well. This scenario – a reflection of 'frailty' – is a common reason for admission to hospital.

Part of the reason why hospital admissions are sometimes necessary is that the care which may enable a person to stay at home is not available. Some people will have family and friends who can visit several times a day, fetch food, help dress, and bathe, while others will not. Part of the problem is in who meets the cost. The House of Commons Health Committee reported in 2012 that the means testing many people undergo in the assessment for home care is often a 'shock', and that the reality of the complexity of the care needed by older people in 'trying to define NHS care and social care as two separate and indistinct things will only make matters worse for older people'.[276] Part of the problem is the fragmentation of stressed services both in the NHS and in the third sector; who is to take charge, and when?

As an example; imagine an elderly person, with mild dementia, who needs new medication urgently. The visiting GP phones and asks the care worker to visit to collect the prescription and give it to the patient. But the care-co-ordinator reports that the carer has done her visits for the day. The patient's daughter lives too far away to visit today. The district nurse is no longer allowed to collect the prescription under the terms of her contract. The pharmacy, who deliver medications, have also finished their round where a car delivers medicines to people not able to get to them. The gaps in the person's care begin to open up as it is unclear who, exactly, has responsibility to help (and in the end, the GP in this case drove to the pharmacy, then back to the patient, delivering the medication herself – meaning that the work of visiting other sick patients at home did not get done until later.)

Indeed, elderly people living in care homes have the lowest amount of admissions to hospital compared with people being cared for in the community. When we consider that people in care homes are generally there because they are frail and have more diseases, they would ordinarily be considered at highest risk of needing hospital care. But the constant care given by nursing homes means that admissions into hospital are not needed as often.[277]

It is likely that some hospital admissions are able to be avoided because of the ability of care homes to provide constant, hands-on monitoring and nursing expertise. I can think of many instances where the inability to provide this kind of high level of specialist care has resulted in the admission of an elderly person to hospital. Sometimes admission will still have been needed – for example, if urgent diagnostic blood tests, x-rays or CT scans are required. Other times, admission to hospital will not be in the best interests of the patient, who, removed from home, may become bewildered and disorientated, his normal surroundings being replaced by an alien, fluorescent ward. Even worse, the admission may not have been needed if there had been enough of the right kind of care at home. But because the basics of care are classed as 'social' not 'health', they are allowed to go unmet. Even though a lack of social care results in a distressing experience for the patient and an expensive hospital admission, the funding gap persists.

A study from 2008 examined two years' worth of data from 150 English local authorities examining the relationship between local social care resources and problems for patients needing hospital care – delayed discharges and emergency. The bottom line was that 'richer' social care resulted in lower levels of delays for people to be discharged from hospital – and reduced subsequent admissions to hospital. It concluded that social and healthcare services were 'interdependent'.[278] In other words, trying to improve health is also about improving social care: and improving social care is expected to have a positive impact on health.

This may sound logical and obvious, but it is also based in evidence. It remains to be seen whether the most recent proposals to ensure ceilings on funding across health and social services will be accepted and workable.[279]

The caring budget

Professionals do have time off work – unlike the family and friends caring for an individual at home. These carers need breaks and support too. We have already seen how the funding for care services which are provided by local councils can result in the bare minimum of home care for people.

Can we really not afford better? Let's examine what is and isn't funded by the government. The NHS has four homoeopathic hospitals, fully funded. Millions are spent on inpatient beds, outpatient appointments and medical and nursing staff.[280] Homeopathy has no basis in science. In contrast, the people struggling with a bare minimum of home care may find, with few resources and scarce time, that it is hardly possible to protest or argue the case for better funding for themselves.

Or drugs funding? A vaccine against shingles for older people was rolled out in 2013 at a cost of £250 million.[281] The vaccine itself is not perfect – it reduces the risk of shingles by around half in people in their 60s.[282] This translates to a reduction in the annual risk of getting shingles in adults aged between 70-79 from 0.88% a year to 0.44% a year.[283] Cost-benefit analyses have suggested that the QALY results – a reduction in nerve pain, a nasty side effect of shingles, and the avoidance of rare deaths due to it – are favourable,[284] even though this is based on estimates, not real-life evidence.[285] Still, the NHS is happy to fund that.

Then there are drugs such as vemurafenib, for malignant melanoma, the most serious form of skin cancer and which has been approved by NICE. It costs £1,750 for a week's supply and costs around £50,000 to produce one QALY.[286] Although described as capable of 'melting tumours away within weeks'[287] the evidence suggests that it can produce, on average, an improvement of overall survival of three months.[288]

Home and social care are low tech, quiet and do not do much evolving. Medications are new, funding is fought over, and are described with dramatic language. When, initially, NICE said that vemurafenib was not cost-effective, one campaigner told the *Daily Telegraph* that 'This is another truly devastating blow to all melanoma patients and their families, many of whom are very young and with young families' and said that NICE's decision was 'tantamount to passing them a death sentence'.[289] When the decision was reversed, after the manufacturer applied a discount (making the cost lower and thus the cost-effectiveness higher) the decision was treated with delight, with talk of it being a 'great stride forward' and a 'brilliant example' of the new generation of cancer drugs.[290]

Clearly, no one would want to dismiss the usefulness of any drug capable of improving the quality of life of a terminally ill person. The threshold of QALY becoming cost-effective is rightly ambiguous at the end of life. But there is a strange dichotomy between what we are, and are not, prepared to fund in our last years.

Vemurafenib will be available to around 1,000 people per year in the UK, at a cost of £91 million. In December

2013, the Warm Homes Healthy People scheme was axed.[291] Costing £20 million – just over a fifth of the drug budget for vemurafenib – it provided emergency boiler repairs, snow clearing and emergency food supply in cold weather for older and vulnerable adults. It had been appraised by the Health Protection Agency (HPA) earlier the same year. They found that cold living environments contributed to heart disease, stroke, pneumonia, as well as worsening arthritis and mental illness. Children living in cold homes were more likely to have conditions like asthma compared to warmly housed children, and were less likely to achieve at school. Unlike drug interventions for cancer, Warm Homes was not tested under trial conditions. However, when the HPA went to ask community councils whether they thought it was a good idea, there was 100% agreement that the fund was useful, especially, as one respondent said, it is offered 'at a time when budgets for this work are otherwise non-existent'. Two hundred thousand people were estimated to have received help from the budget, via emergency heaters, warm meals, blankets, duvets or home checks.[292]

This is not an argument against expensive cancer drugs. Rather, it is a demonstration of the variation in funding available depending on whether the intervention is classed as social or healthcare. The divide, as we have seen, is artificial – one affects the other. In terms of quality of life, the separation of social and healthcare need is nonsensical.

The Warm Homes system is not the only area of social care squeezed out. The cuts to social care in the UK as part of the 'austerity budget' in the 2010s was examined in a report from the academic Personal Social Services Research Unit. They found that £890 million less was being spent on social care for adults in 2012/13 compared with 2005/6. This meant that over a quarter of a million fewer older individuals were receiving social care – a 39% drop.[293] Again, we lack direct causal evidence, but in older people, there was an association between higher social care costs and lower hospital costs at the end of life.[294] When more was spent on social care, less

> Reducing unnecessary use of acute hospitals by people at the end of their life could make additional resources available for expenditure on end of life care. At least 40% of people who died in an acute hospital in the Sheffield in October 2007 did not have medical needs which required them to be admitted. These patients used 1,500 bed days, costing approximately £375,000, with nearly a quarter of them having been in hospital for over a month. Over the course of a full year, this could make around £4.5 million available for investment in community services.
>
> House of Commons Public Accounts Committee. **End of life care: Nineteenth Report of Session 2008–09.** Stationary Office, 2009. www.publications.parliament.uk/pa/cm200809/cmselect/cmpubacc/99/99.pdf

tended to be needed on hospital care.

This cuts to the sharp end of general practice, where a person at the end of life is struggling at home with a worsening of a chronic illness. If enough social care cannot be quickly rallied, or a bed in a hospice obtained, the person often ends up admitted to hospital.

At the end of life, up to a third of people are admitted to hospital when they 'could' have been cared for in the community.[295] But without wraparound social care, it would be unsafe and uncaring to leave patients at home if they need on-hand nursing and comfort. Our media reacts in horror when expensive cancer drugs are denied. Yet the injustice over a lack of social care funding which would allow adequate care at home at the end of life seems to be silently accepted.

Part of the problem of trying to get fair funding for social care may be the lack of robust research in many areas, meaning that, for example, it was not possible to say whether the Warm Homes scheme had definitely improved health. The solution may be to trial and test social care interventions, which might perhaps lead towards equity of funding and fairness for people whose needs are more 'social' than 'health' care but are just as effective as the latest blockbuster drug.

But if we do need better evidence to make the health case for social care, this should not trump the more pressing need for us all, whether lonely, ill or dying. If someone has just been discharged from hospital, we do not need a randomised controlled trial to tell us that it is humane and kind to ensure that she is warm, has enough food, and the reassurance that someone will be looking in on her.

The technology 'solution'

The political response to the lack of such wraparound social care and the rising needs of elderly and frail people has been to promote telehealth technology widely and voraciously as a 'solution'.

Prime Minister David Cameron said in 2011: 'We've trialled it, it's been a huge success, and now we're on a drive to roll this out nationwide. Dignity, convenience and independence for millions of people. And this is not just a good healthcare story. It's going to put us miles ahead of other countries commercially, too.'[296] The press release sent out from the Department of Health claimed that telehealth could 'deliver' a 45% reduction in mortality rates, a 15% reduction in A&E visits, and a 20% reduction in emergency admissions. Cameron was clear that 'This is going to make an extraordinary difference to people.'[397]

The definition of 'telehealth' is somewhat loose, as indeed it was in the telehealth trial Cameron referred to. It was known as the 'whole system demonstrator' trial, published in the *BMJ* in 2012. But what exactly did it test? 'Choice of telehealth devices and monitoring systems varied across the trial and there was no attempt to standardise these technologies across sites.'[398] In other words, there was no consistent device under test.

Some telehealth devices are 'smart boxes' which run along with equipment like pulse oxygen meters, worn by the patient, where the data is sent to a control centre for analysis. Other uses of telehealth are simply the ability to send data – for example, sugar readings to someone who has diabetes – to a nurse. In the WSD (Whole System Demonstrator) trial, even the results from weighing scales were used as a 'telehealth' reading – which was surprising to me, since weighing scales have been used for decades for people with heart failure as a way to monitor how much extra fluid they are carrying and to adjust their diuretics (water pills) accordingly.

What supposedly made this 'telehealth' (as opposed to standard practice) was the means of communication. Often the plan of what to do for weight change is held by the patient, who knows the medication adjustments to make and who to contact if advice is needed. Sometimes the monitoring is done by a specialist pharmacist or nurse, who will visit or speak on the phone to the patient regularly; sometimes, especially if patients have severe or unstable heart failure, this is done by the GP. Yet this is standard practice, and it seems a stretch to call this 'telehealth'. Similarly, in rural areas, the use of video consultations and telephone calls have been used for decades for patients to consult with specialists, without having to make onerous avoidable journeys.[399]

Monitoring chronic conditions like diabetes or chronic bronchitis is standard practice. Most people with stable symptoms are reviewed every year or so. Even then there is a debate about what's useful to measure and how frequent return appointments should be. It's difficult, therefore, to know the value of collecting frequent monitoring data in people who are getting on fine, and how best to react to it.

Cameron praised his project in December 2011. The research paper the comments were based on was not published until June 2012. In November 2011 the Department of Health, in their Operating Framework for the NHS in England, told local authorities that they 'should spread the benefits of innovations such as telehealth and telecare as part of their ongoing transformation of NHS services'.[300]

The cut in death rates claimed in the Department of Health press release had been based on relative risks – to know how big a 45% cut in death rates really is, you have to know what the number of deaths was to start with. And the trial did show a difference in death rates. The group who had telehealth had a 4.6% death rate at one year compared to the control group, at 8.3%. But the reasons for this may be more complex again. Staff were diverted from their usual posts to monitor the output of telehealth devices, meaning that fewer staff would have been available for patients in the 'usual care' group.[301] Telehealth did not clearly reduce hospital admissions.

It is hard to know not just what was being tested, but also if telehealth led to truly positive benefits. Were the control group inadvertently receiving poorer than 'normal' care? Or was more contact with health professionals (which the evidence, as we have seen, and quite separately from telehealth, would support)? Large contracts had already been issued to telehealth companies from the NHS in 2010, well before the results of the WSD were filed, meaning that money had been put into buying the technology even before the data had been analysed.[302]

Cochrane reviews have found mixed results on telehealth. One review found poor assessment of potential harms and little advantage for patients.[303] For people with heart failure, telemonitoring did reduce death rates and hospital admissions, but so did straightforward regular telephone call reviews.[304]

What works? Frequent contact between doctors, nurses and patients who know each other? Or the technological black box? In Mid Staffordshire, as nursing numbers were cut, the government were setting up contracts to deliver telehealth technology; was the roll out more about expanding a section of commercial industry rather than getting the best human care to patients?

What of quality of life – given the claims by our politicians that it was going to make an 'extraordinary' difference to people's lives? On the government's *3millionlives* website, which lists multiple telehealth companies as 'contributors', claims are made that it can bring 'full control of my life' 'more confidence' and 'retention of dignity' for patients.[305] Quality of life evidence was published from the WSD trial in 2012 from a subsection of patients in the WSD study. But it found no improvement in quality of life or psychological outcomes with telehealth at all.[306]

Telehealth is an expensive zombie policy, based on fallacy. Since when did an expensive high-tech telehealth box help someone to the toilet?

The bureaucratic 'solution'

The other political reply to the demand on the NHS has been to contract GPs to create 'advanced care plans' (ACPs). These are targeted at the patients with the highest chance of needing admission into hospital. The plan has to be discussed and a pre-set form filled in after a discussion between staff and patient.[307] In England, this is called an 'unplanned admissions enhanced service'.[308]

The original idea – thought up far from the machinations of the Department of Health – was to encourage discussions about what is wanted, and not wanted, at the end of life. This is an excellent ideal. Thinking, talking and planning what we want to happen to us can be useful to patients and families. Careful dialogue is the essence of ensuring that people don't have things done 'to them' but 'for them'.

This is a subtle process. One document about using care plans in terminal care states:

> Initiation of ACP discussion by a care provider requires careful consideration: ACP is voluntary and should not be initiated simply as part of routine record keeping or care. The care provider may respond to 'cues' which indicate a desire to make specific wishes known eg worries about who will care for them. ACP should not be initiated as a result of outside pressure eg family wishes or organisational pressures.... No pressure should be brought to bear by the professional, the family or any organisation on the individual concerned to take part in ACP...[309]

... the nurse turned up 45 minutes late but I suppose the elderly have all the time in the world to sit about waiting.

A chirpy, determined to be cheerful, very pleasant, younger edition of Gracie Fields appeared and ploughed through a form. Every single item (except 2) of information required to fill the form could have been pulled off practice data or social services records...

Two questions. Oh yes... here's one.

'Where would you like to die...'

It came as a bit of a shock. The Duchess thought 'at home'. I said Hawaii. Can we get the tickets on an FP10?

Here's cracking question number two:

'... if you ever need cardiopulmonary resuscitation do you agree to Do Not Resuscitate.'

Bang! Right between the eyes! Out of the blue, no warning... do you want to be flat-lined?

Lilley R. **Where's no-man?**
nhsManagers.net myemail.constantcontact.com/Where-s-No-Man-.html?soid=1102665899193&aid=W9FRJ7f7GQk

This is important: it isn't fair or kind to push people into end-of-life planning if they are still coming to terms with the shock of a diagnosis. The doctor or nurse should be listening to their patient. When people say things like 'I'm scared about what will happen to me' or 'I really don't want to go back into hospital', it's a prompt to listen and talk. Similarly, the doctor, realising that a patient is now so frail and unwell that they are at high risk of dying soon, may be able to find a way to broach the subject in a way that acknowledges the current circumstances and is supportive rather than frightening.

Gentleness and humanity are needed to talk about future life and death. ACPs, sometimes called 'anticipatory care' plans, should be a 'work in progress'. In real life, such consideration, reflection and discussion, of what kind of medicine, social care and medical interventions are wanted – should ideally be natural and normal general practice. The idea of introducing a target for GPs to complete was out of a belief that this would reduce hospital admissions and save money. However if the government is reckoning on spending money on care plans in order to save money on admissions, they will be in the red: there is evidence that they make no difference.[310]

The consequences of pushing doctors into meeting targets are two-fold: firstly, time that could have been spent allowing a natural and nuanced conversation to unfold is pushed into binary tickboxes and administration – resulting in nurses being sent to ask stark questions of patients they had no ongoing relationship with. In 2013 the British Medical Association polled GPs and asked about the effect of the contract on their workload. Ninety-seven per cent of doctors said that paperwork distractions were increasing; Chaand Nagpaul, the chair of the GP committee, concluded that 'an increase in bureaucracy, box ticking, and administration has damaged GP services and patient care... we particularly need to see how we can free up more time to deliver the personalised care that patients deserve and meet the challenges from an increasing number of older patients who need coordinated and effective care.'[311] In other words, GPs like me want to take their eyes off the computer and listen to their patients.

To do this, we have to make time by stopping doing things that don't work. The nature of general practice is of an hour-long consultation of listening and thinking which takes place, piecemeal, over a year. The rigmarole of form-filling for an advance care plan is alien to such a relationship.

Entitlements and illness

This is not the only harmful bureaucracy. In December 2013, a 53-year-old named Tim Salter died by suicide. The coroner reported that he was depressed, agoraphobic, and with failing eyesight, when his incapacity benefit was stopped, a decision which resulted in 'leaving him almost destitute'.[312] Mark and Helen Mullins described a 12-mile hike to a food bank in November 2011 after they fell into poverty after Helen's benefits were stopped, after Helen, who had learning disabilities, was advised to apply for incapacity benefit, not unemployment benefit, and, seeming to fall between government departments, went hungry. They made a pot of soup with vegetables given from the food bank to last a week. In November 2011, their deaths were 'unexplained'.[313, 314]

The benefits system in the UK has been frequently derided for being too generous, with naming and shaming of 'benefits cheats' in the popular press.[315] Yet the government's own figures suggest that 0.9% of claims are underpaid in error – and only 0.7% are fraudulent claims.[316] The vast majority of people receiving benefits are therefore receiving them lawfully. Conversely, many people who are entitled to receive disability allowance (now called PIP, personal independence payments) or carer's allowance are reluctant to claim either.[317] Often people feel that they should be able to manage without financial support, or they don't deserve it. It's hard to disengage the stigma perpetuated by the media against people receiving benefits from the reasons why people don't claim them – and who struggle on instead. Indeed, the Institute for Social and Economic Research has estimated that only around 65% of people entitled to carer's allowance actually receive it.[318]

A bigger problem than benefit fraud is, realistically, of people being under-served by the benefits system. Even the tests, such as the work capability assessment, which are designed to assess people as to whether they are medically fit or not, have been shown, at judicial review, to place people with mental illness at a disadvantage.[319] Run by Atos, a private company, the criteria for judging when people are medically unfit enough to be allowed benefits has been persistently opaque. Thirty-eight per cent of people who appeal against the decision have it reversed at appeal – a process costing the state £50 million.[320]

The stress generated by the Atos system in people who are already ill has been one of the most shameful episodes

...I had to telephone the 0845 number again, wait another 30 minutes for the call to be answered, and tell the representative that the forms had been wrongly completed. I asked if it were possible to send the forms back with amendments, but that was not acceptable. Instead, I had to write a covering letter pointing out the errors and discrepancies and providing the correct information.

I was also asked to produce my original birth certificate, marriage certificate, and medical certificate of sickness and to provide details of any pensions or sickness insurances that I had paid for privately. These documents had to be sent by recorded delivery to the local Jobcentre office to process my claim.

I was shocked by the bureaucracy of a system that is supposed to be a safety net for people who fall sick through no fault of their own and have paid national insurance contributions all their lives. Fortunately, I am not reliant on receiving any state benefits for my living expenses because I have sufficient private provision, but I am sure that many of my patients are not in such a lucky position. Furthermore, I do not feel ill or unwell as such, otherwise I might not have had the strength and perseverance to persist with my claim. And nor do I have hearing loss or a speech impairment, which would make a telephone interview impossible. I am also organised enough to know where to find my birth and marriage certificates and so on.

It is a scandal that the system is so complicated: it is likely to fail the very people who are most in need of help. I suspect this may be a deliberate government ploy to reduce the number of benefit claims and reduce the overall cost of welfare. If so this should be publicised and shown for what it is: the government withholding funds from sick and needy people through a bureaucratic claim system.

Dyson AE. **It is too difficult for ill people to claim benefits.** *BMJ* 2012; 345: e7209 www.bmj.com/content/345/bmj.e7209

in recent British social history. One GP, writing about her patient who had no insight into her mental illness, and another man with learning difficulties, diabetes and alcohol addiction, wrote simply 'I am fearful that more of my patients will be put at risk of homelessness and suicide by this brutal new system.'[321]

The divide between social care and healthcare could not be more stark. The NHS offers to treat people 'who are ill or believe themselves to be ill'. A doctor can be struck off for choosing not to treat the sick patient in their consulting room. No one in need can be turned away by the NHS.

Yet when it comes to welfare and social care, judgement and stigma hang over a patient at every complicated form, as the state's system decides whether or not people will be given money. Fraud is played up by the media; yet the people who are deserving but not claiming are often invisible. People must prove they are deserving, through a system which is faulty, flawed and expensive. There is no presumption of people telling the truth; instead even the act of smiling during an interview with Atos is taken to mean that a person does not have severe depression.[322]

Where is the kindness and compassion, the human care for ill people who also need social care? How can we hope to give and receive humane care when the systems which are meant to provide them are so stressed and distressing themselves?

Targets and trust

At the end of life, there are many uncertainties; the time frame in which death is likely, the mode of death, the amount of medication required to bring relief from pain or anxiety, their side effects, the patient's wishes; their relatives' wishes. Healthcare staff may feel as though they are treading water, constantly trying to ensure they are doing the right thing. Decisions are based on delicate, often difficult conversations with the patient and their family, who are facing the enormous stress of the death of a loved one. It should go without saying that the conversations should be underpinned with the trust that the best interests of the patient are at heart.

And then we bludgeon what should be a carefully realised dialogue with the imposition of financial targets. In 2012, Freedom of Information requests revealed that 85% of NHS hospital trusts had received financial payments – totalling around £12 million – for reaching specific numbers of patients who died on the Liverpool Care Pathway (LCP).[323] Financial incentives to trusts for hitting specific targets had been increasing since 2009.[324] Typically, a trust had under 10% of deaths coded as 'palliative' in 2008 before rising to between 30 and 40% after the target was placed in 2012.[325]

What are we to make of this? For many families, the conclusion was obvious – their relative had been placed on the LCP and treated as 'palliative' in order for the hospital trust to collect the money for meeting the target. Some journalists stated: 'reports have suggested that doctors have been establishing "death lists" of patients to put on the pathway'.[326] 'Hospitals bribed to put patients on pathway to death' ran one headline.

How must this have felt to families whose relative was, or had recently been, terminally ill? The temptation to think that a child, mother, father, sister or brother had died earlier in order to reap financial reward for the hospital was pricked by a media looking to blame. Targets in healthcare offer rewards for specific behaviour, when surely patients and families have a right to expect that the behaviour of healthcare staff is motivated only by the need to do their best for them.

It is like shining a light at different parts of the same elephant. We want personal care for people who may – or may not – be approaching the end of life, delivered by trustworthy people, who have time to care, who explain, who communicate, who listen, and comfort. We want to know that a doctor suggests a course of action, not because a manager has told her to do so in order to meet a target, but because it is the best course of action and more likely to bring comfort to the patient.

We should want doctors who listen, who act with the best interests of their patients at heart, and who respond to the individual, despite the uncertainty faced by all parties. These are exactly the qualities which conflict with a politically driven NHS, and which fails to prize the need for hands-on, eye-to-eye, person-to-person, human healthcare.

We should design health services to help healthcare staff concentrate on just this. Financial rewards thwart trust – and subvert professionalism.

Chapter 6

The Myths Of CPR

Most people – 67% – want to die at home, pain free, with their family and friends, and with dignity – but 60% of these would change their mind if there was not enough support to allow them to do so.[327] We need the right kind of care, staff, treatments and equipment available at home as rapidly as it was needed. But, as we have seen, it would also mean withdrawing or stopping some treatments, such as chemotherapy, or choosing not to have such interventions such as CPR.

Anyone who has seen cardiopulmonary resuscitation will have a flavour of its drama. A monitor shows that the heart stops, or the patient may collapse, becoming rapidly comatose. An alarm sounds, and there is noise and bustle as a team of doctors and nurses rush in. The head rest is pulled down flat. The chest is compressed repeatedly, by hands forcing the ribcage up and down in a rapid, regular rhythm. A finger sweeps the mouth to remove anything obstructing the passage of air, and the head is tilted back. The lungs are inflated by mouth-to-mouth breathing, or via a face mask. Tubes may be inserted into the windpipe to inflate the lungs. This is done manually as the chest continues to be pumped. A line is put in a vein, either in the arm or the neck, and drugs are injected through it. The heart is monitored for signs of life. Pads are placed on the bare chest wall to distribute an electric shock to the heart. The staff stand back as the body convulses. The monitor is watched, and further shocks, or chest compressions, continue. This continues until no sign of life can be detected, or until the heart starts to beat again. If it does, the patient is usually transferred to intensive care for further treatment.

In my own experience, I have seen impressive success with CPR – the clearly life-saving resuscitation, for the father who weeks later walked out of hospital holding his toddler daughter's hand. It's hard to forget the failures. The harsh, visceral crunch as my fingers broke fragile ribs, the bruising of papery skin, the family members pushed aside to watch the traumatic clinical struggle of CPR from the edge of the room, needles, tubes, electric shocks and 'stand clear'.

The kind of CPR that occurs in popular media is very different. A survey of what happened in fictional US television programmes was published in the *New England Journal of Medicine* and found that most patients – almost 70% – survive to discharge.[328] The authors concluded 'In a subtle way, the misrepresentation of CPR on television shows undermines trust in data and fosters trust in miracles'. An assessment of UK television scenarios concluded that they gave a 'falsely high expectation to the public'.[329] This is reflected in surveys where most patients rate their chances of surviving CPR as 80% or better – indeed, almost a quarter of older patients believed their chance of survival was 90% or better.[330]

The real-life outcomes are, sadly, very different. In the US, when people are resuscitated outside hospital, most do not survive. Taking the whole population, including young and old people, just 9.6% of people resuscitated outside hospital make it to discharge home.[331] When it comes to people who need resuscitating inside hospital, 17% survived to be able to be discharged from hospital.[332] CPR fails far more often than it saves lives – it is not a miracle cure. Even doctors and nurses overestimate the chances of successful CPR for their patients.[333]

Additionally, CPR can be successful in that the person survives – but unsuccessful in terms of the quality of life it results in. In a study published in the *New England Journal of Medicine* in 2013 looking at older adults, out of 6,972 patients who had survived CPR in hospital, a fifth died within 30 days. The older the patient, the less likely their survival.[334] Meantime, when patients were resuscitated in hospital, although 84% had been admitted to hospital from their homes, only 51% were able to return there.[335] Being dependent on others for care, or having dementia, or metastatic cancer, all make successful CPR less likely.[336]

Indeed, for patients with metastatic cancer, a review published in 1991 found that no patient with advanced metastatic cancer survived and went on to be discharged from hospital.[337] Similarly, in another series, 243 patients had cancer and were in hospital when they had a cardiac arrest and CPR. One hundred and seventy-one of these cardiac arrests were anticipated – these patients were recognised as dying. The remaining 73 patients had a sudden and unexpected arrest. Of the 171 patients who were already ill and deteriorating, none survived to be discharged from hospital. Of the 73 patients who suddenly arrested, 16 survived to be able to be sent out of hospital – though only 6 went home, with the remainder going to other hospitals or hospices.[338] In other words, CPR does not help those people who are unwell, and clinically deteriorating, in hospital with metastatic cancer. Resuscitation can, uncommonly, help people who have cancer and who have a cardiac arrest – the 6 out of 73 getting home after a cardiac arrest may be a poor result, but is not far off the average outcome.

Consent and usefulness

From this data, the rationale for professionals to feel justified in not offering CPR is clear. In most situations it is not at all likely to work, and when it does sustain life, it is likely to result in brain damage and/or an invasive, unpleasant death. Far from decrying a lack of CPR, professional concerns have been of doctors applying CPR too often and too indiscriminately. Indeed, from the *Journal of Medical Ethics*: 'Beneficence supports use of CPR when most effective. Non-maleficence argues against performing CPR when the outcomes are harmful or usage inappropriate... Autonomy restricts CPR use when refused but cannot create a right to CPR.'[339] Thus, doctors should not, and cannot ethically be forced to perform a useless or harmful procedure on a patient even if the patient wants it. In fact, this is simply in keeping with any other medical intervention. Just as patients should not be able to legally force doctors to perform, say, brain surgery for no good reason and with attendant risks, so CPR should not be performed without firm appraisal of the probability of a good outcome – and consideration of the potential, harmful downsides.

This should be no less straightforward than any other discussion of risk and benefit, but the legal and media climate in which CPR is, or is not, performed, is perilous. In 2011, a woman who had terminal cancer broke her neck in a car accident. The doctors treating her had entered a 'DNR' (do not resuscitate) notice into her notes, which meant that she was not to have cardiopulmonary resuscitation were her heart to stop. It was removed after a family member objected, but reinserted when she was very ill a few days later. However this was not discussed with the patient herself but her family.[340] The husband of the patient told the BBC 'It was my wife's wish, she did not want a DNR. She was quite clear, and it was not my decision to make. It was hers. It was her life.' The NHS Trust has said that on the second occasion, the patient did not wish to discuss whether or not the DNR order should be replaced, and it was discussed with the family instead.[341]

The harsh reality is that, from the reported facts, survival from CPR in a woman with metastatic lung cancer and a broken neck would, from a reading of the evidence, be negligible to zero. The treating doctors may have felt that chest compressions and intubation would have been more likely to result in distress together with a minimal or no chance of CPR working.

Similarly, in 2012, a case was brought against an NHS Trust after a patient had a DNR form placed in his notes. The man had Down's syndrome and dementia, he was unable to swallow, and had a feeding tube placed in his stomach. While learning disability should never be used as a reason to withhold CPR, it seems that in this case the patient was chronically and significantly unwell, and had been bedbound for some time.[342] Again, with dementia being a risk factor for CPR being ineffective,[343] the evidence would suggest that the chance of survival after CPR would be minimal.

These cases were reported widely in the press, with much legal comment being passed over the unacceptable 'power' that doctors wielded. The *Daily Mail* ran a headline 'Do not resuscitate: They're the fateful words meaning doctors won't try to save you if you collapse in hospital. But could they go on your file without you being asked?'[344] Recurrently, media horror is expressed if the choice of CPR is seemingly not being offered. The *Daily Telegraph* even printed a list of patients who had died, without being resuscitated, after a DNR instruction had been placed in the notes and without the family being aware of it. One relative said 'To have a situation where a doctor can put a DNR order without telling the patient, his family or anyone else is callous and arrogant.'[345] A commentator in the *BMJ* told doctors that 'Do not resuscitate orders at any age, without discussion, are unethical.'[346]

While official NHS guidance makes it clear 'individuals do not have the right to demand that doctors carry out treatment against their clinical judgement' they compound this by saying 'the person's wishes to receive treatment should be respected wherever possible'. It's always 'possible' to perform CPR – the question is whether or not this is a useful, dignified or kind intervention for patients to have.

If a patient declines CPR, the NHS says that this decision is to be 'clearly documented in the medical and nursing notes after a thorough, informed decision with the individual and possibly their relatives'.[347] The risk is seen to be that of *not* having CPR. There is no such equivalent form for patients to consent into CPR, explaining the hazards and side effects. Patients may also find it difficult to recall crucial aspects of information around it – one small study has found that, in people who had CPR explained to them, only a small minority recalled the risk of brain damage.[348]

The result of this policy, where I practise, is that each person with a terminal illness has to have a form filled out to document that consent has been obtained for CPR not to be performed. It's obviously vital that all the people caring for the family – nurses, physiotherapists, doctors, ambulance staff – know that CPR is not appropriate. But the forms are also in order to mitigate against the charge that in not performing CPR, we healthcare workers do not get sued. When planning the care of a dying person, there are often frequent visits where we explain the roles of painkilling medication – a drug infusion, or painkilling patches. We often tell family members what death can be like – how breathing can falter or seem to stop before it finally does. We explain about how to keep the mouth moist, and the skin moisturised, and our district nurses will be coming over twice a day or more to assist with turning the patient, monitoring pain, and supporting the family.

It has always seemed to me incongruous and self-protectionist to find the opportunity to discuss the role of a DNR form and to seek the family's consent for the form to be signed and left in the hallway. In these circumstances, the patient and their family know that death is near; the spoken plan has been for a peaceful, calm death. I have a duty as a doctor to be honest, and would never wish to lie or cover up the fact that CPR would be unhelpful and harmful. Yet raising a 'thorough, informed decision' can often seem like raising unnecessary pain. After all, we do not ask patients or their families to sign consent forms for CPR.

Spelling out the risks of such inappropriate CPR may

be honest. At the end of life, it may also be insensitive and harmful to patients and their families. In reality CPR is an intervention which can do just as much harm as the delivery of any other unwise medicine. Additionally, it can place relatives under pressure to feel that agreeing to a DNR order will make them subsequently responsible for their relative's death. As another doctor told the BMJ: 'Recently, in the space of a fortnight, two of my inpatients have complained when cardiopulmonary resuscitation was sensitively discussed with them by a doctor. Both patients felt that these decisions should have been made by the medical profession without their involvement and they both felt that by discussing resuscitation with them the doctor thought they were likely to die. Both patients were discharged home.'[349] While medicine should not be paternalistic, secretive or presumptuous, it should also be practised flexibly with discretion and kindness. While the default position should be one of complete transparency and clear communication between patient, carers, family and healthcare professionals, protocols and guidelines should not overstep individual conversations, discussions, and the need for care and subtlety. The National Audit on Death and Dying in 2014 reported that only about half of family members were told what to expect. This is far from ideal. There is a need for ongoing informative conversation, based on what families and patients want and need to know, and can absorb at a particular time. There is far more to helping families through a death than offering brutal statistics in order to please the binary tick boxes on a form.[350]

Kindness and resuscitation

As a junior doctor I encountered a new policy, encouraging senior doctors to discuss CPR orders with their patients. The result was that frail patients at the end of life were given an unexpected discourse from their doctor on whether they wanted to be resuscitated or not if they were to collapse without a pulse. From the evidence, and because the ward

I was working on was for a group of very old patients with severe, ongoing illnesses, CPR would have been extremely unlikely to be successful – and very likely harmful. I remember a wife asking why the discussion had been had at all – why, she wondered, when it was already clear that her husband was at the end of his life? Couldn't we see how distressed the conversation made him? Her hurt was apparent; it had been salt rubbed in raw wounds. She told me later that she felt the discussion had provoked a low mood in her partner which lasted until he died, a few days later, in hospital. The need to protect the hospital against law suits seemed to have overtaken the need to sensitively choose when and if it is appropriate to have a conversation at all.

In early 2013, there was an international outcry when the tape recording of a nurse calling for emergency services in the US was broadcast. The nurse on the phone said that she could not perform CPR. The emergency dispatcher on the phone pleaded with her to do so. It was policy in the facility for CPR not to be performed. The dispatcher went on: 'I understand if your boss is telling you, you can't do it, but, as a human being, is there anyone that's willing to help this lady and not let her die?'[351] The patient was 87 years of age and died, after the emergency phone call, of a stroke. Her chances of survival after CPR, from the medical details publicly available, would have been slender. Many commentators wrote of how important CPR was[352] or of the need for a criminal investigation,[353] or who was liable.[354] Crucially, her family afterwards released a statement saying 'It was our beloved mother and grandmother's wish to die naturally and without any kind of life-prolonging intervention. We regret that this most private and personal time has been escalated by the media. Caregivers, nurses and other medical professionals have very difficult waters to tread in the legal and medical landscape of our country today.' [355] The family were at peace with a carefully thought out and long-standing decision. Yet much of the media seemed unable to accept that it was possible or wise for her to have done so.

Essentially it seems that not performing CPR – whether the family or patient has requested it or declined it – is liable to set the media rabidly loose on finding a party to blame.

We are invited into an exquisite dilemma. There is a wish that 'everything possible' is done; yet 'everything possible', if we are terminally ill, is very likely not to help and instead rob us of a peaceful death. There is no protocol or calculation that can entirely predict the outcome of CPR. Instead we have to

> Among the forms was one that mattered: the DNR – do not resuscitate – order. Dr No's mother was dying, and in the event of her collapse, attempts to resuscitate her would be both futile and burdensome, an officious yet pointless striving to keep alive. The original purple order was placed near her, at the front of her notes, and the order propagated through the system, to the out of hours and emergency services, to forestall unnecessary heroics.
>
> Or so we thought: in fact, it wasn't. When Dr No's mother collapsed in the early hours one morning, her live-in carer (Dr No was at home, taking a rest after four days of chaos), previously frustrated by the dallying ways of 111, understandably dialled 999. Red lights went on, and blue lights started flashing. Paramedics were dispatched, police called to the scene, and the 999 operator gave immediate orders to start cardio-pulmonary resuscitation. Instead of being allowed, as intended, to die peacefully, Dr No's mother was subject to the panoply of a response befitting the unexpected collapse of a fit twenty year old, all because of an IT failure. The DNR order, intended to forestall unnecessary heroics, had got lost; and the live-in carer, lest you be in any doubt about the gravity of the situation, was ordered to assault – assault, because that is technically what it was, if Dr No's mother was still alive – Dr No's dying mother, an act as unkind as unfair to both carer and patient.
>
> Dr No. **The ghastly passage.**
> *Bad Medicine blog*, 1 March 2013
> www.badmed.net/bad-medicine-blog/2013/03/ghastly-passage.html

rely on the professional opinions of the healthcare workers looking after us. We have to pay attention to analyses finding that 13% of people resuscitated survive to discharge – but also note that all of those people were described as 'otherwise healthy with reversible conditions who experienced a sudden and unexpected arrhythmic [heart rhythm] event'.[356] CPR can work for the basically healthy who have a sudden cardiac problem. It is not a successful treatment for people who are frail and declining.

The prediction of death, as we have seen, is inexact and difficult. Add this to the emotional pain of a parent or sibling dying, and decisions for a family can be fraught. The default position should be for patients and their families to know what is written in the notes, and to be aware of the most likely outcomes of CPR. While the institution of medicine has power, the only real power medicine has over expected deaths is to make the process more bearable through comfort, the relief of pain, nursing care, explanation and consolation. What's compassionate care? Does it include insisting that patients or their relatives must know and approve plans not to offer ineffective treatments? Who is being protected – the patient or their doctors?

Choice and professionalism

In fact, many medical interventions are not routinely offered to patients when it is likely they would do more harm than good, like organ transplantation or kidney dialysis. If we want to follow the NHS instructions that 'the person's wishes… should be respected wherever possible' it would reverse the means which medicine uses to protect people from ineffective interventions. It would mean that doctors would be obliged to give antibiotics for sore throats if the patient wanted them (no matter if the infection was viral and the antibiotics would be more likely to cause diarrhoea and antibiotic resistance) or sick notes for people who requested them, even if they were well and capable of employment. Medical professionals routinely use their clinical judgement about the appropriateness of what they offer and indeed are criticised when they prescribe excessive antibiotics[357] or give sick notes liberally.[358]

Interpreting what choices are acceptably safe, practicable and advantageous for patients is a key professional skill. These sets of clinical judgements are part of the covenant of professional practice. Medicine cannot be a safe commercial transaction because of the harms that unchecked free choice of medication, monitoring or surgery would incur. Nor are privately made decisions which patients and doctors make insulated against their wider impact. The practice of doctors in the care of one individual will also affect the broader community, be it in the development of 'superbugs' due to thoughtlessly prescribed antibiotics causing resistance, or the societal cost of fraud in the welfare system, were sick notes to be signed recklessly. Similarly, professional practice means that doctors should not have a choice as to who they treat. Doctors have an obligation to care for people who are not 'easy' or 'profitable' – who may have alcohol or drug addiction, who are dirty, or who smell, or whose treatments are expensive or time consuming to deliver. Doctors are also obliged to treat people whose past experiences or current distress may make them angry, be frustrating to interact with, or simply unpleasant and rude. The reality of medical 'choice' has limits to its safe freedom.

So how do we find the balance between cherishing the principle of autonomy for patients against the need of doctors to ensure that resources are used wisely and without undue harm? The professional covenant held by doctors does not negate the need for transparency, or for patients to take the lead on the decisions to be made. This covenant does not lend itself to paternalism, the 'doctor knows best' attitude that has caused much suffering where patients, for many years and in many instances, have hardly had a voice. It should mean that doctors must advocate for their patients with compassion. But none of this means that doctors must follow patients' requests for useless or even actively harmful treatment 'wherever possible'.

In May 2014, the Council of Europe published their *Guide on the decision-making process regarding medical treatment in end-of-life situations*.[359] The report comments:

> 'Autonomy does not imply the right for the patient to receive every treatment he or she may request, in particular when the treatment is considered inappropriate. Indeed, health-care decisions are the result of a reconciliation between the will of the patient and the assessment of the situation by a professional who is subject to his or her professional obligations and, in particular, those arising from the principles of beneficence and non-maleficence as well as justice.'

The NHS decree of 'whenever possible' is not very helpful. 'Whenever useful' would be better. And, if we define 'goodness' in medicine as a phenomenon which needs listening, wisdom, care and compassion, 'whenever good' would be better again.

Saying no

If our decisions are to be 'good', then we need to know we can have confidence in receiving professional advice. If we are given the information that an expensive treatment is no good, for example, we should be able to trust that this is factually correct, and not because less treatment means less bother or profit for the doctor. Nor should patients feel that they or their medical needs are a burden to healthcare professionals or resources. We have to be able to trust the ability of professionals to help us make 'good' choices. This does not excuse patronising healthcare which excludes or dismisses the patient. As Onora O'Neill said in her 2002 Reith Lecture: 'Trusting is not a matter of blind deference, but of placing – or refusing – trust with good judgement.'[360]

When it comes to decisions around DNR orders, decision making is placed more formally into a relationship in law, rather than of, primarily, trust and professionalism. This brings a new set of dilemmas. While CPR is a dramatic event, the myriad other, quieter decisions which patients and doctors make are no less important – from offering and accepting help to stop smoking, to the decision to take aspirin after a stroke – may have just as much effect over when death occurs. Yet we do not insist on the same legal documentation to be agreed, signed and stored for each of those choices. Instead, it seems that contemporary concerns about a perceived lack of resuscitation have overwhelmed our ability to take careful stock of its limitations and hazards, and have compelled the use of law, rather than professionalism, to safeguard it.

And has the effect of a legal framework protected patients? Time and again, healthcare professionals in North America cite fear of being sued as a reason for performing CPR which they know to be futile.[361] While this may lessen some doctors' fear of being sued, it will have changed the nature of many deaths from peaceful to spectacles of failed heroic medical interventions. This may perhaps have kept some doctors out of the law courts, but is it really a fair exchange for quality of death for the dying and their families?

Indeed, for healthcare professionals, not performing CPR can be seen as the riskier inaction. A paper from Canada published in 1999 looked at how likely paramedics were to give CPR to terminally ill patients. The fact that patients had made a prior instruction not to have CPR made no difference as to whether or not the patient received it.[362] A lack of formal documentation can also be seen as a reason to resuscitate. In one US study, only half of patients who did not want to have resuscitation had it formally documented, meaning that they could still be subjected to it despite their wishes to the contrary.[363] And in questionnaire surveys, about a third of German doctors said they would perform CPR against patient wishes.[364]

What of the opposite? Rarely, reports have emerged of doctors being sued because they did not follow a patient's advance directive not to have CPR. In April 2013, in the US, a 90-year-old lady with dementia was increasingly confused and septic when she collapsed. The ambulance crew were apparently not aware of her DNR form, and proceeded to CPR, the insertion of a breathing tube and a line going into the jugular vein, together with drugs to temporarily paralyse her. She was given artificial ventilation and a feeding tube before her daughter intervened. She was then placed in a palliative care unit, where she died a few days later. To add insult to injury, her daughter was sent a medical bill for all the interventions she had but which she had said, in advance, that she didn't want.[365] Her daughter's complaint was that her mother had been 'robbed of her natural death and instead suffered from prolonged dying in a manner that was contrary and repugnant to her expressed wishes'.[366]

Sure, there's nothing intrinsically good about 'natural'. Meningitis, measles and ricin are all potentially fatal but also pretty 'natural'. Nevertheless, it's understandable that in the US, the Hospice Patients Alliance has written of the alternative code to DNR – 'allow natural death' or AND. 'As most of us in the medical field know, asking for a DNR does not mean that we have stopped care. What it means is that we have simply changed the goal of treatment.'[367] This 'allow natural death' instruction has been taken up by some hospitals in the UK.[368] Yet still there is little explanation of how ineffective CPR will change the nature of a death. The form-filling culture ensures that clinical staff, patients and families may still feel like risk takers for not doing CPR.

Then there is the additional misconception around DNR orders: the perception that once the form has been filled in, the patient is 'written off', the prognosis is hopeless, and care will not be delivered as dutifully. This has been perpetuated by many media reports whose headlines have suggested that a DNR means that doctors have 'given up', that useful treatments will be taken away, and that death is near. These are incorrect. In truth, medicine has only ever been able to cure a precious few conditions, and most medical offerings can only aim to prolong life, reduce suffering, or improve the quality of our existence. When resuscitation is not performed, the aims of medical care do not change.

In Cleveland, Ohio, in 1999, 'Comfort Care Orders' were placed on statute allowing people to choose not to have CPR in the future. However, crucially, the legal framework emphasised that attending emergency crews would still care and support the patient.[369] Thus, patients at the end of life are still given analgesia, or drugs for nausea, or secretions removed from the throat if there is difficulty breathing. 'DNR' clearly is not equivalent to inaction. It means plentiful, kind and compassionate care.

What may seem at first glance as 'medical power' to 'deny' CPR is more about the aching futility of much of medicine in the face of death. Should every patient have to give their consent *not* to have CPR? CPR remains the default option. And while it is undoubtable that CPR has delayed the deaths of many people and should continue to be judiciously used, it clearly does not work when people are already terminally ill.

Chapter 7

War, Truth and Lies at the End of Life

Bravery and battles

Medicine is inexact, often messy, and what happens in the last weeks and months of life may be down to chance, not a predictable power of medicine. Doctors will get prognoses wrong, even when relying on the best available evidence and long careers filled with experience in caring for people in similar situations. This can work in our favour – or against it.

These hinterlands are cloaked in uncertainty. Decisions are often being made by patients, families and healthcare professionals with different aims in mind. When is a treatment worth it, especially when there is no hope of a cure? Is delaying death always best no matter the cost in side effects or time spent in hospital? And what, then, is the role of 'hope'?

Time and again people with serious diseases are encouraged to 'be positive, be full of hope, be ready to fight'. That particular phrase was plastered onto billboards across Glasgow in 2014, calling for donations to the local cancer hospital. Being hopeful and willing to do battle are seen as essential weapons in the 'war' on cancer. Conflict has become a powerful metaphor in medicine – there are 'magic bullets' of treatment, which are offered to 'blast' tumours – and I read, sadly, many times in an obituary, that someone 'lost the fight'. People are 'victims', drugs are 'powerful', and doing 'battle' with disease is a common description even in the most gentle of people.

A US oncologist is quoted as saying in the cyclist Lance Armstrong's book about testicular cancer: 'We're going to hit you with chemo, and then hit you again, and hit you again'. His reaction to hearing this was of 'shell shock'. Armstrong promptly changed oncologists.[370] Clearly, offering a vision of future bodily assault as treatment can alienate and harm, rather than help, patients.

The war metaphor may suit some. Stephen Sutton, a young man who died of bowel cancer, was widely lauded for his spirited efforts to raise money for charity at the end of his life with an uncomplaining, upbeat attitude. He wrote about how he valued each day of life, and that, aged 18 'in the last three years I have been fighting cancerous tumours in my bowel, knee, groin and pelvis'.[371] He was treated with multiple rounds of chemotherapy. Perhaps some people may draw a plan or a mindset which they find useful in framing the delivery of unpleasant treatments, or in accepting side effects which are hard to tolerate.

But the end problem is this: battles have winners and losers, and if we depict illness as a battle, then deciding not to have unpleasant but rarely effective treatments becomes not a rational decision about quality of life, but a choice of the patient to 'lose'. This is unfair to the person and their family. These people are not 'losers'; nor do they lack bravery or courage. Nor is there any evidence that people with cancer who have a 'fighting attitude' live longer or have less recurrences of their illness.[372] Additionally, in a small study, researchers noted that patients felt doctors promoted a 'positive attitude' which 'meant resisting the expression of emotional distress rather than the disease. By encouragement to "fight" and "be positive", clinicians may therefore collude with patients' emotional suppression.' Doctors urging patients to fight and be positive may end up with patients and their families unable to talk about their fears, desire to stop active treatment or accepting and planning death.[373]

A culture of 'war on cancer' and of valuing bravery in illness may therefore prevent patients from discussing feelings about nearing death. It may also make it more difficult for some people to decide to stop, or not to take interventions they are offered. It is natural to be afraid of what might happen, of whether the treatments will work, or of what the side effects might be. Patients and their families will naturally also wonder what the future will hold, and how long life might now last.

Doctors must be honest, but this necessity may mean disclosure of a great deal of unsureness. It is rare for doctors to be able to offer a prognosis of complete certainty. Even when it is highly likely that a person will never have a recurrence of their breast or bowel cancer, it is uncommon for anyone to be told they are 'all clear', for example. These grey areas, with their lack of absolutes, married with fear and hope, create a potent combination that can be hard to live with. It is not just the purveyors of the alternative therapies who promise cures for cancer through esoteric, non-evidence-based, and often expensive scams. False hope can be delivered just as badly by conventional doctors.

Mrs Nancy Wolf, an American, was diagnosed aged 79 with lung cancer, after an x-ray done as a screening test was performed by her doctor. After her death, her children – who included a medical historian, an actuary and a health journalist – wrote an essay describing and evaluating their mother's and their decisions.[374] Nancy's family doctor, who was responsible for ordering the x-ray (a screening test, which was not part of an evidence based programme), told her 'how sorry he was'. Nancy 'laughed as she recalled his words... He acted like I'm dying.' She then met a surgeon, who thought he could remove the tumour, and proceeded to operate. She then met an oncologist, who recommended chemotherapy. Two of her children were present at the appointment. The oncologist told them that half of patients with Nancy's stage of disease could survive for five years, and this could be increased with chemotherapy to 60 to 65%. But Nancy was 79. Would this make a difference, the children asked? Yes.

> He then revised downward his five-year-survival-without-chemotherapy estimate, to below 50 percent. When the two actuaries pointed out that as a seventy-nine-year old, Nancy's prognosis was also likely bleaker than studies indicated even *with* chemotherapy, Dr. O1 offered anecdotal evidence supporting treatment. He noted that a current patient, now 77, was still alive one year after four rounds of chemotherapy.

This use of anecdotal evidence by the oncologist is powerful. It can humanise statistics which otherwise appear as two dimensional objects, and create a powerful and hopeful image (and, mea culpa, I have used this tool by telling stories illustrating this book.) But anecdote can also mislead, because one form of cognitive bias – recall bias – is capable of filtering out our memories of the bad things that happened. For example, we may not remember patients dying sooner than we thought they would and recall only our exceptionally good success stories.

Nancy went on to have chemotherapy, despite the later finding by her children – who studied the research literature – that it would improve her chances of survival, three years after treatment, from an average of 40% to 45%. She also had radiotherapy to her brain to treat metastatic tumours but described these as treatments that would 'make my brain inhospitable to cancer'. Her children noted her saying 'Maybe I can live twenty years and it won't recur.' Nancy went on to have further treatment with drugs and regular scans but her cancer had spread, aggressively. Her cancer was clearly at a late stage with death being near, but she did not understand this because the messages she got from her doctors emphasised treatments that might help her. Her daughter Jackie had discussed a friend with the same type of cancer with her. Nancy said:

But Nancy did not understand she was about to die. Instead she believed, as she kept telling friends and family, that WBRT [whole brain radiotherapy] would make her brain 'inhospitable to cancer.' Indeed, she assumed that WBRT would add many productive years to her life...

Yet Dr. R never hinted that the chance of Nancy surviving beyond a few months was slim. To the contrary, he spoke of 'years' of survival without debilitating effects and explicitly stated that whole brain radiotherapy would ward off the brain tumors' detrimental effects...

Nancy completed the thirteen WBRT treatments that Dr. R recommended but stopped the radiation treatments on her neck at eight because she was barely able to talk or swallow after the eighth treatment. In fact, the pain became so intense on April 9 that she and Herb went to the emergency room of their local hospital...

Nancy asked Dr. R about hospice as an alternative to the radiation that was now causing her so much discomfort. In individual phone calls to their children shortly after their appointment with Dr. R, Herb and Nancy reported that Dr. R responded angrily to Nancy's query about hospice. Hospice was 'fine', he told them, 'if you want to spend the rest of your life on opiates, doped into oblivion, lying in your own BMs [bowel movements].' Herb, age eighty-three, told his children that he and Dr. R almost came to blows.

Everything that Dr. R insisted would be prevented by WBRT occurred within four weeks of the treatment's end. Nancy became incontinent. She could not shower or dress herself. She could walk only in a slow shuffle, leaning heavily on another person, measuring progress in inches. She was unable to make simple decisions.

Wolf JH, Wolf KS.
The Lake wobegon effect: are all cancer patients above average?
The Millbank Quarterly 2013; 91 (4): 690-728.
www.oucom.ohiou.edu/hpf/pdf/bios%20april%202014/Volume91_Issue4_Are_All_Cancer_Patients_above_Average.pdf

'But her cancer is completely different from mine'...
'Oh?' Jackie asked. 'Her cancer isn't non-small-cell?'
'No, it is.' Puzzled, Jackie pressed her mother. 'So how is it different?'
Nancy responded impatiently, '*Her* cancer is terminal.'

Jackie was stunned. She said nothing, unsure of how to contradict her mother's interpretation of doctors' messages.

Nancy's mistaken belief in the chances of success of her treatment is not isolated. A study published in the *New England Journal of Medicine* in 2012 found that 81% of patients being treated with chemotherapy for metastatic bowel cancer did not understand that this treatment was palliative, to try and control symptoms, and with no expectation that it would cure their cancer.[375]

Additionally, in the UK, there is evidence that many people at the end of life are not recognised by their doctors as dying – and don't get offered the palliative care that could improve their last days.[376, 377]

Clearly, even though Nancy was surrounded by professionals as well as her caring family, she did not get the information that the treatments weren't likely to help. She wasn't able to use this knowledge to protect herself from the side effects of treatment or, perhaps, to use her last months away from hospitals and in the way that she wanted to. Her doctors kept offering her hope that treatments would cure her.

However this kind of hope was not realistic. It would likely have been more evidence based – and better for Nancy – to introduce palliative care early, to improve her pain control and talk about the feasible goals of treatment. The goal could not have been, in all honesty, to cure. Is it not better to have the hope of living one's remaining life as fully as possible, and to use medicine to help the person feel and live better?

What doctors choose for themselves

Ken Murray, a retired US doctor, wrote in 2011:

> Years ago, Charlie, a highly respected orthopedist and a mentor of mine, found a lump in his stomach. It was diagnosed as pancreatic cancer by one of the best surgeons in the country, who had developed a procedure that could triple a patient's five-year-survival odds – from 5% to 15% – albeit with a poor quality of life.
>
> Charlie, 68 years old, was uninterested. He went home the next day, closed his practice and never set foot in a hospital again. He focused on spending time with his family. Several months later, he died at home. He got no chemotherapy, radiation or surgical treatment... As for me, my doctor has my choices on record. They were easy to make, as they are for most physicians. There will be no heroics, and I will go gentle into that good night. Like my mentor Charlie... Like so many of my fellow doctors.[378]

This anecdote reflects real life. The John Hopkins Precursor Study has followed a group of doctors who qualified in the US between 1948 and 1964. They have been asked what treatments they would want in the future. By 2008, the vast majority – 92% – didn't want CPR, and 88% wouldn't have chemotherapy for cancer. Additionally, two thirds had written an advance directive making clear what interventions they didn't want.[379, 380]

A medical career gives insight into both the usefulness – and not – of medicine at the end of life. It's striking that so many doctors would choose not to have supposedly 'lifesaving' interventions. The question is whether citizens without a medical career have access to the same kind of information that doctors do – and whether they would make different choices were they to have it.

Alternative untruths

In the alternative medicine sector, false hope in general, and in terminal illness in particular, is just as prolific. Media reports regularly name people who have chosen to eschew evidence-based treatments for the false hope of alternative therapies. It's easy to find therapists online who promise not to use evidence-based treatments but instead focus their efforts on unproven (and often expensive) diets, dietary supplements, vitamins and treatments. Gerson Therapy offers a special diet, coffee enemas, and supplements with the claim that it is used 'as a treatment for degenerative diseases such as skin tuberculosis, diabetes and, most famously, cancer'.[381] There is no trial evidence to suggest this is the case.[382]

One woman described how she decided to reject evidence-based medicine:

> Did I want my path through cancer to be passive or something I was actively involved with, where everything I did was focused on health? I didn't want to give my body chemicals and poisons. My body had created this problem, so if I gave it good things, de-stressed, detoxed, then I felt that I should be able to undo it.
>
> When I rang the radiotherapy department to cancel my treatments, they were confused. They asked if I'd spoken to my doctor and told me they would have to inform him. My husband and daughters trusted my judgment – but the rest of my family found it difficult to understand and thought I was crazy.
>
> I call what I did a 21st-century version of Gerson therapy. I had four juices a day, 120 supplements, homoeopathic injections and four coffee enemas. I also did yoga, meditation, reiki – a holistic approach. It's not an easy option. The treatment is a full-on, full-time job, and there's no room for anything else.[383]

The woman concerned now works as a 'holistic health specialist'. For all her efforts, there is no evidence that what she has done (except for the standard, orthodox advice for a healthy diet, weight and exercise) will improve her outlook.

Making good decisions depends on high-quality evidence and full admissions of uncertainty over the treatments offered. But this uncertainty means that it is possible for alternative therapists to claim a 'victory' over a cancer 'battle' when their successes would have happened anyway – and without their therapy.

Famously, the Burzynski clinic in the US has been accused of offering cancer treatments with no evidence behind them. This clinic, run by a doctor with no formal training in oncology[384] says they use the 'natural biochemical defense system of our body, capable of combating cancer with minimal impact on healthy cells'.[385] In the UK, in November 2011, an uncle wrote about his need to raise £200,000 to send his niece for treatment for a brain tumour to this clinic:

> Is it impossible for her to survive? No, as it turns out. Sam and Terri very quickly found out about a pioneering treatment at the Burzynski Clinic in Texas for children with DIPG [Diffuse Intrinsic Pontine Glioma]. The estimated cost is £200,000. It is not available in this country, it is new and there are no guarantees. When you are faced with a decision like that, what can you do? It's like Monopoly money and when we realised we would have to raise this amount, it seemed ridiculous. Especially as there's only a slight chance that the treatment might work.
>
> But it might save her life. So you have got to try. It was a relief to finally do something.[386]

The phenomenal effort that families will go to in order to assist is done, rightly, out of love. This can make us vulnerable to false hope. It is here that we need health professionals to be honest about the treatments – and not to be mere advertising agents. This is not the family's fault, but the fault of the promoters of treatments who did not make the limited or non-existent evidence for their alternative treatments clear. Ridiculously, critics of the clinic, who wanted to point out the distinct lack of evidence for the treatments offered, were threatened with legal action by people acting for the clinic.[387] For the family, as the child's uncle explained, it was more simple:

> Her parents know it is unproven, but there are other families in this country who were told by their hospital that their condition was terminal and nothing could be done for them, but were then treated at the clinic and survived. Knowing this, Billie's parents felt they couldn't sit back and do nothing if there was a small chance this treatment would save her life.[388]

Sadly the little girl, Billie, died in June 2012.[389] Burzynski, meantime, has claimed that he can cure half of certain cancers – well in excess of what conventional medicine can honestly offer[390] – despite the Texan Medical Board trying to remove his licence because of 'unprofessional and dishonourable conduct that is likely to deceive or defraud the public'.[391] And while the scale may be different – he is alleged to have falsified records, making it appear that the

In the United Kingdom, it is illegal to advertise cancer treatments under the Cancer Act (1939). Breaches of the Cancer Act should be reported to Trading Standards. Details of your local office may be found here.

To my mind, it is impossible to overstate the harm that can be done by 'miracle' cancer cures. They can drive a wedge between patients and their families just when they need them the most. They can give false hope to the desperately ill, persuading them to live out their days on complicated and punishing dietary regimes. Some people with treatable cancers will even refuse surgery and medication.

Jones. J. **The Cancer Act: who to report to.** Sense about Science. 25 September 2013 www.senseaboutscience.org/blog.php/65/the-cancer-act-who-to-report-to

treatment was working when it wasn't[392] – the selling of false hope can be just as toxic whether it appears in the alternative or mainstream medical sector.

In the UK, there are the rare convictions under the Cancer Act (1939) which seeks to protect people against quackery; one such was Errol Denton, who offered cures for cancer, diabetes and HIV 'caused by lifestyle and curable through lifestyle treatments and herbs'.[393] This was mainly as a result of a campaign from blogging activists who were concerned about persistently misleading advertising.[394]

However the Cancer Act alternative therapists still offer things that 'might help' or 'can assist'. Yet the expense, and time – especially if the patient's lifespan is now limited – are the additional hugely important costs of false hope.

The meaning of hope

It's clear from the popularity of these clinics that what they offer appeals to many people with serious illness. Certainly there should be regulation sufficient to expel healthcare professionals who offer treatments whose evidence for their advertising does not exist. But honesty also has the potential to be hurtful and cause harm – for example, a doctor advising a patient that death is likely in days rather than the expected years may cause enormous distress. So where should 'hope' exist in serious illness where life expectancy is very limited? One relative has written of her distress when 'hope' seemed to be removed from her sister.

> Some weeks later, at another hospital, she was diagnosed as having stage 4 ovarian cancer. It was a tough summer, with Militza undergoing further tests and chemotherapy. Her morale did not improve when a bright, young gynaecologist told her straight out: 'You have only a few months at best.'
>
> Again, she was left reeling and started having regular nightmares, also uncontrollable feelings of terror. When I tackled this doctor, she stood her ground. 'I was asked the question,' she told me. 'That is my obligation according to

> GMC [General Medical Council] guidance.' Yet I believe that whatever my sister had asked, she was not looking for a final departure date.
>
> As next of kin I had been privately warned that, at best, treatment offered only a 25 per cent chance of any improvement. I pleaded with her consultant that, while it was important to be open, Militza should not be frightened out of her wits. Despite the poor outlook, she needed something to work towards, even if it was a small chance that chemotherapy would help.
>
> After several sessions of chemotherapy, she was alone in her room in July when another registrar, again in his late 30s, came in and said: 'I have to tell you that the chemo has not worked. You now have three weeks to three months at the very best. We are sending you to a hospice right away.'
>
> She was moved within two hours. All hope was now gone: she was hit by the utter finality. Her nightmares increased in ferocity. She experienced a sense of rushing into a large, white wall and crashing into it.[395]

Was it right that doctors apparently told Militza that treatment hadn't worked? The charge is that removal of the 'hope' that Militza's disease might somehow still be cured was devastating to her. Conversely, telling someone that death is now nearing and inevitable may be kind and humane. I've come across situations where a husband doesn't want a wife to know her prognosis and vice versa. This leads to tremendous energy being used to create and maintain falsehoods, and the loss of an opportunity for the relationship strengths of families and friends to allow time to say things they need to, and a gentle death.

Professionals are also afraid of 'destroying hope' or outlining a bleak future.[396,367] Medical training is often about how to do and fix things: being able to offer no cure and feeling that they have no solution to offer can make doctors and nurses feel hopeless themselves. It is easy to feel inadequate as a doctor, especially when death is clearly premature – a young person or a child, for example. Doctors

> I have waited in the door of the clinic room for the inevitable return of a grown up child who needs to ask, out of earshot, how long their parent has left, as if knowing and planning and sorting will somehow hold things at bay... I have huddled with relatives of dying patients in corridors, in stairwells, in car parks and explained in simple terms the most complex of ideas – that the person they love is leaving forever. I have dragged myself wearily up the stairs to the ward after a long clinic to talk to the families of patients who are too unwell or confused to know who their children are... And I have sat in my office and wept for the times when I know in my heart of hearts that we haven't done the best we could. We haven't been as open or as honest as we should have been. We have let our desire for a 'good outcome' cloud our acceptance of a poor one. We have failed to diagnose dying until it's too late.
>
> Lowri E. **Dying Matters.**
> Elin Lowri's blog. 11 May 2013. elinlowri.wordpress.com

are given training in how to 'sound out' patients for the information they want – or think they might want. 'Cues' are listened for – a signal from a patient that they want to talk about the future. For example, a patient might say 'I've been wondering if I will be able to go on holiday', which might be a way of indicating that he or she wants to talk about when they might be expected to die.

Some information which doctors have a duty to offer will be distressing no matter how skilfully it is given. Yet it would also be cruel to force patients to hear poor prognoses when they are not ready to do so, or if they are already distressed, alone, or dealing with significant problems elsewhere in their lives. There may be no easy way through. In a review paper published in *Palliative Medicine*, it was found that not enough information about prognosis caused stress, anxiety and frustration for patients; there was, though, a clear wish from patients that professionals should be 'playing it straight'.[398]

For all that, research suggests that the majority of patients do want realism about their illness and not 'false hope'. One

> Clinicians are often uncomfortable discussing prognosis and possible treatment options if the information is unfavourable. The evidence suggests that this is due to a number of reasons including:
>
> - Uncertainty about the patient's expectations
> - Fear of destroying the patient's hope.
> - Fear of their own inadequacy in the face of uncontrollable disease.
> - Not feeling prepared to manage the patients anticipated emotional reactions.
> - Embarrassment at having previously painted too optimistic a picture for the patient.
>
> National Council for Hospice and Specialist Palliative Care Services. **Breaking Bad News: Regional Guidelines.** Department of Health, Social Services and Safety, Belfast, February 2003. www.dhsspsni.gov.uk/breaking_bad_news.pdf

US study found that 98% of patients who had widespread cancer wanted their doctors to give realistic views on what would happen to them – and 82% said they did not want their doctors to use euphemisms around death.[399] In a German study of patients who were severely affected by multiple sclerosis, 76% wanted to discuss the likely future pattern of their illness, and 64% wanted to talk about their future death and dying.[400] Another UK study of people who have heart failure found that 'prognostic uncertainty and high risk of sudden death lead to EOLC [end of life care] conversations being commonly avoided'.[401] We can never get rid of uncertainty, and the researchers suggested that discussions about the future could be introduced as 'hoping for the best, but preparing for the worst'. Making this better, though, is not simply about staff training. It's also about making it a priority within the system we work in. Staff being pressed for time is constant and 'normal'. One doctor described to me the feeling of knowing that it is going to be necessary to talk about death with a patient he felt sure was nearing the

> I think sometimes the transition from an intervention to palliative care sometimes can be pretty daunting for me as a consultant... I certainly find it difficult, and you may have to take a softly softly approach, one step at a time, and then say look the outlook looks grim so we may have to move from there, we need to discuss it with everyone else, with the relatives and everyone else and see how you can take this forward. I mean it's very difficult.
>
> Gott M, Ingleton C, Bennett MI et al.
> **Transitions to palliative care in acute hospitals in England: qualitative study.**
> *BMJ* 2011; 342: d1773. www.bmj.com/content/342/bmj.d1773

end of his life but 'the patient wants to talk about his tablets, and has an insurance form needing to be filled out, and I still have six patients to see in clinic, and a theatre list starting in an hour. I know I should. But I don't have time to start that conversation.'

What about 'too much' honesty? The Palliative Medicine review[402] – stated that 'for a proportion of patients, hope and realism were irreconcilable when presented with detailed or unequivocal information. Professionals have a responsibility to provide information to patients, but also to respect the need to maintain some ambiguity about the future, if that is a patient's wish.' And while this is laudable, it can create enormous conflicts – for example, of continuing to administer treatments which are causing only side effects and no chance of a longer life. I am not sure it will ever be possible to get the balance of information entirely right.

Hope for the best, plan for the worst

Instead it's helpful to examine what 'hope' means to patients. In the earlier part of the twentieth century, healthcare professionals would routinely not tell a patient he was dying in order to preserve 'hope'.[403] Now, these attitudes smack of paternalism, secrecy and a lack of human honesty.

> I was just summoned into the room of an actively dying patient who'd been in the ER for several hours. Both the emergency physician had seen her, as well as her admitting doctor. All they told... the family was that she was 'very, very sick' and that they would put her in hospital to try to treat this. So where did this leave the family? All they heard was 'sick and 'treat'... I gathered her son to my side and with great respect, I got right to the point. 'Sir, I am Dr. Murphy and I know that I have not been involved in the care of your mother, but your nurse has very kindly asked me to come speak with you. I know your mother is about to be transported upstairs to the room right now and I also know that her wishes are to have a Do Not Resuscitate order in place. But I'm concerned that no one has told you that your mother is actually dying right now and I'm sorry you have to hear this so abruptly and from a stranger.' I grabbed his hand to ease the blow. Then, I continued, 'Furthermore, frankly, I don't want to move her from this room. I think it would be best if you called any children and family you want to be with her.'
>
> With a gesture of gratitude, he grasped my shoulder and said, 'Thank you for telling me ...' and he immediately made phone calls and sent text messages.
>
> Within 15 minutes the room was filled with children and grandchildren. One of the children who worked in the hospital came up immediately — he was so grateful that the nurse and I had identified the dying moment so that he could be with his mom... Small grandchildren climbed up on the bed to kiss their grandmother's cheek while adult children held her hands. A hand-made blanket was draped over her legs. There were sweet whispers and loving goodbyes.
>
> Williams-Murphy M. **Doctors cannot speak about the reality of death and dying**. *KevinMD.com* blog, 6 September 2014. www.kevinmd.com/blog/2014/09/doctors-speak-reality-death-dying.html

Crucially, however, having 'hope' does not necessarily mean hope for a cure. It is possible to be expected to live for only days or weeks but still feel hopeful. In the US, patients with metastatic, incurable cancer were asked to define hope. Patients expressed it as a feeling 'that you can still enjoy a good quality of life even if life expectancy is uncertain' or 'a feeling or expectation that things can go well' or 'To get on with life, make sure you make the most of it for as long as you can; set a distant goal and work like hell to get there.' Only 8% defined 'hope' as 'they may find a cure or extend my life'.[404] In terms of who helped them to feel hopeful, only 9% cited 'advances in cancer care'. Most thought that families, friends, or spiritual beliefs produced hope for them. Hope is important for patients at the end of life – but might not have the same meaning for professionals or family as it has for the patient.[405] In other words, 'hope' mainly does not mean that patients are chasing cures or prolonged life. Indeed, when children are terminally ill, parents can feel hopeful even when they have been told that their child's expected lifespan is short.[406] When people with terminal illnesses are asked about hopes for the future, and what is 'most important to achieve?' the answers are usually about basic things; being free of pain or experiencing simple pleasures, for example 'I want to be able to sit on my front porch and watch the farm go by.'[407]

We can also reasonably hope for a good death. It is often hard to find the words to talk frankly about how poor treatments are likely to be and how near death is. But not talking means it's possible to be misled into accepting treatments that are not going to help, by people acting with all kinds of motives, good and bad. But 'hope' for a cure is not the only kind of hope. We can hope to be cared for well, to spend time doing things we take value from, and to have a gentle death. We need to find a way of joining up these values in a way that gives us the honesty we need and the care we want to die well.

So what should 'good' care in the last days or weeks, in delivery, look and feel like? Sometimes it is clear that death is likely. It's often less certain. Even extremely old, frail people who have become very unwell with a urine or chest infection can bounce back quickly with treatment. I get this wrong a lot. On many occasions, I have raised the possibility that we are reaching the end of life with the patient or his or her relatives. Two days later, the patient is sitting up in bed, drinking tea and cracking jokes, and it is plain that their doctor is guilty of a big over-reaction. Though in my defence, and as we have seen, making the correct call that death is near is an inexact science.

This means a problem. Ignoring the possibility that death is near means that it is possible to miss the point. Instead of prioritising comfort, pain relief and familiar surroundings, hospital admission, invasive tests and unpleasant treatments can get in the way.

Here's a story from the US. A patient with cancer has been admitted to have fluid drained from his lung. The surgeon has asked another doctor, a specialist in oncology, to see him. She visits the patient, in his hospital bed. But her 'immediate impression is that he's dying.' She speaks to him:

> 'I hear you are having an operation,' I say.
>
> 'Yes, they need to get this fluid off my chest.'
>
> 'Are you in pain?'
>
> 'Yes, it hurts like hell, doc. Every time I breathe, it stabs me.'
>
> The resident hands me the sheet of inadequately charted pain relief. 'His kidneys are not great, so they've gone easy on the drugs,' she says.

His pain relief has been cut because his kidneys are not able to excrete the drugs, making the risk of side effects higher. She goes on.

> Outside the room, we run into the surgeon, whom I know well. He's about to meet the patient before the operation.
>
> 'We're done,' I say. 'By the way, he looks dry and needs better pain management, which I've attempted to fix.'
>
> I pause, hoping for a sign of a reservation granting me

> permission to unleash my own mounting ones. But he simply says, 'I think the VATS will give the poor man relief. He's been struggling for days.'
>
> We part ways, but when he's out of earshot, I tell my resident, 'I can't believe they operate on such patients; he just doesn't look right.'

However, the operation has complications, and the man ends up in intensive care. After a few days of struggle, he dies. His doctor asks:

> Is this really the best we could have done? I think not. For though we probably couldn't have changed the fact of his death, we held the circumstances in our hands. We could have cancelled the surgery, aggressively controlled his pain, and called an urgent family meeting to ascertain his wishes and be guided in shared decision making. But this model, to which we aspire, went astray, as it often does.
>
> Days later, I speak to the surgeon. 'I feel so sorry that he died,' he reflects. 'I thought we could help him, but he was clearly too unwell to have an operation.'
>
> The nagging voice returns to my head. Banking on our rapport, I say, 'I keep wishing that I had mentioned my doubts to you that morning. He looked like he was dying.'
>
> Seizing on my comment, the surgeon asks, 'Why didn't you tell me?... If you had so much as mentioned your fears, I would have stopped…' [408]

This story is not simply about the problems when doctors don't communicate well with each other. It is also about how hard it can be for doctors to stop offering useless treatments and for patients and their families to tell doctors they don't want them. In this case, the patient was offered surgery when it might have been kinder to treat his pain at all costs – even if it meant that his kidney function suffered. In retrospect – and it is always easier in retrospect – it would have been more compassionate to plan for his death instead. This shift in goals may mean difficult, time-consuming conversations. It might mean dying a few days sooner – but it might have allowed him to die at home with family around him rather than bleeping monitors. We have to start valuing a good death – even if that comes with some kind of cost.

How we manage to find the balance of delivering the right kind of care is fundamentally difficult. No doctor would want to under-treat a patient or offer palliation where another active intervention would be more helpful. The charge is often made of ageism – that older people are written off on the basis of when they were born. Of course, age alone should be no barrier to good medicine that aims to delay death. Rapid treatment for broken hips, arteries being quickly unblocked in heart attacks and strokes, or surgery and chemotherapy for cancer are medical staples which can produce extra months and years of good health and life. It's absolutely possible for a person in their eighties and even nineties to be biologically fitter than a 40-year-old. And just because a decision for 'DNR' is in place does not mean that antibiotics or fluids cannot be given or that x-rays or CT scans cannot be ordered. For example, if a patient who has widespread cancer and is in pain, unrelieved with medication, has a DNR instruction in place, they can and should still be treated as appropriate with other helpful interventions like radiotherapy or even nerve-blocking surgery.

We need perspective; palliative care, aiming to relieve symptoms like pain, nausea, or fatigue, and not aiming for a 'cure', is capable of giving patients just as much time as standard care. This still requires fine judgement – when should the aim of treatment be not to delay death but to comfort – even welcome – its passage?

The distinction is important; treatments may conflict. In the example above, fear about kidney failure prevented the patient from being given high enough doses of pain medication to bring relief. Swallowing fluid or food may bring one of few available pleasures. But if the gag reflex is not working properly, food can end up in the lungs, causing pneumonia. If death is now inevitable, the risk that the comfort of food brings may be an entirely reasonable risk. If, however, the odds of survival are to be raised at all costs, then a feeding tube, either via the nose or directly into the stomach, could be inserted. Both types of tube can fall out. Those inserted via the nose may be easy to insert, in a conscious person able to co-operate. Or it may be difficult, uncomfortable and distressing to manoeuvre the tube into the correct position in someone already confused and disorientated. If this was to effect a better quality of life and death; fair enough. But if it simply slows death down and makes the final days more painful or difficult, we should question what the purpose of the feeding tube is. Is it to protect the healthcare professionals – or family members – from accusations of a lack of caring, or mistreatment? Or is the tube to improve the quality of life of the patient?

Thirst and dehydration – not the same

The context for this dilemma is of charities interacting with the media and producing widespread critical coverage. 'Dehydration and malnutrition led to 2,162 deaths since 2003'[409] ran *The Guardian*, covering a freedom of information enquiry made by the Alzheimer's Society. Their director told the *Daily Telegraph* 'How can we call ourselves civilised when people are left to starve or die of thirst?' under the headline 'More than a thousand care home residents die thirsty'.[410]

The article went on:

> The real figures are likely to be far higher because residents who died while in hospital were not included. Campaigners said the disclosures raised serious concerns about the way vulnerable elderly people were treated and why the Government had failed to decrease the numbers dying of thirst after more than three years in office. Dot Gibson, general secretary of the National Pensioners Convention, said the care system needed an urgent overhaul. 'It is not good enough for ministers or the care regulator to talk about

> making improvements by 2015 when, in the meantime, older people are dying from neglect. The public would be outraged if animals were treated in the same way – we need to show the same compassion when it comes to caring for our elderly loved ones, she added.

Certainly, dehydration may have been the cause of death – but it is not possible to equate this with either dying of thirst, or being due to neglect. Death certificates record the cause of death in a stepwise fashion. So the first cause of death may indeed be 'dehydration'. The cause leading to this may be dementia, and another recorded contributing cause may be pneumonia. The pneumonia may have caused low blood pressure, worsening confusion, and semi-consciousness, which will have impacted on the person's ability to swallow. A decision may have been taken that the chances of survival were so low, and the distress caused by a shift from a care home to a hospital bed for intravenous fluids so great, that comfort care – ensuring that the lips and mouth are moistened – should be offered. The severity of the pneumonia may have been made worse through the dementia; and dementia can cause an impaired sense of thirst.

The enormous misunderstanding is equating a death caused by dehydration as a death caused by thirst. It is the rare exception, not the rule, that fluids should be restricted out of medical necessity. For example, some people who are being treated with dialysis because of kidney failure are advised to limit how much they drink between dialysis sessions, whereas, if someone is thirsty and at the end of life, there should be no reason not to meet that need.

But in reality, when the end of life draws near, thirst is uncommon. In one study of 32 patients with terminal illness, and who were mentally alert and fully aware, two thirds experienced no hunger, with all but one of the remainder experiencing hunger initially only. Similarly, two thirds experienced no thirst, or thirst initially only. In the remainder, small amounts of fluids to sip, ice to suck, or putting moisturising cream over the lips took any remaining thirst symptoms away.[411] Another study co-authored by Dame Cicely Saunders, the mother of modern hospice care, found that thirst as a symptom was unrelated to clinical dehydration as shown by blood tests.[412] People at the end of life who are dehydrated through a lack of drinking or intravenous fluids do not routinely experience thirst. If they do, it can be reliably relieved, as a symptom, by good basic nursing care.

Feeding tubes absolutely have a role for many patients, for example, after major bowel surgery. But what of using feeding tubes when it is likely that the end of life is very near? A common reason for considering feeding is because of the poor appetite which people with advanced dementia often have. Often, even prompts and encouragement to eat don't make much of an impact. A US study found that in people with advanced dementia, around half had a feeding tube inserted when admitted to hospital. When the patients were followed up, half were dead within six months. But the risk of death was just as high for patients who did not have a feeding tube inserted – in other words, having a feeding tube inserted did not reduce the chances of dying.[413] Other research has pointed out that people with dementia who had feeding tubes placed because of swallowing or choking problems (which are common in severe dementia) are more likely to die sooner, a counter-intuitive finding.[414] Tube feeding in these circumstances cannot, therefore, be used as an evidence-based way to prolong life. Doing without a feeding tube in these circumstances can thus hardly be deemed to be negligent or uncaring.

In fact, it is absolutely possible to die of dehydration, but comfortably, without thirst, and with dignity. Comfort and caring for the patient who is at the end of life does not require feeding by nasogastric tube. Even intravenous fluids given via a drip in order to hydrate a person are not necessarily kind either. A body whose kidneys are failing, for example, is not able to get rid of fluid efficiently, meaning that the fluid can simply build up and cause uncomfortable swelling in the legs and abdomen.

The misinformation perpetuated around death and hydration can mean enormous emotional pain for relatives. Our culture loves food, and celebrates high days and holidays through feasting with families and friends. We are a society that gives presents of chocolate, cake and alcohol. Food is a synonym for love. No wonder that the possibility that a loved one will be allowed to 'dehydrate' or 'starve' to death has such appalling meaning. As a wife said of her husband: 'What happens when Pete can no longer swallow? Will he just starve to death? I don't want him suffering.'[415]

However, pointedly, the dying body does not experience thirst or hunger as a healthy person does. Treatments with artificial hydration do not work in the same way, and are not usually necessary. It may comfort us, the relatives or friends, to feed or give fluids to our loved one. It may be difficult to accept that this act is likely to comfort us, the relative, more than the patient.

Prolonging death and life

When fluids or nutrition are given at the end of life, the good intention may be to comfort, but, as we have seen, they are not likely to extend life and may not give much pleasure for the recipient. Could the delivery of other medical interventions be delivering harm?

Many doctors have felt that it is possible for them to prolong life artificially by medical means only for the patient to suffer for longer. In 1984, there was huge controversy in Colorado, when a governor said that old and terminally ill people 'had a right to die and get out of the way... We are approaching a time of almost technological immortality when the machine and the tubes and the drugs and the heart pacemakers... literally force life on us. I believe we really should be very careful in terms of our technological miracles that we don't impose life on people who, are in fact, suffering beyond the ability for us to help.'[416] While some expressed

> 'I have spent countless nights in the Intensive Care Unit (ICU) trying to gently convince families that most interventions we do to critically ill, elderly patients are of little benefit. They will only inflict unnecessary suffering,' wrote Jason Weatherald, a fellow of the University of Calgary's Division of Respirology. 'These pleas often fall on deaf ears. We have been conditioned, as a society, to want to preserve life at all costs. We believe that our family members are "fighters" and can make it through serious medical emergencies. [As a result], it is often the family members we are treating with heroic measures. Not the patient.'
>
> Kay J. **Canadian doctors explain why so many of us die badly**. *National Post*, 11 July 2013. fullcomment.nationalpost.com/2013/07/11/jonathan-kay-canadian-doctors-explain-why-so-many-of-us-die-badly

outrage, others spoke in support. 'When I can't digest my food, when I can't breathe on my own, when my heart can't beat on its own, it could just be that God is trying to tell me something.' An octogenarian responded 'My doctor and I have a compact that if I reach the "point of no return" – no prospect of getting back to any kind of meaningful life – he will not take any artificial means to prolong my life.' And 'As a clergyman for 60 years, with a large proportion of my time spent in hospitals and nursing homes, I have seen endless human situations where the cost of keeping a helpless, senile person alive is tremendous – not only financially but also in terms of the woeful condition of the person himself and the day-to-day strain on members of his family.'[417]

It may attract little publicity, but it is relatively common for people to decide to forego medical interventions which they know will shorten their life – but because it may also make the last days better. Kidney dialysis is a life-saving and life-prolonging treatment for many people, but the older and more unwell a person is, the shorter their life expectancy is likely to be while receiving it. There comes a point for many people where the ongoing need to be hooked up through their bloodstream to a machine for four hours, three times a week, with all the attendant travel, tests, and fatigue from doing so, will no longer make sense. Stopping dialysis may lead to death sooner, but release one's limited time to increase the quality of existence in the days left.

Art Buchwald, the famous US satirist and journalist, did just this. He chose to stop dialysis and receive palliative care only, saying 'If you have to go, the way you go is a big deal.' He recorded his own video obituary for the *New York Times*, beginning, with a big smile, 'I just died.'[418] He was initially told that he would have weeks left. In fact, he had much longer, and spent several months with his friends and family, writing a great deal, and left the hospice he initially stayed in to take a holiday.[419] We have already seen that an accurate prediction of death is very difficult, and the extent of Buchwald's achievements is unusual. However many people choose to stop dialysis when they are approaching the end of life. Around a fifth of deaths in patients who are on dialysis in the UK are because patients make a decision to stop it.[420] A similar proportion is seen in other European countries.[421] In the UK, this is seen as a humane decision reached with patients and their families using 'judgement, sensitivity and good communication. A shared view, between patient, family and carers, and all members of the multidisciplinary team, with respect to the patient's current situation and likely prognosis, is key, with increasing age and dependency, progression of underlying medical conditions, or the emergence of new medical problems, life on dialysis may become difficult to bear.'[422]

In the US, making choices around dialysis at the end of life has been described differently. One renal specialist described it: 'I view it as being driven by a culture of "life at any cost". It used to be that families wanted to stop and doctors wanted to go on... now it's the reverse, and courts have basically decided that families have the right to request therapy even if it's futile. Meanwhile, the populace has gotten less frightened, less bewildered by the technology of medicine. It doesn't trouble them as much as it once did. So grandma has six feeding tubes and seventeen IVs and a respirator and a whatever – bring it on.'[423]

One UK study examined what happened when a group of patients aged over 80 and with kidney failure made a decision, after discussion, either to have dialysis, or to have 'conservative' – symptomatic, or palliative – care instead. Once the patients who had the highest levels of fitness were removed from the equation, there was no difference between the two groups in terms of how long people survived.[424]

Another US study found much the same thing. Three-hundred and twenty-one patients were assessed for renal dialysis; 258 were recommended it, and 63 others recommended, because of frailty or other ongoing conditions, palliative care instead. However some patients recommended for palliative care did opt to have dialysis anyway. Yet there was no difference between when the people recommended for palliative care died, whether or not they chose to have dialysis.

Furthermore, 65% of the patients in this study who were recommended for palliative care but had dialysis died at

Treatment Burdens

Dialysis, especially haemodialysis, can be stressful and exhausting. Most of three days each week may be spent travelling to and from dialysis, receiving the treatment, and recovering from it. Heart disease and some other conditions may make the treatments particularly difficult for some. Patients who are easily confused (e.g. suffering from dementia) may find dialysis frightening or confusing, and may have difficulty with necessary medicines and restrictions.

No dialysis and stopping dialysis.
From EdREN, the website of the Renal Unit of the Royal Infirmary of Edinburgh. renux.dmed.ed.ac.uk/EdREN/EdRENINFObits/NoRRT.html

home compared with 27% of patients treated palliatively.[425] It thus seems possible to identify people who are nearing the end of life and will not live longer with dialysis. Rather than doctors 'playing god', the facts, compassionately presented, may enable some people to know that dialysis is unlikely to help them live longer. Instead, they can plan to spend their last days at home doing what they choose rather than attached to a machine. This increases the chances – should it be wished – of dying at home.

Similarly, the effects of chemotherapy in people who are terminally ill with cancer is questionable – and can do unintended harm. Such palliative chemotherapy is not offered with the expectation that there will be a cure, but rather is used when treatment has failed with the hope that it will do 'something' useful. An editorial in the *BMJ* in 2008 noted that

> ...chemotherapy is increasingly being given closer to the end of life, and patients are having to decide whether or not to have this treatment at the same time as facing the harsh realities of dying... Several studies have highlighted the link between the desire to maintain hope and the use of chemotherapy in advanced disease... In one study, maintaining hope was one of the most important aims of second line chemotherapy for breast cancer, and another commentated that patients may be given chemotherapy because of the need to do something active even if they were unlikely to benefit.[426]

So who does the palliative chemotherapy help? Does it make patients feel better – or their doctors?

It's possible that palliative chemotherapy may make doctors feel better about doing 'something' – but while simultaneously doing harm to patients. In a *British Medical Journal* paper published in 2014, people in the US whose cancer had spread and who were judged by their doctors to be terminally ill were entered into a study to compare the difference from palliative chemotherapy. The patients who

Kate Granger, a doctor diagnosed with terminal cancer at the age of 29, decided to have palliative chemotherapy. She wrote of her dilemma:

'Having only just survived my second battering with chemotherapy and still suffering ongoing consequences, I think the decision to refuse further treatment in future may be easier. However, when someone is offering you more life on a plate it is difficult to refuse. Choosing the more time option does run the risk of ruining the quality of life during any remaining time, and this is an aspect I've had many internal battles with. I firmly believe there does come a point in a situation like mine where death has to be accepted; where quality is pursued over quantity, where time at home is valued rather than repeated trips to the hospital. I've always said I wouldn't want to spend my final days lying in a hospital bed hooked up to a drip filled with poison. I hope I will instinctively know when that point is.'

Granger K. **How do you know it's time to refuse treatment for incurable cancer?** *The Guardian*, 16 April 2014. www.theguardian.com/society/2014/apr/16/palliative-chemotheraphy-incurable-cancer

had the chemotherapy were no more likely to die later. However, 11% of them died in intensive care, compared with 2% of the others, and were less likely to die at home, at 47% versus 66%.[427] I don't think it is useful to see deaths in hospital as a 'failure' compared to death at home. But if a routine offer of palliative chemotherapy makes death just as likely and a home death less likely, palliative chemotherapy becomes a systematic failure. It means that doctors offer something that does not help and simply causes more deaths to occur in the harsh clinical environment of ITU rather than the known bed and bathroom of home which most people prefer.

Offering palliative chemotherapy may help doctors to feel that they are offering something – hope. Doctors may feel that they have to continue to offer 'something' medical rather than instead having a difficult conversation to tell a patient and their family that nothing further 'medically' can effect a cure. We need a different kind of 'doing something', one that does not serve to ease the doctors' anxieties, or avoid admittance of the side effects of chemotherapy. Instead we can reconsider what we mean by 'hope'. Rather than hoping to delay death – which the treatment could not promise – would we not be better to invest our hope in a different thing? Thinking and planning about what we want the end of our life to be like, and having hope that our last days and hours should be as we wish – peaceful and quiet, or filled with family and chatter, or accompanied by beer or music?

Stopping treatments that are no longer, on balance, beneficial is therefore common. Many interventions at the end of life hold no value for the patient, and some simply erode the quality of life remaining. Stopping ineffective interventions is simply a humane action.

However, working out what is 'ineffective' can be difficult, and in truth, may often be unclear. A round of treatment in the form of chemotherapy may, for example, be predicted to extend life for a few weeks. But it may mean that much of those weeks are spent in hospital, feeling very unwell, and with 'domino' effects, such as being prescribed intravenous antibiotics, due to an infection caused by the chemotherapy depressing the immune system. Getting the balance between treatments that help versus treatments that are only doing harm can be extremely difficult. Statins, for example, can reduce the risk of a heart attack or stroke over the coming five or ten years. There is therefore little point in taking them when an illness is terminal. If there is a struggle to swallow down all the recommended tablets, stopping them can be a relief – but explaining why they are no longer needed may require enormous tact.

Morphine at the end of life

It's useful to consider the ways in which dying in hospital had sometimes been handled before the Liverpool Care Pathway gave staff a kind of 'official' permission to prescribe opiods in the quantity required to treat pain decently. For example, the *Daily Mail*, who had led the charge against the LCP, published an article in 2004 headlined 'Terminally ill denied right to a good death', explaining that people who wanted to die at home were often left in hospitals.[428] In 2009 the same newspaper described the case of a man who was receiving injections of morphine for pain who would die 'screaming in agony'. He had a 'pointless exploratory operation' that his family objected to; his laboured breathing was treated with oxygen but he 'pulled at his tubes and tried to get out of bed... I had to wrestle him back into bed.' He 'should have been unconscious and pain-free, but he was neither'.[429] He did not seem to have been given regular oral pain relief. This would not have been necessary had his morphine been delivered by a syringe-driven pump. This is a staple of palliative care and means that pain relief is constantly delivered. Had this man been placed on the LCP, it is far more likely that he would have received this type of pain relief.

Similarly, in 2012, the cook Prue Leith wrote about how her brother had died: 'no one can do anything about bone cancer except alleviate the pain. Which is what they spectacularly failed to do.' He was given morphine. 'The blessed relief would last three hours, but the nurses would be unable to give him his next dose for another hour. So out of every four hours, one would be spent in groaning, crying, sometimes begging, agony.' The LCP calls for a continuous dose of morphine to be administered in a syringe driver with the dose 'up-titrated' – increased – as necessary to deal with the pain. This means that regular separate doses of pain medication don't need to be given; pain relief is constant. Leith wrote 'surely all that is needed is something like a hospital protocol that if the patient and the next of kin want to end the misery, and two doctors agree that the patient will be dead in a month anyway, they can increase the drugs to the level sufficient to alleviate the pain, even at the risk of death.'[430]

Yet this is exactly what already should happen. Morphine, closely related to heroin, is a strong analgesic and can be given by mouth, under the skin, or by injection into the muscle or vein. It was previously thought that morphine had a 'double effect'. It gave pain relief but also generated side effects which resulted in acceleration towards death, such as slowing or shallowing of breathing and unconsciousness. This was felt by most within medicine to be acceptable; the primary aim was to relieve suffering, not to quicken death.[431] If the by-product of shortening life was to improve its quality, there was felt to be no ethical issue to answer. Yet the testimony in the newspaper articles is of doctors and nurses afraid to increase morphine doses to alleviate pain, resulting in suffering for the patient. Leith writes of her family's request to increase the morphine dose to relieve the pain. She reports the nurses saying 'If you knew how many times we are asked that! We would willingly do it. All over the country, in and out of hospitals, people are suffering like your dad. It's so unnecessary, but no one admits it's happening.' The impression given is that healthcare staff are afraid of increasing the dose and of being responsible for a faster death.

Additionally, the evidence base disputes the perceived side effects of morphine in hastening death. One Japanese study compared the doses of morphine taken by people who were terminally ill. They could not find a relationship between morphine dose and the survival of the patient – meaning that high doses did not seem to increase the risk of death.[432] Another study of 401 terminally ill people in Germany found that 'none of our patients showed clinical signs of respiratory depression'.[433] This exemplifies the findings of an older study of people with advanced cancer who were receiving more than 100 mgs of morphine a day (a reasonably large dose). Their blood was measured by a researcher to find how much oxygen was being transported through their body. Rather than finding an effect of respiratory depression due to morphine 'the results are surprising... chronic ventilatory failure appears to be neither common or severe'.[434] In fact, palliative care physicians have taken issue with the idea that increasing doses of morphine will result in semi-consciousness: 'morphine is well tolerated and does not shorten life or hasten death'.[435] *Palliative Medicine* published an editorial in 2006 saying 'The doctrine of the double effect is largely irrelevant in everyday practice'.[436]

Again, palliative care is not associated with shortening life, so do we have a problem with how doctors and nurses prescribe and use it? A study from London has examined the amount of opioid prescribing done by GPs at the end of life in almost 30,000 patients. Almost half received some form of the drug, but older people were less likely to do so. Why is this?

Another study, published in 2014, examined the records of patients who had died of cancer and who had been prescribed opioid drugs. The researchers found that use of morphine had been slowly rising since 2000, but in 2005, there was a sudden dip.[437] Why? This was around the time that Harold Shipman, the infamous GP who murdered hundreds of his patients, was brought into full media light. Shipman overdosed and killed his patients with morphine causing their deaths in his surgery and their homes.[438] Did healthcare staff become afraid of prescribing opioids in case their intentions looked suspicious? I can certainly remember at around this time showing my patients the writing on vials before injection, even for something as dissimilar to morphine as a flu vaccination. I was afraid my actions would be misinterpreted.

It seems I was not alone. In a qualitative study published in 2011, researchers interviewed nurses, GPs, and doctors working in palliative care about prescribing in terminal illness. One nurse said 'Working in the community I encounter some GPs who just don't want to prescribe any opioids at all and are actually very frightened to prescribe medication and require a lot of reassurance that it's OK and I don't know if it's because they're worried they'll be perceived as someone who is starting the medication inappropriately or they've had a bad experience where they've been questioned, I'm not sure.' A GP said 'after Harold Shipman, as a GP I'm a bit... apprehensive about giving the high doses.' The study found that teamworking – with palliative care nurses being involved with the patient and their family, and able to offer frequent visits – was vital.[439] The same unease was reported in a 2013 study which examined morphine prescribing in patients who were dying and were breathless. While almost all the doctors were willing to prescribe opiods – which can relieve this distressing symptom – a large proportion had concerns about doing so, especially the risk of side effects.[440] Similarly, patients and their relatives may also have concerns about opioids. An English study found that some patients felt as though taking morphine meant that they were near death: 'I, rightly or wrongly, always associate morphine with the sort of top end of the intervention, meaning the sort of last resort almost' said one patient; another said they would expect side effects 'if they go a bit gaga well what can you expect'. There was a fear of tolerance to the drug and a view that morphine use would shorten life. 'In fact, when my father was dying we were asked if they could increase the dose although it would probably kill him. And we said yes. I mean we didn't want to put him through... he was dying, and so we said yes, and of course they did.' Yet the view that morphine was responsible for an earlier death is not supported by the evidence. The conclusion that the family were responsible for an earlier death may have caused needless distress. The researchers concluded that 'we must ensure that morphine does not remain inextricably linked with death. If this connection stays in place then morphine will continue to be viewed as a comfort measure for the dying rather than a means of pain control for the living.'[441]

Giving human care

The end result of the demise of the Liverpool Care Pathway, together with the mixed messages on morphine use, mean that dying patients and their healthcare professionals are pushed into a gap. Morphine should be liberally used at the end of life in order to prevent suffering, but non-specialist wards no longer have the LCP to guide them. So how can we ensure that professionals can deliver the right sort of care and the right quantities of analgesia that dying people need? Not everyone has close friends or nearby family to help with nursing; and in terms of planning distant relations to visit, we have seen that the timing of death can be difficult to predict.

This can make planning hard. The care that is required is usually quite basic – help to wash, toilet and eat. Companionship and a daily routine, together with a discussion of symptoms, and a plan for how to deal with them, should be part of an ongoing dialogue. So, too, should talking about fears and anxieties. Some people will want to know exactly how they are likely to die. Other people will want reassurance that their pain will be treated with whatever dose of analgesics is required. Others will take consolation from reassurance that they will not be admitted into hospital no matter what. Husbands, wives, children and siblings are also likely to need care and attention too.

Delivering all these things is absolutely possible. There is not much technology required. The kit needed for good palliative care is fairly straightforward – the occasional use of oxygen cylinders or a nebuliser, the need for a syringe driver (a battery-driven pump which dispenses a continuous drip of medication under the skin via a needle), a commode, and a telephone to get extra help. These are relatively cheap and standard issue; a hoist, if required for lifting, is more costly but usually available on a temporary basis from local councils. As we have seen, expensive technology and gadgets like telehealth have not been shown to improve lives. Instead, the limiting step to making care at the end of life work well is simple – time.

Carers are sent from the social services department with mere minutes to help clean, wash, dress and feed people. When we consider what value this offers for people – dignity, nutrition, social interaction – the financial price we are willing to pay (near minimum wages) and the pressure we put employees under to deliver cheaply is shameful.

When nearing the end of life, carers, together with district nurses, will often be the ones, backed up by GPs, providing day-to-day care – dressings, assessing pain levels and setting up medication pumps, inserting catheters, supporting and listening to the family and, of course, the patient. They will hear anxieties and fears, and liaise with their GP. The doctor and nurse can discuss symptom relief, sharing expertise and obtaining advice from the local palliative care team if required. The doctor and district nurse will be 'on call' for the family, able to respond quickly to a request for assistance.

This quiet service is carried out with little publicity or much media appreciation. It allows people to die at home with professional support. Ironically, just as we might reasonably consider that our population, ageing and with more chronic diseases, might need more district nurses, district nursing staff levels are actually falling. There are fewer staff, with more patients, and less time to see and treat them. In 2003, there were 12,620 district nurses in England, but 6,656 in 2013 – a reduction of almost half. [442] No wonder that in 2011, 90% of district nurses said their workload had increased, along with stress levels, and this was associated with a concomitant decrease in morale and the quality of care being delivered.[443]

This is a tragedy in slow motion. Our district nurses are the standard bearers for good end-of-life care; many district nurses will start early and finish late to make time to visit dying patients two or three times a day ('just passing'), supporting a family and ensuring comfort. Such intimate, caring relationships are absolutely possible and some of the most important work that goes on in primary care. Yet what value is attached to this hard, frontline work by policymakers who decide on diminishing staffing levels? How can nurses, their time spread thinner over a larger population, serve patients well enough?

The charitable sector has provided hospices and some nursing staff for patients at the end of life (although, notably, Macmillan cancer nurses 'do not carry out routine nursing tasks, such as personal hygiene, changing dressings and giving medicines, and do not focus on non-cancer patients').[444] This means, in effect, that while fundraising might help with some of the support needed at the end of life, it does not guarantee to provide holistic, hands-on care for all dying patients. This task falls to the diminishing numbers of district nurses.

And supposing this care is not enough? In most areas the Marie Curie charity is the only organisation which provides nursing support present constantly in the home. But again, and similar to hospital care, because these organisations exist in the main outwith the NHS, there is no statutory provision. This means that if a nurse, or a bed, is not available, the alternative is instead for an 'acute medical' NHS hospital bed. The overspill for patients for whom there is no space is contained typically in a corridor in an A&E department. This is sadly not surprising – the number of beds available in England has fallen from 141,477 in 2010 to 135,602 in 2012;[445] a similar decline is evident in Scotland;[446] and Wales – where they had a 17% decrease in bed numbers between 2000 and 2010.[447]

Now, sure, some modern procedures that used to require prolonged inpatient stays (such as gallbladder removal) can now be done via less invasive telescope procedures, meaning a shorter hospital stay and less need for beds. But this does not excuse the calamity of the combined reduced capacity in hospital. A report from the Royal College of Physicians in 2012 found that bed numbers had fallen by a third over the previous quarter of a century; yet in the last decade there has been a rise of almost 40% in emergency admissions. The pressure is felt on medical staff, with consultants reporting working more hours and having less time to supervise their trainees.[448] In particular, the report highlighted the wish to help patients make quality decisions, such as whether to accept CPR; the time to do so was in short supply.

Again, time is the limiting factor. Staff are present and willing, but they are struggling against the increased pressing on their time. An extra fifteen minutes per patient to discuss CPR adds up to almost a day's work alone across a ward of 30 people.

Again, time is pressing on general practice. In 1995, the average person consulted their GP just under four times a year. By 2008/9, it was almost 5.5. That's – roughly – an extra 90 million consultations being required annually across England alone.[449] Additionally, as our needs get more complicated – having more than one chronic condition, a mixture of psychological and physical health problems, and increasing frailty – the length of GP consultations has changed from 8.4 minutes in 1992 to 11.7 minutes in 2007. This is good – but multiplied by millions, means thousands of extra hours of consultation time need to be found.[450] Yet the funding that has gone into primary care over the last decade to meet this demand has remained virtually static and is predicted to fall.[451]

Time with our doctors, nurses and carers is exactly what we should want – human, hands-on care. We cannot reasonably hope that technology will ever reduce the need for healthcare professionals to spend time with dying people. The time needed to help a dying person eat or wash cannot be safely or humanely compressed. The minutes of conversation required to talk about pain, and how it should be treated, should not be pushed into a tick box and charted. The unfolding, difficult, perhaps liberating, often painful discussion about what the end of life should be like should not be abbreviated because the staff are lacking in the time to do so. As a friend who is a consultant told me: 'Knowing that I have an outpatient clinic starting in 20 minutes, that I am running almost an hour late already – I know I should be talking to my patient about the end of life. But I'm afraid to start that conversation. I don't have time.'

Assisted suicide

Against the ugly backdrop of what financial value we ascribe to the person who will clean and wash the dying person, physician-assisted suicide has become legal in Belgium, Luxembourg, the Netherlands, Switzerland, Oregon, Washington and Montana.[452] The longest standing law is in the Netherlands, where some studies have suggested that up to 2.9% of the population die by physician-assisted suicide.[453] In some countries, the illness does not have to be terminal, but unbearable, and with no prospect of improvement; minors, too, are legally allowed to seek assisted suicide in Belgium. In the Netherlands, Belgium and Luxembourg, euthanasia is legal under admissionable circumstances.

What's the difference? In euthanasia, the doctor deliberately administers drugs designed to cause immediate death. In assisted suicide, the drugs are given to the patient, who then uses them to cause their own death.

This creates a conflict in the role of doctor. We expect that our doctors should act for us, and in our best interests. If the patient decides that her best interests are served by being dead, should we not therefore expect our doctor not to abandon us but to assist us? Yet doctors are charged with preserving life, comforting if not curing.

James Rachels, in the *New England Journal of Medicine* in 1975, famously argued that there is no difference between acts of omission – like not doing CPR, which he would term 'passive euthanasia' – compared with a deliberate act of killing – 'active euthanasia'.[454] However, this essay, written by a philosopher and not from clinical experience, would mean that any death which was not treated with every possible medical intervention (no matter the hazards or side effects) was essentially 'active euthanasia'. This is absurd, for it would mean that no one's heart should be allowed to stop peacefully, but would have to be attacked by a resuscitation team with defibrillators and syringes of drugs. Enforcing this kind of death has its own immorality.

Clearly, deliberate intention to end life through the action of a doctor is different again. Doctors must help patients make rational decisions about what interventions are useful. Doctors, nurses and healthcare staff are constantly trying to deliver the right amount of the right kind of medicine. Does allowing patients the legal right to have euthanasia or assisted suicide administered or facilitated by a doctor help?

In a recent study of a series of patients in Oregon who requested physician-assisted suicide, a minority – 35% – went on to receive the prescriptions for fatal doses of medication. The prescription – which is issued 15 days after it has been agreed – was even then not taken by everyone, with some people saying that they simply wanted to know that it was there if they needed it. Legally, in Oregon, to have assisted suicide the person has to be within six months of expected death. It is entirely in keeping with the difficulty of predicting the time of death that a small minority lived beyond the six months. Most gave 'loss of autonomy' as their reason for seeking an earlier death; a fifth told of pain or a fear of pain in the future.[155]

Giving a prescription for a lethal dose of medication, with the intention that it will cause death, is different from the perceived double effect dose of morphine. A lethal prescription has a single purpose. This places the doctor in a different role; that of deliberately ending life via an act of commission. Indeed, while pain, or a fear of pain, was a factor in a fifth of people requesting assisted suicide, it was the loss of autonomy which motivated people to seek assisted suicide the most.

This I can understand. I can see why many patients and healthcare professionals are afraid of losing all control over their life and its end.

The most recent call to legalise assisted suicide in the UK would make doctors the judge of which patients should be allowed access to it. But as we have seen, doctors are often poor judges of quality of life. We do not have much data about the wider effects of legalising assisted suicide on how it changes attitudes to death or to doctors' roles in death. Imagine an elderly lady, who has dementia and pneumonia. Antibiotics aren't helping, and it has become more difficult to persuade her to take them. She is merely taking sips of tea after a great deal of encouragement and is now semi-conscious. But she is comfortable in her care home, though becoming dehydrated. Morphine is used to keep her comfortable. She is taking medication for heart failure and is very frail. One option is to admit her to hospital for a rehydrating drip, but it is very unlikely that she will survive that. Her daughter is worried about her becoming disorientated and being taken away from her familiar environment and carers. But she asks, 'is this euthanasia? Am I doing everything I can? Doctor, are you effectively delivering an (unrequested and unauthorised) assisted suicide?'

My own experience is that it has been frequently useful to be able to distinguish acts of medical humanity (morphine for pain and distress) from deliberately accelerating death (prescribing a fatal dose of medication with no other purpose than ending life).

As for autonomy, if a doctor forces a legally competent person into taking food or fluid, they are guilty of assault. Similar to assisted suicide, a person cannot be deemed 'competent' to make the decision if they are, for example, depressed, or affected by drugs or illness such that they have lost the ability to reason. Should a person wish to decline food and fluid, the doctor can, of course, continue to administer drugs to alleviate pain or distress. In other words, if a terminally ill person is determined to die by suicide, it can be completed without recourse to a medical practitioner. Indeed on several occasions in Oregon, taking the prescribed lethal medication did not result in immediate death though

> At less than $300, assisted suicide is, to put it bluntly, the cheapest treatment for a terminal illness. This means that in places where assisted suicide is legal, coercion is not even necessary. If life-sustaining expensive treatment is denied or even merely delayed, patients will be steered toward assisted suicide, where it is legal.
>
> Golden M. **The danger of assisted suicide laws.** *CNN* 14 October 2014 edition.cnn.com/2014/10/13/opinion/golden-assisted-suicide

death followed a day or two later. We cannot guarantee that a lethal prescription supplied by doctors for the purposes of physician-assisted suicide will result in a rapid death.

What are the wider effects of such a change in the abilities of doctors' legal abilities? Why are the rates of assisted suicide so different – from 0.1% in some countries and up to 2.9% in others? What effect does this have on people who are themselves ill, and need care from others? Does the wider acceptability of assisted suicide mean that more people will consider it – and does this meet a previously unarticulated wish or create a desire that was not already there? And are the legal frameworks enough?

On the wider societal effects, there is little or no robust research allowing confident conclusions to know the answers. On the legal frameworks operated by doctors, there is far more concern. Setting aside any debate about abortion itself, the current 1967 UK abortion law requires two doctors to sign a form declaring that the woman meets the legal requirement for abortion (in practice, usually mental distress; the law says 'that the termination is necessary to prevent grave permanent injury to the physical or mental health of the pregnant woman'.)[456] However, an investigation by the Care Quality Commission in 2013 found widespread pre-signing of the forms within the private sector and the NHS, meaning that only one doctor assessed the patient.[457] The General Medical Council took the decision not to prosecute any of the doctors involved.[458] While this cannot prove that the terms of an assisted suicide law would be equally poorly followed by doctors, it does raise questions about how closely legal requirements for a medical intervention are followed in practice. Would the law be followed in the real medical world?

And of course, the question is why people who are terminally ill wish to accelerate their death. If, as the research suggests, it is a fear of pain or a forthcoming loss of dignity, that is a failing on us all. We should be able to look to the end of life with at least the knowledge that our society will ensure that everyone will have the funding for hands-on, personal care, that hospice care would be statutorily funded, and that choices in treatment could be offered even if it meant that the time of our death would be accelerated. If we are fearing our death, let us at least not fear for the things that we as a society can and should provide.

Living wakes

At the beginning of the book, I cautioned against planning for a 'perfect death', simply because, just like birth plans full of whale music and bans on pain relief, it can offer an opportunity for the last days or hours of life to be reframed as a failure if it 'gang aft agley'.[459] The same problem holds true for people who plan an assisted suicide or euthanasia; how much can we control our life, or our death?

In medicine, one of the hardest tasks is to account for and live with uncertainty. Seldom are we sure that what we are doing is right; at best, I can only ever feel that there is reasonable certainty. The feeling that perhaps I'm wrong is common and pervasive. One of the key points in learning to be a general practitioner is living with this inevitability, and not becoming stressed and anxious as a result. (I haven't achieved this.) As we've seen, it can be very hard to know when death is near, even with lots of statistical information about a patient's illness. Is a death via assisted suicide better for the person or their family? Is the sense of control over the timing of our death something which helps or hinders the person – and their family afterwards? Here, we do not know.

One of the roles of family doctors is of bearing witness. Birth, death and weddings are pivotal points of human gathering. We have got quite good at individualising birth and weddings – but not so much at death. When I have witnessed 'death beds' I have been struck with their humanity, joy and sadness; a coming together of family and friends around a dying person, with food, alcohol, music, laughter, tenderness, and memories. Vigils which can comfort and soothe, invigorate and support; the dying person is celebrated and loved. When family members are scarce or friends absent, it is even more important that a dying person can rely on nurses, doctors and social workers, and does not fear pain, indignity or loneliness. This is simple, humane care, and until each dying person can live with the knowledge that they will be cared for like this at the end of life, we have failed.

The goodness of death

Our attempts to push death back with medicine are often highly successful. Surgery and intensive care are at their best when they attempt to reset bad luck – a road traffic crash, septic shock from meningitis, a faulty heart valve. Medicine is also our friend when it offers a specific treatment for a particular problem – a kidney transplant, an artificial hip. Vaccination is an astoundingly successful example of true preventative medicine.

But then there are the uses of medicine to support life, to reduce the risk of complications, and increase the chances of living longer. So we use drugs to lower blood pressure or cholesterol, tablets to strengthen the bones, medication to reduce the chances of blood clotting and resulting in a heart attack or stroke, and tablets to attempt to slow dementia. Rather than medicine being a relatively clean, temporary intervention, it is medicine for the rest of life. It can bring advantages, but also side effects and hazards. And still, it will not stop death.

Much of the media reporting about healthcare focuses on new discoveries, new technology, and the latest medication. Our expectations of what medicine makes possible have been ramped up such that every death can feel like a failure – not just to patients and their families but to doctors and nurses. In an NHS that too often appears to be fuelled by blame, justifying why a test or treatment was done will be easier than justifying why it wasn't.

Embracing or welcoming death may only be possible for a few people and their families. For many others it will be more of an acceptance, which may be difficult or even traumatic. The humanness of our fate can provide much solace.

Accepting death as our shared destiny is powerful. It allows us to call to mind what is important and can help us decide what we would not want. It's clear to me that old and very old people seldom fear death itself, but fear being alone, or in pain, or becoming dependent on others. Death can be a relief, it may be the end of a life well lived, it may come unbidden in a cruelly and unfairly short life. Accepting its inevitability may make it easier to choose a path that gives us more of what we want – peace, being at home, being relaxed with pain relief, stopping hospital tests and treatments that are unlikely to prolong our life. For healthcare staff, too, accepting that death is near should make it easier to make it a more peaceful, gentle time – relaxing visitor restrictions, stopping drawing blood, focusing on palliative care – pain relief, skin and care of the bowels and bladder – the things which we have already seen make the passage of death easier.

If we want to do this – and we should – healthcare needs to be less about technology, targets, and hugely expensive drugs which deliver only marginal improvements. Instead, healthcare needs to be about humanity and human care, the continuity of hands-on care from staff who are working free of management stress and media blame, driven by a vocational desire to help people. The resources are there. But the political will is not. The end of life is full of uncertainties and difficulties – but getting it right is an immense gift. A good death gives easier remembrance by children and siblings, and is the final kindness that human beings can give one another. Witnessing a good death can show family members, friends and colleagues that there is a safe passage for themselves ahead.

If we know the limits of medicine's power, the uncertainties it contains, and the value of people to one another as we enter into our final weeks or months, death could be less about conflict, and more defining what values our community holds. We could choose to lay aside regret, and share our human and humane values. In making death better, we could also make living better.

Things to think about

- If I could plan my death, what would I want? Where would I want to be? Who with?
- Would I trade extra days alive for the potential discomforts of treatments?
- What does quality of life mean to me?
- What balance of risk and harm do I want from preventative medication? Do I want everything – no matter the side effects? Or do I want to avoid all – or most – side effects – and at what cost?
- Do I want to register as an organ donor? This can be done online; tell family and friends of your decision.
- Would I want to know everything about my illness? Would I prefer conversations over time? How much detail do I want? Who would I want with me – if anyone? Would tape recorded consultations with health professionals help?
- When it comes to the last days or weeks of life, what would I want? If I had the choice, where would I want to be, what would I like to do? What would be important to me and my family? What would I hope for – and is this something to share with the professionals involved?
- Would I want to have CPR, or be admitted to ITU? Your family, friends, GP, hospital doctors would want to know.
- If I am offered entry into a clinical trial, would I accept? Good information about how to tell good trials from bad can be found at **testingtreatments.org**.
- If I have a terminal illness, how much information do I want? Do I want to discuss how I might die? Will there be a better time to talk about what might happen? This can be a conversation, and can take a while.

- What kind of things would be most important to me when I am dying? Do I have strong views about being at home or in hospital? Would there be any treatments I would or wouldn't want? What would be my priorities? Is there anything I definitely wouldn't want to happen?
- What are the chances of the treatment I am offered working towards the end of life? It's easy to present statistics in a way designed to persuade one way or another. To make sense of the numbers, ask what the expected success would be without the treatment compared to with the treatment. And what are the side effects?
- Are there any decision aids I can use to help me choose the best course of action? For example **adjuvantonline.com** helps to outline the pros and cons of cancer treatment, and **sdm.rightcare.nhs.uk** can help you to make choices for many treatments in the NHS.
- Who do I consider my next of kin? Should I consider conferring legal rights to them in the event of my incapacity, and give them a power of attorney? (These can only be made when the person has the mental capacity.) It's a good idea for everyone to have a legally appointed power of attorney who can act for you if you become incapable. This saves later legal expense but more importantly appoints someone who can act for you if you become unwell.
- Some people want to plan their funerals. There are good tips and thoughts on the Dying Matters website: **dyingmatters.org**, and **bestendings.com**
- Writing a will is a good idea – dying without a will means that your wishes will not be carried out, and can create all sorts of hassles for your family. And you don't have to be dying to write a will.

Edward and Rosa: Take 2

The following is absolutely not a tale of what I personally can do, or do do. It is rather a story about what might happen if health services were pointed at and resourced for people who might benefit best from them. As for my bias: this is the kind of death that I would like to have.

Rosa has cancer. She is seventy two years of age. She wears her long, white hair in a knot, tucked into the nape of her neck. She is slender, her skin hanging loosely on the tendons of her arm and the bone of her jaw; she smiles, slowly, as she recognises me, and her eyes carefully follow me across the room. The flat is festooned with photographs, merrily cluttering the sideboards, bookshelves and television. The carpets are worn and the lights are weak. She is wearing loose clothing, whose drapes do not disguise the weight she has lost. Edward stands to her left, one hand – all knuckle and muscle – resting on her shoulder, and his other hand gestures for me to sit.

I sit on the chair, rest my medical case on the floor, and the brown folder of her medical notes on my knee. The coffee table is piled with books, magazines, and in the middle, a tray. This tray is stacked with packets of tablets and bottles of medicine, neatly lined up. Edward sits beside his wife and aligns his hand with hers; Rosa leans herself backward into a cushion, biting her lip against pain. The morphine is almost finished. I am here to discuss how to proceed.

* * *

'How are you, Rosa?'

'Well,' she says, 'the pain is still there. But the nausea is better.'

'Is the pain the same?' I ask. 'Same place?' She nods. 'And did the bigger dose of the sevredol do anything for it?'

'Not really. If I'm honest.' I had hoped the bigger dose of morphine might have settled the pains in her shoulder and the front of her chest.

'The nights are bad, doctor. They're the worst. She can never get to sleep.'

'Ah, but he won't let me have my whisky, you see doctor... says it's bad for me.' Edward and Rosa exchange a smile.

'It would really help me,' I say, 'if you could explain to me what you understand about your diagnosis and what plans you are making?'

Edward speaks first. 'It's cancer, and it's in the lung. It isn't good, but they seem to think they can do something about it. With the chemo, radiation therapy, and drugs.'

'So I've to have chemotherapy first,' says Rosa. 'To shrink it down. And then, after that, the radiotherapy.'

'And do you know much about it?'

'Just that it stops the cancer cells,' says Edward. 'Stops them from growing, from getting bigger.'

'And what about the cancer itself? What about that?'

'It's there. It's – cancer.'

I take a deep breath. 'Some cancer treatments are very effective, others aren't so good. Do you know how good your one is?'

Rosa is alert to me and what I am getting at. 'I don't expect a guarantee of a cure. They were careful not to say that at the hospital. But how successful this treatment – the chemotherapy is – well, I don't honestly know.'

Edward is holding his wife's arm. 'We know the treatment will make her a good bit better, doctor. We don't expect miracles.'

'Of course, I know. I suppose I'm just wondering how much treatment you'd want, if there were side effects, or problems with it, what your thoughts are.'

'Oh – she needs the treatment, doctor!' interrupts Edward, and I feel guilty, as though I am hastening his wife's death.

'OK,' I say, 'of course, of course, absolutely. It's sometimes just useful for me to know how much treatment you'd want. For how long. That kind of thing.'

Edward is shaking his head, and I fear that I've offended him. I feel stupid and insensitive.

'The other thing I'm thinking about is how to treat your symptoms just now, how we can try and get rid of your nausea and the pain. We have quite a few options.'

I am on safer ground; there is nodding and agreement. We make a plan for increasing medication and new anti-sickness pills. Edward goes into the kitchen to find their appointment card for the hospital so we can try and co-ordinate my appointments with the oncology ones.

'Doctor,' Rosa says, quietly, quizzically, 'when you say 'how much treatment' – what do you mean?'

'Just that it's quite variable, how people get on with chemo. Some people do very well, they don't notice it much. For other people it's very unpleasant. If it's going to make a big difference to the cancer, then it might be worthwhile. But if not, then... well... it might not be.'

We both notice Edward in the kitchen, sorting through papers.

'What do you think of my cancer, then? Be honest. Do you think the chemo will work? Oh, I know you can't say that. Look at it this way – do you think there's a reasonable chance of it working?'

I had swotted up on the statistics for her type of cancer before I got here, just in case she asked me. I tell her; they are not very good. Slowly, she bites her lip.

'Tell me doctor, would you have it? The chemo?'

'I don't know. I might not.'

'My son is very keen for me to have this,' she says. 'He wants me to take every 'fighting chance' he calls it.'

'Do you see it like that?'

'A bit. I don't want to let them down. But I want to think about this. I'm not sure.'

'I have to say – I don't see it like that. The 'fight'... is that the best description? Do you want me to speak to Thomas about you?'

'Would you? Just – just what you said.'

Edward comes back – 'it's next Wednesday, 11.30, up at the clinic.' The doorbell rings: it is Thomas, their son, as planned.

Thomas says, 'I'm very concerned about her. She seems to be giving up.' We stand to one side, as Jane, the carer, has also arrived; Nancy and Edward are pleased to see her and update her on the problem of the commode. Jane has had two different models of bed support in, they tell me, and isn't happy with either. Jane is instantly on her mobile phone, telling the supplies department that they had better send another set of hand rails today to go beside the bed. Edward is laughing at her mock crossness. Ella Fitzgerald is playing in the background.

Tom and I are in the kitchen, speaking quietly.

'What do you know so far, Tom?'

'Just that it's cancer, that there's treatment that works, that she needs to get on with it. She's healthy, really; never smoked, never drank.'

'Do you know much about the treatment?'

'Side effects you mean? Sickness – but there's drugs for that.'

'OK. Do you know – have you talked to her – about how good the treatment is?'

'Well it's better than doing nothing. Isn't it?'

'I suppose... what I'm worried about is how the side effects will affect her, and how much... how much it's worth it.'

'Really?'

'Has she said much about the cancer itself?'

'Just that it's in her liver. And one or two in her bones.'

'I'm just concerned that once it's spread, this type of cancer... chemotherapy is a holding measure, really, not a cure. It might give her a few extra weeks, it might not, it's not a cure. If you see what I mean.'

'Yes, OK. We didn't expect a cure. I know that. But still, a chance...'

'I suppose... it's how big a chance. And how bad the side effects are.'

'You don't sound optimistic, doctor?'

'I'm sorry. It just might not be as good a treatment as it sounds... Might be one to talk to her about?'

We agree.

When I leave, Jane is also finishing her duties, promising that she'll bring in a picture of her latest grandchild to show them. Rosa says, 'I'll be in touch, doctor, thank you very much.' I walk Jane out.

'I don't think she's that keen on the cancer treatment,' Jane says. 'She says she knows her number's up. Just wanting to enjoy her time, now. I would. Wouldn't be spending it in that hospital, anyway. See you.' She is in her car and I am gone, back to the surgery, after over half an hour of talking.

* * *

Rosa phones me about a week later.

'I had a chat with the consultant. Actually, she was lovely. Says I can have the chemotherapy, but actually, if it's pain relief I want, the radiotherapy will be better, if we can't get on

top of it with the morphine.'

'So what do you think you'll do?'

'I can't say Edward is happy. The verdict is that chemotherapy might give me a few extra months. But it might not. It has side effects and I can't see how being in and out of hospital will be a nice way to spend them. And to be honest, the extra medication you gave me seems pretty good.'

She pauses for a moment. We had added in a couple of different long-acting types of pain medication which had been gradually increased. Rosa sounds like herself.

'I still remember my grandmother dying. She took to her bed. She must have been in her late nineties. I must have been seven or eight. I was taken up to see her – she was like a queen, with pillows propping her up and a knitted bedjacket on. My mum and her aunties, they took turns reading to her, her favourite Jane Austens and Charles Dickens. She was a great reader. She liked scones, so we baked lots of scones. She had brandy at night, to get to sleep – and sherry too. I remember my mum mopping her brow with cold water from the outside tap. I don't remember seeing a doctor. She passed away in the bed she'd been born in, with all of us in the house. We had the wake at the house, it was filled with people, and we played hide and seek. If I could have that... well, I'd die happy.'

* * *

Rosa and Edward come into the surgery. I am surprised; I thought she would have been at the hospital.

'We were out anyway,' she explains. 'We're planning a trip to Inverness. First holiday we ever had was up there, would love to go back. Just for the weekend.'

'So how are you?'

'Edward was a bit annoyed with me. Weren't you?' (He nods.) 'And so was Thomas. But we went back to speak to the doctor, Dr Fornly, and she was very supportive. She said

we could have the chemotherapy if we wanted, but that she thought we were right – I'm feeling much better, in terms of pain, and have been out every afternoon this week.'

She is wearing a well pressed skirt suit, in a 1970s faded orange, and though still thin and pale, she has set her hair and is wearing her usual blusher and lipstick.

'She's done very well, really. I keep telling her to rest but she's not having it,' said Edward, smiling at her.

'If I'm feeling fine, why not?' she asks. 'What I do want to discuss is my bowels and my sleep.'

We plan an adjustment of medication and a date for review. I sign the forms, wondering if their trip will go smoothly.

'Can I ask something?'

'Of course.'

'I'm wondering... quite often, when people have cancer that's spread, they want to make decisions about what should happen if they get worse.'

'We've talked about that, actually, the two of us.'

'Oh?'

'Edward wants me to have full treatment for everything...'

He squeezes her hand. 'It's only because I love you...'

'I'm thinking of things like going into hospital in an emergency, or CPR – you know – resuscitation.'

'I think I'd like to be at home.'

'Even if – even if you live less long?'

'Yes.' She pats Edward's hand. His eyes are glistening. 'I want to die like my grannie did.'

'OK. You want to stay at home, if possible?'

'Absolutely.'

'Have a great trip.'

* * *

It doesn't go smoothly. The day before they are due to leave, Edward calls me to their home.

Rosa is in bed. Her breathing is rapid; she is sweaty and clammy. Her abdomen feels hard and she is tender when I press upon her kidneys. Her blood pressure is low and her chest noisy; meaning a build up of fluid.

I am conflicted. This could be treatable. Diuretics to remove fluid, antibiotics to treat infection; she would be better in hospital for close monitoring. And her abdomen is rigid, meaning a problem there; the biggest concern is for her kidneys. If they are being blocked off due to cancer, they would need drainage, else she would die from the effects of renal failure. If I leave her at home, am I allowing her to die of an easily treatable condition? If I don't admit her to hospital, am I accelerating her death through my inaction? Supposing she just needs a day or two of intravenous treatment – surely that wouldn't be so bad? She could still come home to die when the end really was near. And what about her kidney function – could it be deteriorating, meaning that her pain medication doses should be reduced?

'Rosa, how are you?'

'Terrible. The pain is back. It's worse, when I breathe. I feel awful.'

'What about going into hospital? Would you consider it? They might be able to make you feel better, quicker, and with more monitoring than we can do at home.'

'I really don't want to. I want to stay here.' She looks at Edward imploringly, and Edward nods his assent.

'We could try treating you here, if you wish,' I say, 'with tablets to try and get rid of the fluid. I'm worried about infection too. We could give you antibiotics, and see…'

'As long as I don't have to go into hospital.'

'OK. I'll phone Jane and see if we can get a bit more assistance at home, see if we can get the nurses in a couple of times a day?'

We agree. On the subject of pain, I am even less sure as to what to do.

'If we use bigger doses of morphine, I think that'll help. It might make you drowsy at first, though. Or we could arrange some radiotherapy.'

'I'd have the radiotherapy. But only if I'm fit for it. Otherwise I'm staying here.'

I notice a small bottle of brandy at her bedside. She is happy to have one blood test to check her kidney function, which will allow me to adjust her pain medication as needed.

* * *

I phone the following day. She is brighter, her breathing is easier, but the pain in her side is worse. The blood test shows worsening kidney failure and we readjust the medication doses; the district nurses will sort this out this afternoon. She agrees that I can phone Dr Fornly. She recommends an ultrasound, to assess what is happening in the kidneys – she, too, is concerned about renal failure. She also offers to set up radiotherapy.

We arrange for an ambulance to take Rosa to the hospital that afternoon.

* * *

Edward phones.

'She's got a tumour around her kidney. They've offered to put a tube in and drain the kidney that way, but she's not having it.'

'Really?'

'You know my Rosa. She's coming back home tonight. They've put up her morphine again. The nurses are calling in too. I don't think we're going to get to Inverness, doc.'

* * *

I visit Rosa the following day. She is sitting against dozens of pillows. She is wearing lipstick. Outside her room, I can hear her friends talking, with the occasional burst of laughter. The record player is sounding Ella Fitzgerald, and there is the smell of fresh baking.

'I'm fine,' she says, 'and not sleepy, just... content, I think. It's a bit sore when I turn. The nurses have been great. Jane is in most of the time. You'll look after my Eddie, won't you?'

* * *

Four days later I am asked to certify Rosa's death. She died at home, overnight. Edward, who was sleeping lightly beside her, became aware of her breathing changing. They called Thomas, and a district nurse, who stayed with them. 'She was at peace,' said Edward. Thomas is distraught, but says that she had 'what she wanted'. On the bedside, the brandy is missing a bit. I tell them that I was privileged to look after them. Later the district nurse phones me, and we talk, a little tearfully, about Rosa. I call Dr Fornly, who says that she will phone them too; she knew about Ella Fitzgerald. Apparently, they saw her at the Apollo, Rosa and Edward's first date.

Epilogue

There is guilt in the writing of this book, because there have been many times when I've looked back over my own role in the death of a patient and been aware that I could have done better. I could have opened a conversation about dying, I could have been more honest in describing the likely outlook. I should have asked the person to talk to their relatives about what they did, and didn't, want to happen to them. I don't remember being too pessimistic – and that's usually a good time for a doctor to be wrong – but I do remember being too optimistic. I also can think of many times when I, selfishly, have been worried about increasing morphine doses, in case I would be blamed later on. I've been afraid of starting discussions but then running out of time, of opening a deep emotional well that I am scared that I can't contain, of being asked difficult questions. I will still fail, but writing this book has made me want to at least try to fail better.

I think that times are slowly changing, thanks to the Dying Matters charity, who have promoted discussions about dying amongst the living, and individuals like Dr Kate Granger who have tirelessly campaigned for better deathcare. There is an insistent permeation of the idea that while death will remain inevitable, our approach to it could make life easier. We could take an active part in planning our choices, and understanding the limits of medicine and the interventions we would and wouldn't want to have. We could have a good death, and a good death is not a failure.

However, we will not produce such better deaths, and better lives after a death, unless we prioritise the things we need to care well for dying people. Primarily, this means human, hands-on, care, with enough time to do it well. It's entirely within our grasp to do this, but it will need patients and their families to tell health and social care services what it is that they want. Fundamentally, healthcare professionals, patients and families need to be on the same side, each helping the other to the end.

References

Introduction

1. *Deaths Registered in England and Wales in 2010, by Cause.* Part of mortality statistics: deaths registered in England and Wales (Series DR), 2010 release. Office for National Statistics. 28 October 2011. www.ons.gov.uk/ons/rel/vsob1/mortality-statistics--deaths-registered-in-england-and-wales--series-dr-/2010/stb-deaths-by-cause-2010.html
2. *A Century of Change: Trends in UK statistics since 1900.* Research Paper 99/11. House of Commons Library. 21 December 1999. www.parliament.uk/documents/commons/lib/research/rp99/rp99-111.pdf
3. Barnett K, Mercer SW, Norbury M et al. Epidemiology of multimorbidity and implications for health care, research, and medical education: a cross-sectional study. *The Lancet* 2012;380(9836):37-43. press.thelancet.com/morbidity.pdf

Chapter 1: The modern death

4. *Deaths Registered in England and Wales in 2010, by Cause.* Part of mortality statistics: deaths registered in England and Wales (Series DR), 2010 release. Office for National Statistics. 28 October 2011. www.ons.gov.uk/ons/rel/vsob1/mortality-statistics--deaths-registered-in-england-and-wales--series-dr-/2010/stb-deaths-by-cause-2010.html
5. *Deaths in Older Adults in England.* National End of Life Care Intelligence Network. October 2010. www.endoflifecare-intelligence.org.uk/resources/publications/deaths_in_older_adults
6. McCartney G. Illustrating health inequalities in Glasgow. *Journal of Epidemiology and Community Health* 2011;65:194. jech.bmj.com/content/65/1/94
7. Gomes B, Calanzani N, Higginson IJ. Reversal of the British trends in place of death: time series analysis 2004-2010. *Palliative Medicine* 2012;26(2):102-107. pmj.sagepub.com/content/early/2012/01/17/0269216311432329.abstract
8. Gomes B, Higginson IJ. Where people die (1974-2030): past trends, future projections and implications for care. *Palliative Medicine* 2008;22:33. pmj.sagepub.com/content/22/1/33
9. Ahmad S, O'Mahony MS. Where older people die: a retrospective population-based study. *QJM* 2005;98(12):865-870. qjmed.oxfordjournals.org/content/98/12/865.full
10. Cowie MR, Wood DA, Coats AJS et al. Survival of patients with a new diagnosis of heart failure: A population based study. *Heart* 2000;(83):505-510. heart.bmj.com/content/83/5/505.long
11. Hobbs FDR, Roalfe AK et al. Prognosis of all-cause heart failure and borderline left ventricular systolic dysfunction: 5 year mortality follow-up of the Echocardiographic Heart of England Screening Study (ECHOES.) *European Heart Journal* 2007 28(9):1128-1134. eurheartj.oxfordjournals.org/content/28/9/1128.long
12. *National Diabetes Audit 2011/2 Report 2 Complications and Mortality. Health and Social Care Information Centre.* www.hqip.org.uk/assets/NCAPOP-Library/NCAPOP-2013-14/NDA2011-2012Report2ComplicationsMortalityINTERACTIVEPDF26-11-13.pdf
13. Leal J, Gray AM, Clarke PM. Development of life-expectancy tables for people with type 2 diabetes. *European Heart Journal* 2009;30(7):834-839. www.ncbi.

nlm.nih.gov/pmc/articles/PMC2663724

14. Mulnier HE, Seaman HE, Raleigh VS et al. Mortality in people with type 2 diabetes in the UK. *Diabetic Medicine* 2006;23(5):516-521. www.ncbi.nlm.nih.gov/pubmed/16681560
15. Evans JMM, Barnett KN, McMurdo MET, Morris AD. Reporting of diabetes on death certificates of 1872 people with type 2 diabetes in Tayside, Scotland. *European Journal of Public Health* 2008;18(2):201-203. eurpub.oxfordjournals.org/content/18/2/201.full
16. Rait G, Walters K, Bottomley C et al. Survival of people with clinical diagnosis of dementia in primary care: cohort study. *BMJ* 2010;341:c3584. www.bmj.com/content/341/bmj.c3584
17. Newens AJ, Forster DP, Kay DWK. Death certification after a diagnosis of presenile dementia. *Journal of Epidemiology and Community Health* 1993;47:293-297. jech.bmj.com/content/47/4/293.full.pdf
18. Alderson A, Mendick R, McElroy D. Revealed: Libya paid for medical advice that helped Lockerbie bomber's release. *The Telegraph*. 5 September 2009. www.telegraph.co.uk/news/worldnews/africaandindianocean/libya/6143073/Revealed-Libya-paid-for-medical-advice-that-helped-Lockerbie-bombers-release.html
19. Lockerbie bomber Abdelbaset al-Megrahi dies in Tripoli. *BBC News Africa*. 20 May 2012. www.bbc.co.uk/news/world-africa-18137896
20. Nicholas S. Told they had terminal cancer and had as little as weeks to live, the miracle survivors' club have proved the doctors wrong. *Mail Online*. 22 January 2011.www.dailymail.co.uk/femail/article-1349105/Told-terminal-cancer-little-weeks-live-miracle-survivors-club-proved-doctors-wrong.html
21. Christakis NA, Lamont EB. Extent and determinants of error in doctors' prognoses in terminally ill patients: prospective cohort study. *BMJ* 2000;320(7233):469-473. https://www.ncbi.nlm.nih.gov/pmc/articles/PMC27288
22. Glare P, Virik K, Jones M et al. A systematic review of physicians' survival predictions in terminally ill cancer patients. *BMJ* 2003;327:195. www.bmj.com/content/327/7408/195.long
23. Barnett K, Mercer SW, Norbury M et al. Epidemiology of multimorbidity and implications for health care, research, and medical education: a cross-sectional study. *The Lancet* 2012;380(9836):37-43. press.thelancet.com/morbidity.pdf
24. Barnes S, Gott M, Payne S et al. Predicting mortality among a general practice-based sample of older people with heart failure. *Chronic Illness* 2008 4(1):5-12. chi.sagepub.com/content/4/1/5
25. Gill TM, Gahbauer EA, Han L, Allore HG. Trajectories of disability in the last year of life. *New England Journal of Medicine* 2010;362:1173-1180. www.nejm.org/doi/full/10.1056/NEJMoa0909087
26. Fried LP, Tangen CM, Walston J et al. Frailty in older adults evidence for a phenotype. *Journals of Gerontology Series A* (Biological Sciences and Medical Sciences) 2001:56 (3):M146-M157. biomedgerontology.oxfordjournals.org/content/56/3/M146.full
27. Hall FM, Griscom NT. Gestalt: radiology's Aunt Minnie. *American Journal of Roentgenology* 2008;191(4):1272. www.ajronline.org/content/191/4/1272.full
28. Hastings SN, Purser JL, Johnson KS et al. A frailty index predicts some but not all adverse outcomes in older adults discharged from the emergency department. *Journal of the American Geriatrics Society* 2008;56(9):1651-1657. www.ncbi.nlm.nih.gov/pmc/articles/PMC2676906

29. Tiernan E, O'Connor M, O'Siorain L, Kearney M. A prospective study of preferred versus actual place of death among patients referred to a palliative care home-care service. *Irish Medical Journal* 2002 95(8):232-235. www.ncbi.nlm.nih.gov/pubmed/12405498
30. Brazil K, Howell D, Bedard M et al. Preferences for place of care and place of death among informal caregivers of the terminally ill. *Palliative Medicine* 2005;19(6):492-499.www.ncbi.nlm.nih.gov/pubmed/16218162
31. Tang ST. When death is imminent: where terminally ill patients with cancer prefer to die and why. *Cancer Nursing* 2003;26(3):245-251. www.ncbi.nlm.nih.gov/pubmed/12832958
32. Gomes B, Calanzani N, Higginson IJ. *Local preferences in place of death in regions within England in 2010.* Cicely Saunders International. August 2011. www.csi.kcl.ac.uk/localpref.html
33. Kulkarni P, Kulkarni P, Anavkar V, Ghooi R. Preference of the place of death among people of Pune. *Indian Journal of Palliative Care* 2014;20(2):101-106. www.ncbi.nlm.nih.gov/pubmed/25125864
34. Fukui S, Yoshiuchi K, Fujita J et al. Japanese people's preference for place of end-of-life care and death: a population-based nationwide survey. *Journal of Pain and Symptom Management* 2011;42(6):888-892. www.jpsmjournal.com/article/S0885-3924(11)00242 9/abstract
35. Brazil K, Howell D, Bedard M et al. Preferences for place of care and place of death among informal caregivers of the terminally ill. *Palliative Medicine* 2005;19(6):492-499. pmj.sagepub.com/content/19/6/492
36. Seamark DA, Thorne CP, Lawrence C, Gray DJ. Appropriate place of death for cancer patients: views of general practitioners and hospital doctors. *British Journal of General Practice* 1995;45(396): 359–363. www.ncbi.nlm.nih.gov/pmc/articles/PMC1239299
37. Townsend J, Frank AO, Fermont D et al. Terminal cancer care and patients' preference for place of death: a prospective study. *BMJ* 1990;301(6749):415-417. www.ncbi.nlm.nih.gov/pmc/articles/PMC1663663
38. Jack B, O'Brien M. Dying at home: community nurses' views on the impact of informal carers on cancer patients' place of death. *European Journal of Cancer Care* 2010;19:636-642. onlinelibrary.wiley.com/doi/10.1111/j.1365-2354.2009.01103.x/full
39 Gomes B, Calanzani N, Higginson IJ. Reversal of the British trends in place of death: time series analysis 2004-2010. *Palliative Medicine* 2012 26(2):102-107. pmj.sagepub.com/content/early/2012/01/17/0269216311432329
40. End of Life Care Strategy. Promoting high quality care for all adults at the end of life. Department of Health. July 2008. www.gov.uk/government/publications/end-of-life-care-strategy-promoting-high-quality-care-for-adults-at-the-end-of-their-life
41. End of life care strategy. *Dying Matters*. www.dyingmatters.org/page/end-life-care-strategy
42. The gender gap in unpaid care provision: is there an impact on health and economic position? Office for National Statistics, 16 May 2013. www.ons.gov.uk/ons/dcp171776_310295.pdf
43. Shah AJ, Wadoo O, Latoo J. Psychological distress in carers of people with mental disorders. *British Journal of Medical Practitioners* 2010;3(3):a327. www.bjmp.org/content/psychological-distress-carers-people-mental-disorders

Chapter 2: The quality problem

44. Rothwell PM, McDowell Z, Wong CK, Dorman PJ. Doctors and patients don't agree: cross sectional study of patients' and doctors' perceptions and assessments of disability in multiple sclerosis. *BMJ*;1997; 314:1580. www.bmj.com/content/314/7094/1580?linkType=FULL&resid=314/7094/1580&journalCode=bmj
45. NICE glossary. National Institute for Health and Care Excellence. https://www.nice.org.uk/glossary
46. Višnjić A, Veličković V, Milosavljević NS. QALY – measure of cost-benefit analysis of health interventions. *Scientific Journal of the Faculty of Medicine in Niš* 2011;28(4):195-199. wwwserver.medfak.ni.ac.rs/Acta%20Facultatis/2011/4-2011/1.pdf
47. Singer P, McKie J, Kuhse H, Richardson J. Double jeopardy and the use of QALYs in health care allocation. *Journal of Medical Ethics* 1995;21:144-150. jme.bmj.com/content/21/3/144.full.pdf
48. Williams A. Discovering the QALY. Or how Rachel Rosser changed my life. In: Oliver A (ed). *Personal Histories in Health Research*. London: Nuffield Trust, 2005., www.york.ac.uk/media/che/documents/Williams%20on%20disovering%20the%20QALY.pdf
49. Dolan P, Olsen JA, Menzel P, Richardson J. An inquiry into the different perspectives that can be used when eliciting preferences in health. *Health Economics* 2003;12(7):545-551. onlinelibrary.wiley.com/doi/10.1002/hec.760/abstract
50. Normand C. Setting priorities in and for end-of-life care: challenges in the application of economic evaluation. *Health Economics, Policy and Law* 2012;7(4):431-439. journals.cambridge.org/action/displayAbstract?fromPage=online&aid=8722103
51. Palliative care for the terminally ill in America: the consideration of QALYs, costs and ethical issues. *Medicine, Health Care and Philosophy* 2012;15(4):411-416. link.springer.com/article/10.1007%2Fs11019-011-9364-6
52. Donaldson C, Baker R, Mason H et al. The social value of a QALY: raising the bar or barring the raise? *BMC Health Services Research* 2011;11:8. www.biomedcentral.com/1472-6963/11/8
53. Collins M, Latimer N. NICE's end of life decision making scheme: impact on population health. *BMJ*;2013;346:f1363. www.bmj.com/content/346/bmj.f1363
54. Round J. Is a QALY still a QALY at the end of life? *Journal of Health Economics* 2012 May;31(3):521-527. www.eurohex.eu/bibliography/pdf/Round_2012-2897810690/Round_2012.pdf
55. NICE central to value-based pricing of medicines (press release). National Institute for Health and Care Excellence. 22 April 2014. www.nice.org.uk/News/Article/nice-central-to-valuebased-pricing-of-medicines
56. Raftery J. NICE proposes alternative for value based pricing of medicines. *BMJ Blogs*. 25 February 2014. blogs.bmj.com/bmj/2014/02/25/james-raftery-nice-proposes-alternative-for-value-based-pricing
57. Fisher C, Freris N. Neuromuscular degeneration. *BMJ* 2012; 345:e6880. www.bmj.com/content/345/bmj.e6880
58. Wright RA, Flapan AD, McMurray J et al. Scandinavian simvastatin study (4S). *The Lancet* 1994; 344(8939):1765-1768. www.thelancet.com/journals/lancet/article/PIIS0140-6736(94)92906-8/fulltext
59. Clark JA, Inui TS, Silliman RA et al. Patients' perceptions of quality of life after treatment for early prostate cancer. *Journal of Clinical Oncology* 2003;21(20):

3777-3784. jco.ascopubs.org/content/21/20/3777.full.pdf

60. Palermo T, Rawat R, Weiser SD, Kadiyala S. Food access and diet quality are associated with quality of life outcomes among HIV-infected individuals in Uganda. *PLoS ONE* 2013;8(4):e62353. www.plosone.org/article/info:doi/10.1371/journal.pone.0062353
61. Cramp F, Byron-Daniel J. Exercise for the management of cancer-related fatigue in adults. *Cochrane Database of Systematic Reviews* 2012, Issue 11. Art. No.: CD006145. onlinelibrary.wiley.com/doi/10.1002/14651858.CD006145.pub3/abstract
62. Bausewein C, Booth S, Gysels M, Higginson IJ. Non-pharmacological interventions for breathlessness in advanced stages of malignant and non-malignant diseases (review). *The Cochrane Library* 2008, Issue 3. www.ipac.org/fileadmin/user_upload/publikation/Bausewein-2008-CR.pdf
63. Legg L, Drummond A, Leonardi-Bee J et al. Occupational therapy for patients with problems in personal activities of daily living after stroke: systematic review of randomised trials. *BMJ* 2007;335:922. www.bmj.com/content/335/7626/922
64. McCleery J, Fox R. Antipsychotic prescribing in nursing homes. *BMJ* 2012;344:e1093. www.bmj.com/content/344/bmj.e1093
65. Prescribing of antipsychotic drugs for dementia patients shows sharp decline. Health and Social Care Information Centre. 17 July 2012. www.hscic.gov.uk/article/2093/Prescribing-of-antipsychotic-drugs-for-dementia-patients-shows-sharp-decline
66. McCleery J, Fox R. Antipsychotic prescribing in nursing homes. *BMJ* 2012;344:e1093. . 211.144.68.84:9998/91keshi/Public/File/38/344-7848/pdf/bmj.e1093.full.pdf
67. Richter T, Meyer G, Möhler M, Köpke S. Psychosocial interventions for reducing antipsychotic medication in care home residents. *Cochrane Database of Systematic Reviews* 2012, Issue 12. Art. No.: CD008634. onlinelibrary.wiley.com/doi/10.1002/14651858.CD008634.pub2/abstract
68. Hoe J, Hancock JG, Livingston G et al. Quality of life of people with dementia in residential care homes. *The British Journal of Psychiatry* 2006;188: 460-464. bjp.rcpsych.org/content/188/5/460.full
69. Lawrence V, Fossey J, Ballard C et al. Improving quality of life for people with dementia in care homes: making psychosocial interventions work. *British Journal of Psychiatry* 2012;201(5):344–351. bjp.rcpsych.org/content/201/5/344
70. Vernooij-Dassen M, Vasse E, Zuidema S, Cohen-Mansfield J, Moyle W. Psychosocial interventions for dementia patients in long-term care. *International Psychogeriatrics* 2010;22(7):1121-1128. www.ncbi.nlm.nih.gov/pubmed/20813074
71. Ó Luanaigh C, Lawlor BA. Loneliness and the health of older people. *International Journal of Geriatric Psychiatry* 2008;23(12):1213-1221. onlinelibrary.wiley.com/doi/10.1002/gps.2054/abstract
72. Tilvis RS, Laitala V, Routasalo PE, Pitkala KH. Suffering from loneliness indicates significant mortality risk of older people. *Journal of Aging Research* 2011:534781. www.ncbi.nlm.nih.gov/pmc/articles/PMC3056243
73. Steptoe A, Shankar A, Demakakos P, Wardle J. Social isolation, loneliness, and all-cause mortality in older men and women. *Proceedings of the National Academy of Sciences* 2013;110(15):5797-5801. www.pnas.org/content/110/15/5797
74. Holt-Lunstad J, Smith TB, Layton JB. Social relationships and mortality risk: a

meta-analytic review. *PLoS Medicine* 2010;7(7):e1000316. dx.doi.org/10.1371/journal.pmed.1000316

75. Ellaway A, Wood S, Macintyre S. Someone to talk to? The role of loneliness as a factor in the frequency of GP consultations. *British Journal of General* Practice;49(442):363–367. www.ncbi.nlm.nih.gov/pmc/articles/PMC1313421
76. Jaremka LM, Andridge RR, Fagundes CP et al. Pain, depression, and fatigue: loneliness as a longitudinal risk factor. *Health Psychology* 2014;33(9):948-57. www.ncbi.nlm.nih.gov/pubmed/23957903
77. Schwarzbach M, Luppa M, Forstmeier S et al. Social relations and depression in late life – a systematic review. *International Journal of Geriatric Psychiatry* 2013;29(1):1-21. onlinelibrary.wiley.com/doi/10.1002/gps.3971/pdf
78. Rodda J, Walker Z, Carter J. Depression in older adults. *BMJ* 2011;343:d5219. www.bmj.com/content/343/bmj.d5219?ath_user=nhsdmcgowan002&ath_ttok=%253CTqAd%252BKPfFJr0LXHw0w%253E
79. Kim ES, Sun JK, Park N, Peterson C. Purpose in life and reduced incidence of stroke in older adults: 'The Health and Retirement Study'. *Journal of Psychosomatic Research* 2013;74(5):427-432. www.sciencedirect.com/science/article/pii/S0022399913000391
80. Kvelde T, McVeigh C, Toson B et al. Depressive symptomatology as a risk factor for falls in older people: systematic review and meta-analysis. *Journal of the American Geriatrics Society* 2013;61(5):694-706. www.ncbi.nlm.nih.gov/pubmed/23617614
81. Wilson RS, Krueger KR, Arnold SE et al. Loneliness and risk of Alzheimer disease. *Archives of General Psychiatry* 2007;64(2):234-240. archpsyc.jamanetwork.com/article.aspx?articleid=482179

Chapter 3: Too many tablets

82. Hippisley-Cox J, Pringle M, Ryan R. *Polypharmacy in the Elderly: Analysis of QRESEARCH Data*. QRESEARCH, 2007. www.qresearch.org/Public_Documents/DataValidation/Polypharmacy%20in%20the%20elderly.pdf
83. Gorard DA. Escalating polypharmacy. *QJM* 2006;99(11):797-800. qjmed.oxfordjournals.org/content/99/11/797.full
84. *Social Prescribing: A model for partnership working between primary care and the voluntary sector*. Age UK. 2012. www.ageuk.org.uk/professional-resources-home/services-and-practice/health-and-wellbeing/
85. More than medicine. New services for people powered health. 2013. www.nesta.org.uk/sites/default/files/more_than_medicine.pdf.
86. Pirmohamed M, James S, Meakin S et al Adverse drug reactions as cause of admission to hospital: prospective analysis of 18 820 patients. *BMJ* 2004;329:15. www.bmj.com/content/329/7456/15
87. Shem S. *The House of God*. Black Swan, 1998.
88. Macdonald S. Aspirin use to be banned in under 16 year olds. *BMJ* 2002;325(7371):988. www.ncbi.nlm.nih.gov/pmc/articles/PMC1169585
89. *Aspirin and Reye's Syndrome: Questions and Answers*. Medicines and Healthcare Products Regulatory Agency, 2003. www.mhra.gov.uk/home/groups/pl-a/documents/websiteresources/con019513.pdf
90. Blower AL, Brooks A, Fenn GC et al. Emergency admissions for upper gastrointestinal disease and their relation to NSAID use. *Alimentary Pharmacology and Therapeutics* 1997;11(2):283-291. www.ncbi.nlm.nih.gov/pubmed/9146764
91. Hernández-Díaz S, Rodríguez LAG. Association between nonsteroidal anti-

inflammatory drugs and upper gastrointestinal tract bleeding/perforation: an overview of epidemiologic studies published in the 1990s. *Archives of Internal Medicine* 2000;160(14):2093-2099. archinte.jamanetwork.com/article.aspx?articleid=485416

92. Hawkey CJ, Langman MJS. Non-steroidal anti-inflammatory drugs: overall risks and management. Complementary roles for COX-2 inhibitors and proton pump inhibitors. *Gut* 2003;52:600-608. gut.bmj.com/content/52/4/600
93. O'Flaherty EJ. Modeling normal aging bone loss, with consideration of bone loss in osteoporosis. *Toxicological Sciences* 2000;55(1):171-188. toxsci.oxfordjournals.org/content/55/1/171
94. Johnell O, Kanis JA. An estimate of the worldwide prevalence and disability associated with osteoporotic fractures. *Osteoporosis International* 2006;17(12):1726-1733. link.springer.com/article/10.1007%2Fs00198-006-0172-4
95. Kanis JA, McCloskey EV, Johansson H et al, National Osteoporosis Guideline Group. Case finding for the management of osteoporosis with FRAX® – assessment and intervention thresholds for the UK. *Osteoporosis International* 2008;19(10):1395-1408. link.springer.com/article/10.1007%2Fs00198-008-0712-1
96. Questions and answers on the study by Green and co-workers (2010) on oral bisphosphonates and oesophageal cancer. Medicines and Healthcare Products Regulatory Agency, 2010. goo.gl/vw24li
97. Bottle A, Aylin P. Mortality associated with delay in operation after hip fracture: observational study. *BMJ* 2006;332:947. www.bmj.com/content/332/7547/947
98. Wells GA, Cranney A, Peterson J et al. Alendronate for the primary and secondary prevention of osteoporotic fractures in postmenopausal women. *Cochrane Database of Systematic Reviews* 2008, Issue 1. Art. No.: CD001155. onlinelibrary.wiley.com/doi/10.1002/14651858.CD001155.pub2/full
99. Vitamin D and vitamin D analogues for preventing fractures in post-menopausal women and older men. *Cochrane Database of Systematic Reviews* 2014, Issue 4. Art. No.: CD000227 onlinelibrary.wiley.com/doi/10.1002/14651858.CD000227.pub4/abstract
100. Wainwright SA, Marshall LM, Ensrud KE et al. Hip fracture in women without osteoporosis. *Journal of Clinical Endocrinology & Metabolism* 2005;90(5):2787-2793. jcem.endojournals.org/content/90/5/2787.full
101. *WHO Study Group on assessment of fracture risk and its application to screening for postmenopausal osteoporosis.* WHO technical report series; 843. World Health Organization, 1994. whqlibdoc.who.int/trs/WHO_TRS_843.pdf
102. How a bone disease grew to fit the prescription. *NPR News.* 21 December 2009. www.npr.org/templates/transcript/transcript.php?storyId=121609815
103. The UK NSC policy on osteoporosis screening in women after the menopause. *UK Screening Portal.* April 2013. www.screening.nhs.uk/osteoporosis
104. Osteoporosis: assessing the risk of fragility fracture. NICE guidelines CG146. National Institute for Health and Care Excellence. August 2012. www.nice.org.uk/guidance/cg146
105. Murphy K. Splits form over how to address bone loss. *International New York Times.* 7 September 2009. www.nytimes.com/2009/09/08/health/08bone.html
106. *WHO Scientific Group on the Assessment of Osteoporosis at Primary Health Care Level*, Summary Meeting Report, Brussels, Belgium, 5-7 May 2004. World Health Organization, 2007. www.who.int/chp/topics/Osteoporosis.pdf

107. Committee of Corporate Advisors, International Osteoporosis Foundation. www.iofbonehealth.org/committee-corporate-advisors-cca
108. National Osteoporosis Foundation. Corporate Opportunities. nof.org/articles/55
109. Policies. The International Society for Clinical Densitometry. www.iscd.org/about/policies
110. ASBMR statement about interactions with industry. American Society for Bone and Mineral Research. www.asbmr.org/About/detail.aspx?cid=721e5a79-7a91-4fcb-9fa2-471a497439da
111. Merck establishes new, nonprofit bone measurement institute (press release). *The Free Library*. PR Newswire Association, 31 August 1995. www.thefreelibrary.com/MERCK+ESTABLISHES+NEW,+NONPROFIT+BONE+MEASUREMENT+INSTITUTE-a017284525
112. Pillbox biography: the creation of a blockbuster drug. *NPR News*. 21 December 2009. www.npr.org/templates/story/story.php?storyId=121585433
113. Patient information: once weekly FOSAMAX® (FOSS-ah-max) (alendronate sodium), tablets and oral solution. Merck Sharp & Dohme Corp, March 2010. www.merck.com/product/usa/pi_circulars/f/fosamax/fosamax_onceweekly_ppi.pdf
114. Khosla S, Burr D, Cauley J et al. Bisphosphonate-associated osteonecrosis of the jaw: report of a task force of the American Society for Bone and Mineral Research. *Journal of Bone and Mineral Research* 2007;22:1479-1491. onlinelibrary.wiley.com/doi/10.1359/jbmr.0707onj/full
115. Shane E, Goldring S, Christakos S et al. Osteonecrosis of the jaw: more research needed. *Journal of Bone and Mineral Research* 2006;21:1503-1505. onlinelibrary.wiley.com/doi/10.1359/jbmr.060712/full
116. Lo JC, O'Ryan FS, Gordon NP et al. Prevalence of osteonecrosis of the jaw in patients with oral bisphosphonate exposure. *Journal of Oral and Maxillofacial Surgery* 2010;68(2):243-253. www.ncbi.nlm.nih.gov/pubmed/19772941 As
117. BMA Quality of Outcomes Framework guidance 2014-2015 according to nation bma.org.uk/practical-support-at-work/contracts/independent-contractors/qof-guidance
118. Moore M, Yuen HM, Dunn N et al. Explaining the rise in antidepressant prescribing: a descriptive study using the general practice research database. *BMJ* 2009;339:b3999. www.bmj.com/content/339/bmj.b3999
119. Antidepressants leaflet. Royal College of Psychiatrists, June 2012, reviewed June 2014. www.rcpsych.ac.uk/expertadvice/treatments/antidepressants.aspx
120. Banerjee S, Hellier J, Dewey M et al. Sertraline or mirtazapine for depression in dementia (HTA-SADD): a randomised, multicentre, double-blind, placebo-controlled trial. *The Lancet* 2011;378(9789):403–411. www.thelancet.com/journals/lancet/article/PIIS0140-6736(11)60830-1/abstract
121. Barbui C, Cipriani A, Patel V et al. Efficacy of antidepressants and benzodiazepines in minor depression: systematic review and meta-analysis. *British Journal of Psychiatry* 201;198(1):11-16. bjp.rcpsych.org/content/198/1/11
122. Wilkinson P, Izmeth Z. Continuation and maintenance treatments for depression in older people. *Cochrane Database of Systematic Reviews* 2012, Issue 11. Art. No.: CD006727. www.ncbi.nlm.nih.gov/pubmed/23152240
123. Fournier JC et al. Antidepressant drug effects and depression severity: a patient-level meta-analysis. *Journal of the American Medical Association* 2010;303(1):47-53. www.ncbi.nlm.nih.gov/pmc/articles/PMC3712503/

124. *Using the Commissioning for Quality and Innovation (CQUIN) payment framework: guidance on new national goals for 2012-13.* Department of Health, 2012. https://www.gov.uk/government/publications/using-the-commissioning-for-quality-and-innovation-cquin-payment-framework-guidance-on-new-national-goals-for-2012-13
125. Armstrong R. General medical services – contractual changes 2013/2014. Letter to Dr Laurence Buckman, Chairman, General Practitioners Committee. 6 December 2012. https://www.gov.uk/government/uploads/system/uploads/attachment_data/file/127319/GMS-Contract-letter.pdf.pdf
126. Dementia diagnosis to be overhauled (press release). Gov.UK. 15 May 2013. https://www.gov.uk/government/news/dementia-diagnosis-to-be-overhauled
127. Lonie JA, Tierney KM, Ebmeier KP. Screening for mild cognitive impairment: a systematic review. *International Journal of Geriatric Psychiatry* 2009;24:902-915. onlinelibrary.wiley.com/doi/10.1002/gps.2208/abstract
128. Mitchell AJ, Shiri-Feshki M. Rate of progression of mild cognitive impairment to dementia – meta-analysis of 41 robust inception cohort studies. *Acta Psychiatrica Scandinavica* 2009;119(4):252-265. onlinelibrary.wiley.com/doi/10.1111/j.1600-0447.2008.01326.x/full
129. Couteur DG, Le, Doust J, Creasey H, Brayne C. Political drive to screen for pre-dementia: not evidence based and ignores the harms of diagnosis. *BMJ* 2013; 347:f5125. www.bmj.com/content/347/bmj.f5125
130. Mitchell AJ, Meader N, Pentzek M. Clinical recognition of dementia and cognitive impairment in primary care: a meta-analysis of physician accuracy. *Acta Psychiatrica Scandinavica* 2011;124(3):165-183. www.ncbi.nlm.nih.gov/pubmed/21668424
131. Russ TC, Morling JR. Cholinesterase inhibitors for mild cognitive impairment. *Cochrane Database of Systematic Reviews* 2012, Issue 9. Art. No.: CD009132. www.ncbi.nlm.nih.gov/pubmedhealth/PMH0048510
132. Birks J, Harvey RJ. Donepezil for dementia due to Alzheimer's disease. *Cochrane Database of Systematic Reviews* 2006, Issue 1. Art. No.: CD001190. onlinelibrary.wiley.com/doi/10.1002/14651858.CD001190.pub2/full
133. Melzer D. New drug treatment for Alzheimer's disease: lessons for healthcare policy. BMJ 1998;316(7133):762-764. www.bmj.com/content/316/7133/762
134. Dementia sufferers 'abandoned', says Jeremy Hunt. *Daily Telegraph*, 15 January 2013. www.telegraph.co.uk/health/healthnews/9800807/Dementia-sufferers-abandoned-says-Jeremy-Hunt.html
135. Boseley S. Campaigners angry as early-stage Alzheimer's drugs on NHS rejected. *The Guardian*. 11 October 2006. www.theguardian.com/uk/2006/oct/11/health.topstories3
136. Couteur David G Le, Doust Jenny, Creasey Helen, Brayne Carol. Political drive to screen for pre-dementia: not evidence based and ignores the harms of diagnosis. *BMJ* 2013; 347:f5125. www.bmj.com/content/347/bmj.f5125h3
137. Rosdahl CB, Kowalski MT. *Textbook of Basic Nursing (Lippincott's Practical Nursing).* Lippincott, Wilkins and Wilkins/Wolters Kluwer Health, 2011.
138. Johnson MH. How does distraction work in the management of pain? *Current Pain and Headache Reports* 2005;9(2):90-95. rd.springer.com/article/10.1007%2Fs11916-005-0044-1
139. *Improving patient outcomes: The better use of multi-compartment compliance aids.* The Royal Pharmaceutical Society, July 2013. www.rpharms.com/unsecure-support-resources/improving-patient-outcomes-through-the-better-use-of-mcas.asp

140. Verhagen AP, Damen L, Berger MY et al. Treatment of tension type headache: paracetamol and NSAIDs work: a systematic review. [Article in Dutch]. *Nederlands Tijdschrift voor Geneeskunde* 2010;154:A1924. www.ncbi.nlm.nih.gov/pubmed/20699021
141. Williams C et al. Efficacy of paracetamol for acute low-back pain: a double blind, randomised controlled trial. *The Lancet*, Early Online Publication, 24 July 2014. www.thelancet.com/journals/lancet/article/PIIS0140-6736(14)60805-9/abstract
142. Grosshans M, Mutschler J, Hermann D et al. Pregabalin abuse, dependence, and withdrawal: a case report. *American Journal of Psychiatry* 2010;167(7):869–869. ajp.psychiatryonline.org/article.aspx?articleID=102360
143. Hawton K, Bergen H, Simkin S et al. Six-year follow-up of impact of co-proxamol withdrawal in England and Wales on prescribing and deaths: time-series study. *PLoS Medicine* 2012;9(5):e1001213. dx.doi.org/10.1371/journal.pmed.1001213
144. Grond S, Sablotzki A. Clinical pharmacology of tramadol. *Clinical Pharmacokinetics* 2004;43(13):879–923. www.ncbi.nlm.nih.gov/pubmed/15509185
145. Iverson L (Advisory Council on the Misuse of Drugs). Letter to: Theresa May (Home Secretary, Home Office, London) and Jeremy Hunt (Secretary of State for Health, Department of Health, London). 13 February 2013. *Gov.UK*. https://www.gov.uk/government/publications/acmd-advice-on-tramadol
146. Pain overview - data focused commentary. National Prescribing Centre, 2010. www.npc.nhs.uk/therapeutics/pain/overview/data.php
147. *Opioids for persistent pain: Good practice.* A consensus statement prepared on behalf of the British Pain Society, the Faculty of Pain Medicine of the Royal College of Anaesthetists, the Royal College of General Practitioners and the Faculty of Addictions of the Royal College of Psychiatrists. The British Pain Society, January 2010. www.britishpainsociety.org/book_opioid_main.pdf
148. Dhalla IA, Persaud N, Juurlink DN. Facing up to the prescription opioid crisis. *BMJ* 2011;343:d5142. www.bmj.com/content/343/bmj.d5142
149. Nüesch E, Rutjes AWS, Husni E et al. Oral or transdermal opioids for osteoarthritis of the knee or hip (Protocol). *Cochrane Database of Systematic Reviews* 2008, Issue 3. Art. No.: CD003115. onlinelibrary.wiley.com/doi/10.1002/14651858.CD003115.pub3/abstract
150. Solomon DH, Rassen JA, Glynn RJ et al. The comparative safety of analgesics in older adults with arthritis. *Archives of Internal Medicine* 2010;170(22):1968–78. archinte.jamanetwork.com/article.aspx?articleid=776448
151. Pain overview - data focused commentary. National Prescribing Centre, 2010. www.npc.nhs.uk/therapeutics/pain/overview/data.php
152. McKee S. Pfizer launches chronic pain campaign. *PharmaTimes* 29 January 2013. www.pharmatimes.com/article/13-01-29/Pfizer_launches_chronic_pain_campaign.aspx
153. Van Zee A. The promotion and marketing of OxyContin: commercial triumph, public health tragedy. *American Journal of Public Health* 2009;99(2):221-227. www.ncbi.nlm.nih.gov/pmc/articles/PMC2622774
154. Risser A, Donovan D, Heintzman J, Page T. NSAID prescribing precautions. *American Family Physician* 2009;15;80(12):1371-1378. www.aafp.org/afp/2009/1215/p1371.html
155. Abraham NS, Hartman C, Castillo D, Richardson P, Smalley W. Effectiveness of national provider prescription of PPI gastroprotection among elderly NSAID

users. *American Journal of Gastroenterology* 2008;103(2):323–332. www.ncbi.nlm.nih.gov/pubmed/18289200

156. Prescribing review October-December 2010: hypnotic drugs. NHS Business Services Authority. www.nhsbsa.nhs.uk/3338.aspx
157. Curran HV, Collins R, Fletcher S et al. Older adults and withdrawal from benzodiazepine hypnotics in general practice: effects on cognitive function, sleep, mood and quality of life. *Psychological Medicine* 2003;33(7):1223-1237. eprints.ucl.ac.uk/14113/1/14113.pdf
158. Reed K, Bond A, Witton J et al. *The changing use of prescribed benzodiazepines and z-drugs and of over-the-counter codeine-containing products in England: a structured review of published English and international evidence and available data to inform consideration of the extent of dependence and harm.* Department of Health, May 2011. www.appgita.com/wp-content/uploads/2011/05/Report-1-NAC-Benzos-and-z-drug-addiction.pdf
159. Barbone F, McMahon AD, Davey PG et al. Association of road-traffic accidents with benzodiazepine use. *Lancet* 1998;352(9137):1331-1336. www.ncbi.nlm.nih.gov/pubmed/9802269
160. Pomara N, Stanley B, Block R et al. Adverse effects of single therapeutic doses of diazepam on performance in normal geriatric subjects: Relationship to plasma concentrations. *Psychopharmacology* 1984;84(3):342-346. rd.springer.com/article/10.1007%2FBF00555210
161. What's wrong with prescribing hypnotics? *Drug and Therapeutics Bulletin* 2004;42(12):89-93. dtb.bmj.com/content/42/12/89
162. Batty GM, Oborne CA, Swift CG, Jackson SH. Development of an indicator to identify inappropriate use of benzodiazepines in elderly medical in-patients. *International Journal of Geriatric Psychiatry* 2000;15(10):892–896. www.ncbi.nlm.nih.gov/pubmed/11044870
163. Glass J, Lanctôt LL, Herrmann N et al. Sedative hypnotics in older people with insomnia: meta-analysis of risks and benefits. *BMJ* 2005;331:1169. www.bmj.com/content/331/7526/1169
164. Billioti de Gage S, Bégaud B, Bazin F et al. Benzodiazepine use and risk of dementia: prospective population based study. *BMJ* 2012;345:e6231. www.bmj.com/content/345/bmj.e6231
165. Gallacher J, Elwood P, Pickering J et al. Benzodiazepine use and risk of dementia: evidence from the Caerphilly Prospective Study (CaPS). *Journal of Epidemiology and Community Health* 2012;66(10):869-873. jech.bmj.com/content/66/10/869.long
166. Barter G, Cormack M. The long-term use of benzodiazepines: patients' views, accounts and experiences. *Family Practice* 1996;13(6):491-497. fampra.oxfordjournals.org/content/13/6/491
167. We need to talk coalition. We need to talk: getting the right therapy at the right time. www.mind.org.uk/media/280583/We-Need-to-Talk-getting-the-right-therapy-at-the-right-time.pdf
168. Benzodiazepine and z-drug withdrawal: clinical knowledge summary. Last revised July 2013. National Institute for Health and Care Excellence. cks.nice.org.uk/benzodiazepine-and-z-drug-withdrawal#!scenariorecommendation:1
169. Vitiello MV. Sleep in normal Aging. *Sleep Medicine Clinics* 1 2006:171-176. faculty.washington.edu/vitiello/Recent%20Publications/Vitiello%20Sleep%20Normal%20Aging.pdf
170. Montgomery P, Dennis JA. Cognitive behavioural interventions for sleep problems in adults aged 60+. *Cochrane Database of Systematic Reviews* 2003,

Issue 1. Art. No.: CD003161. onlinelibrary.wiley.com/doi/10.1002/14651858.CD003161/abstract

171. Watts G. Why the exclusion of older people from clinical research must stop. *BMJ* 2012;344:e3445. www.bmj.com/content/344/bmj.e3445
172. Gorard DA. Escalating polypharmacy. *QJM* 2006;99(11):797-800. qjmed.oxfordjournals.org/content/99/11/797
173. MI – secondary prevention: secondary prevention in primary and secondary care for patients following a myocardial infarction. NICE guideline CG172. National Institute for Health and Care Excellence, November 2013. www.nice.org.uk/guidance/cg172
174. Chronic obstructive airways disease. Management of chronic obstructive airways disease in adults in primary and secondary care. NICE June 2010. www.nice.org.uk/guidance/cg101
175. Hypertension: clinical management of primary hypertension in adults. NICE guideline CG127. National Institute for Health and Care Excellence, August 2011. www.nice.org.uk/guidance/CG127
176. Brown MT, Bussell JK. Medication adherence: WHO cares? *Mayo Clinic Proceedings* 2011;86(4):304-314. www.ncbi.nlm.nih.gov/pmc/articles/PMC3068890
177. Mitchell AJ, Selmes T. Why don't patients take their medicine? Reasons and solutions in psychiatry. *Advances in Psychiatric Treatment* 2007;13(5):336-346. apt.rcpsych.org/content/13/5/336
178. McHorney CA, Spain CV. Frequency of and reasons for medication non-fulfillment and non-persistence among American adults with chronic disease in 2008. *Health Expectations* 201;14(3):307-220. www.ncbi.nlm.nih.gov/pubmed/20860775
179. McHorney CA, Schousboe JT, Cline RR, Weiss TW. The impact of osteoporosis medication beliefs and side-effect experiences on non-adherence to oral bisphosphonates. *Current Medical Research and Opinion* 2007;(12):3137-3152. www.ncbi.nlm.nih.gov/pubmed/17988435
180. Benner JS, Nichol MB, Rovner ES et al. Patient-reported reasons for discontinuing overactive bladder medication. *BJU International* 2010;105(9):1276-1282. www.ncbi.nlm.nih.gov/pubmed/19912188
181. Rosser BA, McCracken LM, Velleman SC et al. Concerns about medication and medication adherence in patients with chronic pain recruited from general practice. *Pain* 2011;152(5):1201-1215. www.painjournalonline.com/article/S0304-3959(11)00091-1/abstract
182. Loke YK, Hinz I, Wang X, Salter C. Systematic review of consistency between adherence to cardiovascular or diabetes medication and health literacy in older adults. *Annals of Pharmacotherapy* 2012;46(6):863-872. www.ncbi.nlm.nih.gov/pubmed/22669802
183. Mauskop A, Borden WB. Predictors of statin adherence. *Current Cardiology Reports* 2011;13(6):553-558. www.ncbi.nlm.nih.gov/pubmed/21947789
184. Munger MA, Van Tassell BW, LaFleur J. Medication nonadherence: an unrecognized cardiovascular risk factor. *Medscape General Medicine* 2007;9(3):58. www.ncbi.nlm.nih.gov/pubmed/18092064
185. Simpson SH, Eurich DT, Majumdar SR et al. A meta-analysis of the association between adherence to drug therapy and mortality. *BMJ* 2006;333(7557):15. www.ncbi.nlm.nih.gov/pmc/articles/PMC1488752
186. GP Workload Survey Results. Health and Social Care Information Centre, 31 July 2007. www.hscic.gov.uk/pubs/gpworkload

187. Salisbury C, Procter S, Stewart K et al. The content of general practice consultations: cross-sectional study based on video recordings. *British Journal of General Practice* 2013;63(616):e751–759. www.ncbi.nlm.nih.gov/pubmed/24267858
188. British Medical Association. *Quality and Outcomes Framework for 2012/13: Guidance for PCOs and practices*. NHS Employers. March 2012. https://www.myhealth.london.nhs.uk/sites/default/files/u1217/gpqofguidance20122013.pdf
189. Heath I. Love's Labours Lost: Why society is straitjacketing its professionals and how we might release them. International Futures Forum, Michael Shea Memorial Lecture, Edinburgh, 10 September 2012. www.internationalfuturesforum.com/u/cms/Iona_Heath_Lecture2012.pdf
190. Hajjar ER, Cafireco AC, Hanlon JT. Polypharmacy in elderly patients. *American Journal of Geriatric Polypharmacy* 2007;5(4):345-351. www.ncbi.nlm.nih.gov/pubmedhealth/PMH0023944/

Chapter 4: Caring not curing

191. Connor SR, Pyenson P, Fitch K et al. Comparing hospice and nonhospice patient survival among patients who die within a three-year window. *Journal of Pain and Symptom Management* 2007;33(3):238-246. www.jpsmjournal.com/article/S0885-3924(06)00724-X
192. Temel JS, Greer JA, Muzikansky A et al. Early palliative care for patients with metastatic non–small-cell lung cancer. *New England Journal of Medicine* 2010;363:733-742. www.nejm.org/doi/full/10.1056/NEJMoa1000678#t=articleResults
193. Connor SR, Pyenson P, Fitch K et al. Comparing hospice and nonhospice patient survival among patients who die within a three-year window. *Journal of Pain and Symptom Management* 2007;33(3):238-246. www.jpsmjournal.com/article/S0885-3924(06)00724-X
194. Smith CB, Nelson JE, Berman AR et al. Lung cancer physicians' referral practices for palliative care consultation. *Annals of Oncology* 2012;23(2):382-387. www.ncbi.nlm.nih.gov/pmc/articles/PMC3265546
195. Cherlin E, Fried T, Prigerson HG et al. Communication between physicians and family caregivers about care at the end of life: when do discussions occur and what is said? *Journal of Palliative Medicine* 2005;8(6):1176-1185. www.ncbi.nlm.nih.gov/pubmed/16351531
196. Wright AA, Zhang B, Ray A et al. Associations between end-of-life discussions, patient mental health, medical care near death, and caregiver bereavement adjustment. *Journal of the American Medical Associatoin* 2008;300(14):1665-1673. jama.jamanetwork.com/article.aspx?articleid=182700
197. Chibnall JT, Tait RC, Harman B, Luebbert RA. Effect of acetaminophen on behavior, well-being, and psychotropic medication use in nursing home residents with moderate-to-severe dementia. *Journal of the American Geriatrics Society* 2005;53:1921-1929. onlinelibrary.wiley.com/doi/10.1111/j.1532-5415.2005.53572.x/abstract
198. Husebo BS, Ballard C, Reidun S et al. Efficacy of treating pain to reduce behavioural disturbances in residents of nursing homes with dementia: cluster randomised clinical trial. *BMJ* 2011;343:d4065. www.bmj.com/content/343/bmj.d4065
199. Husebo BS, Ballard C, Cohen-Mansfield J et al. The response of agitated behavior to pain management in persons with dementia. *The American Journal of Geriatric Psychiatry* 2014;22(7):708-717. www.sciencedirect.com/science/

article/pii/S1064748112001030

200. Richter T, Meyer G, Möhler R, Köpke S. Psychosocial interventions for reducing antipsychotic medication in care home residents. *Cochrane Database of Systematic Reviews* 2012, Issue 12. Art. No.: CD008634. onlinelibrary.wiley.com/doi/10.1002/14651858.CD008634.pub2/full
201. *Liverpool Care Pathway for the Dying Patient: supporting care in the last hours or days of life*. NHS Cumbria, 2009. www.gp-palliativecare.co.uk/files/LCP_generic_version_December_2009.pdf
202. Phillips M. Care? No, this is a pathway to killing people that doctors deem worthless. *MailOnline*. 14 October 2012. www.dailymail.co.uk/debate/article-2217748/Care-No-pathway-killing-people-doctors-deem-worthless.html
203. Doughty S. Top doctor's chilling claim: The NHS kills off 130,000 elderly patients every year. *MailOnline*. 26 October 2012. www.dailymail.co.uk/news/article-2161869/Top-doctors-chilling-claim-The-NHS-kills-130-000-elderly-patients-year.html
204. Pullicino P. Can we predict impending death? The Scientific Evidence [Powerpoint presentation]. PowerPointOnline. https://onedrive.live.com/view.aspx?resid=8163D01F1A1B6118!119&cid=8163d01f1a1b6118&app=PowerPoint&wdo=2
205. *More Care, Less Pathway: A Review of the Liverpool Care Pathway. Gov. UK*. Department of Health, 15 July 2013. https://www.gov.uk/government/publications/review-of-liverpool-care-pathway-for-dying-patients
206. Veerbeek L, Zuylen L van, Swart SJ et al. The effect of the Liverpool Care Pathway for the dying: a multi-centre study. Palliative Medicine 2008;22(2):145-151. pmj.sagepub.com/content/22/2/145
207. Chan R, Webster J. End-of-life care pathways for improving outcomes in caring for the dying. *Cochrane Database of Systematic Reviews* 2010, Issue 1. Art. No.: CD008006. onlinelibrary.wiley.com/doi/10.1002/14651858.CD008006.pub2/pdf
208. Torjesen Ingrid. Bad press over Liverpool care pathway has scared patients and doctors, say experts. *BMJ* 2013; 346:f175. www.bmj.com/content/346/bmj.f175
209. Less than half of dying patients are placed on a nationally recommended care pathway [press release]. *Eureka Alert*. 3 June 2013. www.eurekalert.org/pub_releases/2013-06/bmj-lth053113.php
210. George R, Martin J, Robinson V. The Liverpool Care Pathway for the dying (LCP): lost in translation and a tale of elephants, men, myopia – and a horse. Palliative Medicine 2014;28(1):3–7. pmj.sagepub.com/content/28/1/3
211. Undergraduate Admissions Statement – Medicine. Bristol University. 2013. www.bristol.ac.uk/medical-school/prospective/application/admissionsstatement1213.pdf
212. Admission: Frequently asked questions. Cardiff University School of Medicine. 2014. medicine.cf.ac.uk/medical-education/undergraduate/admissions/frequently-asked-questions
213. "Poor care + patient's comfort & needs not the..." *Patientopinion.org.uk*. https://www.patientopinion.org.uk/opinions/111926
214. "Serious concerns about my mother's care". *Patientopinion.org.uk*. https://www.patientopinion.org.uk/opinions/76188
215. GPs fine hospitals over failure to meet A&E waiting time targets. *Pulse*. 13 February 2012. www.pulsetoday.co.uk/gps-fine-hospitals-over-failure-to-meet-ae-waiting-time-targets/13423958.article#.Uq7bNvRdU40

216. Darley JM, Batson CD. "From Jerusalem to Jericho": a study of situational and dispositional variables in helping behavior. *Journal of Personality and Social Psychology* 1973;27:100-108. faculty.washington.edu/jdb/345/345%20Articles/Darley%20&%20Batson%20(1973).pdf
217. Stephenson J. "Lansley: understaffing is not excuse for 'never events'". *NursingTimes.net*, 1 March 2011. www.nursingtimes.net/nursing-practice/clinical-zones/management/lansley-understaffing-is-not-excuse-for-never-events/5026316.article
218. Smith MD, Birch JD, Renshaw M, Ottewill M. Qualitative analysis of factors leading to clinical incidents. *International Journal of Health Care Quality Assurance* 2013;26(6):536-48. www.ncbi.nlm.nih.gov/pubmed/24003753
219. Nichols P, Copeland TS, Craib IA et al. Learning from error: identifying contributory causes of medication errors in an Australian hospital. *Medical Journal of Australia* 2008;188(5):276-279. www.ncbi.nlm.nih.gov/pubmed/18312190
220. Edwards D, Burnard P, Hannigan B, Cooper L et al. Clinical supervision and burnout: the influence of clinical supervision for community mental health nurses. *Journal of Clinical Nursing* 2006;15:1007-1015. onlinelibrary.wiley.com/doi/10.1111/j.1365-2702.2006.01370.x/abstract
221. Mid Staffs Trust to be prosecuted over death. *Sky News*. 29 August 2013. news.sky.com/story/1134663/mid-staffs-trust-to-be-prosecuted-over-death
222. Francis R. The Mid Staffordshire NHS Trust Foundation Trust Public Enquiry, final report. 2013.
223. NHS heading for crisis as job losses mount (press release). Royal College of Nursing. 20 November 2014. www.rcn.org.uk/newsevents/press_releases/uk/nhs_heading_for_crisis_point_as_job_losses_mount_-_rcn
224. Two-thirds of nurses have considered resigning, says survey. *The Guardian*. 31 August 2013.www.theguardian.com/society/2013/aug/31/nirses-want-resign-two-thirds
225. Schreuder JA, Roelen CA, van Zweeden NF et al. Leadership styles of nurse managers and registered sickness absence among their nursing staff. *Health Care Management Review* 2011; 36 (1) 58-66. www.ncbi.nlm.nih.gov/pubmed/21157231
226. NHS staff: average worker takes an estimated 9.5 working days off sick a year. Health and Social Care Information Centre. News Archive 2013-2014. www.hscic.gov.uk/staffsicknesspr
227. Office for National Statistics. *Sickness Absence in the Labour Market*. April 2012. www.ons.gov.uk/ons/dcp171776_265016.pdf
228. Rafferty AM, Sean P. Clarke, Coles J et al. and Linda H. Aiken. Outcomes of variation in hospital nurse staffing in English hospitals: Cross-sectional analysis of survey data and discharge records. *International Journal of Nursing Studies 2007;44(2):175-182.* www.ncbi.nlm.nih.gov/pmc/articles/PMC2894580
229. Parker PA, Kulik JA. Burnout, self- and supervisor-rated job performance, and absenteeism among nurses. *Journal of Behavioral Medicine* 1995;18(6):581-599. www.ncbi.nlm.nih.gov/pubmed/8749987
230. Aoun SM, Kristjanson LJ, Currow DC, Hudson PL. Caregiving for the terminally ill: at what cost? *Palliative Medicine* 2005;19(7):551-555. pmj.sagepub.com/content/19/7/551
231. University of Leeds. Carers save UK £87 billion per year (press release). 7 September 2007. www.leeds.ac.uk/news/article/430/carers_save_uk_87_billion_per_year

232. Cormac I, Tihanyi P. Meeting the mental and physical healthcare needs of carers. *Advances in Psychiatric Treatment* 2006;12:162-172. apt.rcpsych.org/content/12/3/162.full
233. Addington-Hall J, Karlsen S. Do home deaths increase distress in bereavement? *Palliative Medicine* 2000 14(2):161-162. pmj.sagepub.com/content/14/2/161.full.pdf
234. Christakisa NA, Iwashynab TJ. The health impact of health care on families: a matched cohort study of hospice use by decedents and mortality outcomes in surviving, widowed spouses. *Social Science & Medicine* 2003;57(3):465-475. www.sciencedirect.com/science/article/pii/S0277953602003702
235. Bradley EH, Prigerson H, Carlson MDA et al. Depression among surviving caregivers: does length of hospice enrollment matter? *American Journal of Psychiatry* 2004;161:2257-2262.
236. Savage S, Bailey S. The impact of caring on caregivers' mental health: a review of the literature. *Australian Health Review* 2004;27(1):103-109. www.deakin.edu.au/dhs/publications-archive/Carers%20lit%20review.pdf
237. Ballard CG, Eastwood C, Gahir M, Wilcock G. A follow up study of depression in the carers of dementia sufferers. *BMJ* 1996; 312: 947. www.bmj.com/content/312/7036/947ajp.psychiatryonline.org/article.aspx?articleid=177221
238. Effectiveness and cost-effectiveness of home palliative are services for adults with advanced illness and their caregivers. 6/6/13 Cochrane Review. onlinelibrary.wiley.com/doi/10.1002/14651858.CD007760.pub2/abstract
239. Cormac I, Tihanyi P. Meeting the mental and physical healthcare needs of carers. *Advances in Psychiatric Treatment* 2006;12:162-172. apt.rcpsych.org/content/12/3/162.full
240. Schulz R, Beach SR. Caregiving as a risk factor for mortality. The Caregiver Health Effects Study. *JAMA* 1999;282(23):2215-2219. jama.jamanetwork.com/article.aspx?articleid=192209
241. Charlesworth G, Shepstone L, Wilson E et al. Befriending carers of people with dementia: randomised controlled trial. *BMJ* 2008;336:1295. www.bmj.com/content/336/7656/1295
242. Yeandle S, Wigfield A (eds). *New Approaches to Supporting Carers' Health and Well-being: Evidence from the National Carers' Strategy Demonstrator Sites programme*. Centre for International Research on Care, Labour and Equalities, University of Leeds, 2011. www.sociology.leeds.ac.uk/assets/files/research/circle/151111-6121-circle-newapproaches-complete-report-web.pdf
243. Breakaway for carers - book a volunteer to give you a break when you need it. Hertfordshire County Council. www.hertsdirect.org/services/healthsoc/carersupport/outcare/breakaway/
244. Carer breaks. Richmond upon Thames London Borough Council. www.richmond.gov.uk/carer_breaks
245. Carer's allowance. *Gov.uk*. Last updated 24 September 2014. https://www.gov.uk/carers-allowance

Chapter 5: The politics of death

246. Prescription charges and people with long-term conditions. Prescription Charges Coalition. March 2013. www.prescriptionchargescoalition.org.uk/uploads/1/2/7/5/12754304/paying_the_price_report.pdf
247. Unhealthy charges, Citizens Advice Bureau, 2001. www.citizensadvice.org.uk/index/policy/policy_publications/er_health/unhealthy-charges.htm
248. Birch S. Relationship between increasing prescription charges and

consumption in groups not exempt from charges. Journal of the Royal College of General Practitioners 1986;36(285):154–156. www.ncbi.nlm.nih.gov/pmc/articles/PMC1960399

249. Groves S, Cohen D, Alam MF et al. 2010. Abolition of prescription charges in Wales: the impact on medicines use in those who used to pay. *International Journal of Pharmacy Practice* 2010;18(6):332-340. orca.cf.ac.uk/28397
250. Apply for a needs assessment by social services. *Gov.uk*. Last updated 4 September 2014. https://www.gov.uk/apply-needs-assessment-social-services
251. Allen D, Griffiths, L, Lyne P. Accommodating health and social care needs: routine resource allocation in stroke rehabilitation. *Sociology of Health & Illness* 2004;26:411-432. onlinelibrary.wiley.com/doi/10.1111/j.0141-9889.2004.00397.x/full
252. Elkington H, White P, Addington-Hall J et al. The healthcare needs of chronic obstructive pulmonary disease patients in the last year of life. *Palliative Medicine* 2005;19(6):485-491. pmj.sagepub.com/content/19/6/485.abstract
253. Goreb JM, Brophy CJ, Greenstone MA. How well do we care for patients with end stage chronic obstructive pulmonary disease (COPD)? A comparison of palliative care and quality of life in COPD and lung cancer. *Thorax* 2000;55:1000-1006. thorax.bmj.com/content/55/12/1000.full
254. Agarwal S, J Banerjee J, Baker R et al. Potentially avoidable emergency department attendance: interview study of patients' reasons for attendance. *Emergency Medicine Journal* 2012;29:e3. emj.bmj.com/content/29/12/e3.long
255. Kersnik J, Svab I, Vegnuti M. Frequent attenders in general practice: quality of life, patient satisfaction, use of medical services and GP characteristics. *Scandinavian Journal of Primary Health Care* 2001;19(3):174-177. www.ncbi.nlm.nih.gov/pubmed/11697559
256. Ronalds C, Kapur N, Stone K et al. Determinants of consultation rate in patients with anxiety and depressive disorders in primary care. *Family Practice* 2002;19(1):23-28. fampra.oxfordjournals.org/content/19/1/23.long
257. Appelby J, Devlin N, Parkin D. NICE's cost effectiveness threshold. *BMJ*;335(7616):358-359. www.ncbi.nlm.nih.gov/pmc/articles/PMC1952475
258. NICE. Social value judgements. Second edition. National Institute for Health and Clinical Excellence, 2008. www.nice.org.uk/Media/Default/About/what-we-do/Research-and-development/Social-Value-Judgements-principles-for-the-development-of-NICE-guidance.pdf
259. Court warns CCG over disagreeing with NICE guidance. National Institute for Health and Care Excellence. 6 May 2014. https://www.nice.org.uk/news/article/court-warns-ccg-over-disagreeing-with-nice-guidance
260. Dominiczak P. Jeremy Hunt rejects 'minimum staffing levels' for hospitals. *The Telegraph*. 6 August 2013. www.telegraph.co.uk/health/healthnews/10225226/Jeremy-Hunt-rejects-minimum-staffing-levels-for-hospitals.html
261. Draft NICE guidance underlines the need for a 1:8 nurse/patient ratio. *Nursing Standard* 2014;28(37):7. rcnpublishing.com/doi/full/10.7748/ns.28.37.7.s2
262. Rafferty AM, Sean P. Clarke, Coles J et al. and Linda H. Aiken. Outcomes of variation in hospital nurse staffing in English hospitals: Cross-sectional analysis of survey data and discharge records. *International Journal of Nursing Studies 2007;44(2):175-182.* www.ncbi.nlm.nih.gov/pmc/articles/PMC2894580
263. Kane RL, Shamliyan TA, Mueller C et al. The association of registered nurse staffing levels and patient outcomes: systematic review and meta-analysis. *Medical Care* 2007;45(12):1195-1204
264. Bray B et al. Associations between Stroke Mortality and Weekend Working

by Stroke Physicians and Registered Nurses. PLOS Medicine 19/8/14 DOI 10.1371/journal/pmed.1001705 www.plosmedicine.org/article/info%3Adoi%2F10.1371%2Fjournal.pmed.1001705

265. RCN calls for action on unsafe staffing levels. *This is Nursing*. 22 April 2013. thisisnursing.rcn.org.uk/public/updates/rcn-calls-for-immediate-action-on-unsafe-staffing-levels
266. *Safe staffing for nursing in adult inpatient wards in acute hospitals*. NICE guideline SG1. National Institute for Health and Care Excellence, July 2014. https://www.nice.org.uk/Guidance/SG1
267. *Mandatory Nurse Staffing Levels*. Royal College of Nursing, March 2012. www.rcn.org.uk/__data/assets/pdf_file/0009/439578/03.12_Mandatory_nurse_staffing_levels_v2_FINAL.pdf
268. National Advisory Group on the Safety of Patients in England. A promise to learn – a commitment to act. Improving the Safety of Patients in England. Department of Health. 6 August 2013. https://www.gov.uk/government/publications/berwick-review-into-patient-safety
269. Dominiczak P. Jeremy Hunt rejects 'minimum staffing levels' for hospitals. *The Telegraph*. 6 August 2013. www.telegraph.co.uk/health/healthnews/10225226/Jeremy-Hunt-rejects-minimum-staffing-levels-for-hospitals.html
270. Britain's homecare scandal. *Panorama Special*. BBC One, 9 April 2009. news.bbc.co.uk/panorama/hi/front_page/newsid_7990000/7990682.stm
271. Which? exposes failings in home care system. *Which?* 16 March 2012. www.which.co.uk/news/2012/03/which-exposes-failings-in-home-care-system-281517
272. Annual survey of hours and earnings, 2012 provisional results. Part of annual survey of hours and earnings, 2012 provisional results release. Office for National Statistics. 22 November 2012. www.ons.gov.uk/ons/rel/ashe/annual-survey-of-hours-and-earnings/2012-provisional-results/stb-ashe-statistical-bulletin-2012.html
273. Bennett R. Elderly left at risk by NHS Bidding wars to find cheapest care with reverse auctions. *The Times*. 1 June 2009.
274. Ramesh R. Social care funding cut by £900m last year. *The Guardian*. 14 June 2012. www.guardian.co.uk/society/2012/jun/14/social-care-funding-cuts
275. *Measuring unmet need for social care amongst older people. Population Trends*, No. 145, Autumn 2011. www.ons.gov.uk/ons/rel/population-trends-rd/population-trends/no--145--autumn-2011/index.html
276. House of Commons Health Committee. *Social Care Fourteenth Report of Session 2010-12*. London: The Stationery Office Limited, 2012. www.publications.parliament.uk/pa/cm201012/cmselect/cmhealth/1583/1583.pdf
277. Charlesworth A, Thorlby R. *Reforming social care: options for funding*. Nuffield Trust. May 2012. www.nuffieldtrust.org.uk/publications
278. Fernandeza J-L, Fordera J. Consequences of local variations in social care on the performance of the acute health care sector. *Applied Economics* 2008;40(12):1503-1518. www.tandfonline.com/doi/abs/10.1080/00036840600843939
279. *A new settlement for health and social care*. Final report of the Commission on the Future of Health and Social Care in England. The King's Fund, 2014. www.kingsfund.org.uk/projects/commission-future-health-and-social-care-england
280. Science and Technology Committee, UK Parliament. *Evidence Check 2: Homeopathy. HC 45, Fourth Report of Session 2009-10. Parliament.uk*. 22 February 2010. www.parliament.uk/business/committees/committees-archive/

science-technology/s-t-homeopathy-inquiry
281. Bryant B. GPs' disbelief at £250m shingles jab to save 200 lives. *The Telegraph*. 3 November 2013. www.telegraph.co.uk/health/nhs/10424112/GPs-disbelief-at-250m-shingles-jab-to-save-200-lives.html
282. Gagliardi AMZ, Gomes Silva BN, Torloni MR, Soares BGO. Vaccines for preventing herpes zoster in older adults. *Cochrane Database of Systematic Reviews* 2012, Issue 10. Art. No.: CD008858. onlinelibrary.wiley.com/doi/10.1002/14651858.CD008858.pub2/abstract
283. Shingles (herpes zoster): the green book, Chapter 28a. Public Health England. First published 12 July 2013; updated 23 September 2014. https://www.gov.uk/government/publications/shingles-herpes-zoster-the-green-book-chapter-28a
284. Van Hoeka AJ, Gaya N, Melegaroa A et al. Estimating the cost-effectiveness of vaccination against herpes zoster in England and Wales. *Vaccine* 2009;27(9):1454-1467. www.sciencedirect.com/science/article/pii/S0264410X08017465
285. Joint Committee on Vaccination and Immunisation. Statement on varicella and herpes zoster vaccines. 29 March 2010. webarchive.nationalarchives.gov.uk/20130107105354/http:/www.dh.gov.uk/prod_consum_dh/groups/dh_digitalassets/@dh/@ab/documents/digitalasset/dh_133599.pdf
286. NICE plans to say yes to two breakthrough treatments for skin cancer (press release). National Institute for Health and Care Excellence. 2 November 2012. www.nice.org.uk/news/press-and-media/nice-plans-to-say-yes-to-two-breakthrough-treatments-for-skin-cancer
287. Boseley S. Skin cancer drug Zelboraf gets NHS go-ahead. *The Guardian*. 2 November 2012. www.theguardian.com/society/2012/nov/02/skin-cancer-drug-nhs
288. NICE plans to say yes to two breakthrough treatments for skin cancer (press release). National Institute for Health and Care Excellence. 2 November 2012. www.nice.org.uk/news/press-and-media/nice-plans-to-say-yes-to-two-breakthrough-treatments-for-skin-cancer
289. Smith R. Melanoma drug 'too expensive' for NHS. *The Telegraph*. 15 June 2012. www.telegraph.co.uk/health/healthnews/9331485/Melanoma-drug-too-expensive-for-NHS.html
290. Pickover E. Watchdog approves skin cancer drugs ipilimumab and vemurafenib. *The Independent*. 2 November 2012. www.independent.co.uk/life-style/health-and-families/health-news/watchdog-approves-skin-cancer-drugs-ipilimumab-and-vemurafenib-8276527.html
291. Donnelly L. Ministers scrap £20 million scheme to keep elderly warm. *The Telegraph*. 25 December 2013. www.telegraph.co.uk/health/healthnews/10530467/Ministers-scrap-20m-scheme-to-keep-elderly-warm.html
292. *Evaluation report. Warm homes, healthy people fund 2011/2012*. Health Protection Agency. October 2012. webarchive.nationalarchives.gov.uk/20140714084352/www.hpa.org.uk/webc/HPAwebFile/HPAweb_C/1317136356595
293. Fernandez J-L, Snell T. Wistow G. *Changes in the patterns of social care provision in England: 2005/6 to 2012/13*. PSSRU Discussion Paper 2867. Personal Social Services Research Unit. December 2013. www.pssru.ac.uk/archive/pdf/dp2867.pdf
294. Bardsley M, Theo Georghiou T, Dixon J. *Social care and hospital use at the end of life*. The Nuffield Trust. 2010. www.nuffieldtrust.org.uk/publications

295. Abel J, Rich A, Griffin T, Purdy S. End-of-life care in hospital: a descriptive study of all inpatient deaths in 1 year. *Palliative Medicine* 2009;23(7):616-622. pmj.sagepub.com/content/23/7/616.short
296. Crispin S. DH launches 3m lives telehealth campaign. *EHI ehealth Insider*. 6 December 2011. www.ehi.co.uk/news/ehi/7378/dh-launches-3m-lives-telehealth-campaign
297. Telehealth gets thumbs up from Whole System Demonstrator programme. The Homecare Industry Information Service (THIIS). www.thiis.co.uk/news-snippets/telehealth-whole-system-demonstrator-programme-dec11.aspx
298. Steventon Adam, Bardsley M, Billings J et al. Effect of telehealth on use of secondary care and mortality: findings from the Whole System Demonstrator cluster randomised trial. *BMJ* 2012;344:e3874. www.bmj.com/content/344/bmj.e3874
299. Peel RK. Response re: effect of telehealth on use of secondary care and mortality: findings from the Whole System Demonstrator cluster randomised trial. *BMJ* 2012;344:e3874. www.bmj.com/content/344/bmj.e3874/rr/594124
300. The Operating Framework for the NHS in England in 2012/13. Department of Health, 2011. https://www.gov.uk/government/uploads/system/uploads/attachment_data/file/216590/dh_131428.pdf
301. Steventon A, Bardsley M, Billings J et al. Effect of telehealth on use of secondary care and mortality: findings from the Whole System Demonstrator cluster randomised trial. *BMJ* 2012;344(jun21 3):e3874–e3874. www.bmj.com/content/344/bmj.e3874/rr/592310
302. Tunstall Healthcare awarded framework agreement from buying solutions. *eHealthNews.au.* 11 August 2010. www.ehealthnews.eu/tunstall/2185-tunstall-healthcare-awarded-framework-agreement-from-buying-solutions
303. Currell R, Urquhart C, Wainwright P, Lewis R. Telemedicine versus face to face patient care: effects on professional practice and health care outcomes (review). *The Cochrane Library* 2010, Issue 1. www.thecochranelibrary.com/userfiles/ccoch/file/Telemedicine/CD002098.pdf
304. Inglis SC, Clark RA, McAlister FA et al. Structured telephone support or telemonitoring programmes for patients with chronic heart failure. *Cochrane Database of Systematic Reviews* 2010, Issue 8. Art. No.: CD007228. onlinelibrary.wiley.com/doi/10.1002/14651858.CD007228.pub2/abstract
305. 3million lives: 3millionlives.co.uk
306. Cartwright M, Hirani Shashivadan P, Rixon L et al. Effect of telehealth on quality of life and psychological outcomes over 12 months (Whole Systems Demonstrator telehealth questionnaire study): nested study of patient reported outcomes in a pragmatic, cluster randomised controlled trial. *BMJ* 2013; 346:f653. www.bmj.com/content/346/bmj.f653
307. *Scottish Quality and Outcomes Framework 2013/2014: guidance for NHS Boards and GP practices.* Scottish Government, 1 May 2013. www.sehd.scot.nhs.uk/pca/PCA2013(M)02guide.pdf
308. BMA. Guide to avoiding unplanned admissions. 2014/15 guidance. bma.org.uk/practical-support-at-work/contracts/gp-contracts-and-funding/general-practice-funding/unplanned-admissions/put-care-plans-in-place
309. *Advance Care Planning: a guide for health and social care staff.* End of Life Care, 2008 www.ncpc.org.uk/sites/default/files/AdvanceCarePlanning.pdf
310. Huntley AL, Thomas R, Mann M et al. Is case management effective in reducing the risk of unplanned hospital admissions for older people? A systematic review and meta-analysis. *Family Practice* 2013;30(3):266–275.

www.ncbi.nlm.nih.gov/pubmed/23315222
311. Limb M. Patient care is being damaged by rising bureaucracy, GPs warn. *BMJ* 2013;347:f5732. careers.bmj.com/careers/advice/view-article.html?id=20014602
312. Traynor L. Benefit cuts blind man committed suicide after Atos ruled him fit to work. *Daily Mirror.* 28 December 2013. www.mirror.co.uk/news/uk-news/benefit-cuts-blind-man-committed-2965375
313. Butler P. Do cuts kill? Patrick Butler Cuts Blog. *The Guardian.* 16 November 2011. www.theguardian.com/society/patrick-butler-cuts-blog/2011/nov/16/do-public-spending-cuts-kill
314. Inquiry call over Mark and Helen Mullins deaths. BBC News, 9 November 2013. www.bbc.co.uk/news/uk-england-coventry-warwickshire-15645206
315. Ellicott C. Benefits cheat UK: court sees a staggering 23 cases of welfare fraud in just one day. *Mail Online.* 5 March 2011. www.dailymail.co.uk/news/article-1363162/Benefit-cheat-UK-How-just-day-court-saw-staggering-23-cases-welfare-fraud.html
316. Department of Work and Pensions. Benefit fraud and error: Hard work must continue to cut 3.5 billion loss 9/5/13 www.gov.uk/government/news/benefit-fraud-and-error-hard-work-must-continue-to-cut-35bn-loss
317. Papworth J. Take care you don't miss out on helper's allowances. *The Guardian.* 26 October 2013. www.theguardian.com/money/2013/oct/26/care-allowances-ill-disabled-help
318. Berthoud R. *The take-up of carer's allowance: a feasibility study.* Institute for Social and Economic Research, University of Essex. Report No. 2010-38. 18 November 2010. https://www.iser.essex.ac.uk/files/iser_working_papers/2010-38.pdf
319. Gentleman A. Fitness-for-work tests unfair on people with mental health problems, court says. *The Guardian.* 22 May 2013. www.theguardian.com/society/2013/may/22/fitness-work-tests-mental-health-unfair
320. Fullfact. How many 'fit to work' decisions are successfully overturned. https://fullfact.org/factchecks/ATOS_ESA_assessments_overturned-3135)
321. Pilkington A. 'This brutal new system': a GP's take on Atos and work capability assessments. *The Guardian.* 4 January 2013. www.theguardian.com/commentisfree/2013/jan/04/gp-atos-work-capability-assessment
322. Greenaway H. Nurse makes heartfelt apology after Atos forced her to trick disabled people out of benefits. *Daily Record and Sunday Mail.* 24 September 2012. www.dailyrecord.co.uk/news/scottish-news/nurse-makes-heartfelt-apology-after-1340838
323. Bingham J. NHS millions for controversial care pathway. *The Telegraph.* 31 October 2012. www.telegraph.co.uk/health/healthnews/9644287/NHS-millions-for-controversial-care-pathway.html
324. Commissioning for Quality and Innovation (CQUIN) payment framework. NHS Institute for Innovation and Improvement. www.institute.nhs.uk/world_class_commissioning/pct_portal/cquin.html
325. Donnelly L and Telegraph interactive team. Fears that hospitals are covering up death rates. *The Telegraph.* 27 March 2014. www.telegraph.co.uk/health/healthnews/10728189/Fears-that-hospitals-are-covering-up-death-rates.html
326. Liverpool Care Pathway to be scrapped. *Sky News.* 15 July 2013. news.sky.com/story/1115792/liverpool-care-pathway-to-be-scrapped

Chapter 6: The myths of CPR

327. Shucksmith S, Carlebach S, Whittaker V. *Dying: Discussing and planning for end of life*. NatCen Social Research, 2013. www.natcen.ac.uk/media/84524/dyingfull_report.pdf
328. Diem SJ, Lantos JD, Tulsky JA. cardiopulmonary resuscitation on television — miracles and misinformation. *New England Journal of Medicine* 1996;334(24):1578-1782. www.nejm.org/doi/full/10.1056/NEJM199606133342406
329. Harris D, Willoughby H. Resuscitation on television: Realistic or ridiculous? A quantitative observational analysis of the portrayal of cardiopulmonary resuscitation in television medical drama. *Resuscitation* 2009;80(11):1275–1279. www.resuscitationjournal.com/article/S0300-9572(09)00403-1/abstract
330. Adams DH, Snedden DP. How misconceptions among elderly patients regarding survival outcomes of inpatient cardiopulmonary resuscitation affect do-not-resuscitate orders. *Journal of the American Osteopathic Association* 2006;106(7):402-404. www.jaoa.osteopathic.org/content/106/7/402
331. McNally B, Robb R, Mehta M. Out-of-hospital cardiac arrest surveillance - Cardiac Arrest Registry to Enhance Survival (CARES), United States, October 1, 2005 - December 31, 2010. Centers for Disease Control and Prevention, 2011. www.cdc.gov/mmwr/preview/mmwrhtml/ss6008a1.htm
332. Peberdy MA, Kaye W, Ornato JP et al. Cardiopulmonary resuscitation of adults in the hospital: A report of 14 720 cardiac arrests from the National Registry of Cardiopulmonary. *Resuscitation* 2003;58(3):297-308. www.resuscitationjournal.com/article/S0300-9572(03)00215-6/abstract
333. Wagg A, Kinirons M, Stewart K. Cardiopulmonary resuscitation: doctors and nurses expect too much. *Journal of the Royal College of Physicians of London* 1995;29(1):20–4. www.ncbi.nlm.nih.gov/pubmed/7738875
334. Chan PS, Nallamothu BK, Krumholz HM et al. Long-term outcomes in elderly survivors of in-hospital cardiac arrest. *New England Journal of Medicine* 2013;368(11):1019-1026. www.nejm.org/doi/full/10.1056/NEJMoa1200657
335. RamenofskyDH Weissman DE. www.mcw.edu/FileLibrary/User/jrehm/fastfactpdfs/Concept179.pdfEnd of Life/Palliative Education Resource Center. Fast Facts and Concepts.
336. Ebell MH, Becker LA, Barry HC, Hagen M. Survival after in-hospital cardiopulmonary resuscitation. *Journal of General Internal Medicine* 1998;13(12):805-816. www.ncbi.nlm.nih.gov/pmc/articles/PMC1497044
337. Faber-Langendoen K. Resuscitation of patients with metastatic cancer: is transient benefit still futile? *Archives of Internal Medicine* 1991;151(2):235-239. archinte.jamanetwork.com/article.aspx?articleid=614553
338. Ewer MS, Kish SK, Martin CG et al. Characteristics of cardiac arrest in cancer patients as a predictor of survival after cardiopulmonary resuscitation. *Cancer* 2001;92(7):1905-1912. onlinelibrary.wiley.com/doi/10.1002/1097-0142(20011001)92:7%3C1905::AID-CNCR1708%3E3.0.CO;2-6/full
339. Hilberman M, Kutner J, Parsons D, Murphy DJ. Marginally effective medical care: ethical analysis of issues in cardiopulmonary resuscitation (CPR). *Journal of Medical Ethics* 1997;23(6):361-367. www.ncbi.nlm.nih.gov/pmc/articles/PMC1377578
340. Boseley S, Meikle J. Court blocks judicial review over 'do not resuscitate' orders. *The Guardian*. 21 December 2012. www.theguardian.com/society/2012/dec/21/court-blocks-judicial-review-dnr
341. Addenbrooke's Hospital rejects DNR Janet Tracey case claims. *BBC News*

Cambridgeshire. 7 November 2012. www.bbc.co.uk/news/uk-england-cambridgeshire-20244042

342. Meikle J. Family of Down's patient sue hospital over DNR order. *The Guardian*. 13 September 2012. www.theguardian.com/society/2012/sep/13/downs-patient-hospital-dnr-order
343. Ebell MH, Becker LA, Barry HC et al. Survival after in-hospital cardiopulmonary resuscitation. *Journal of General Internal Medicine* 1998;13(12):805-816. www.ncbi.nlm.nih.gov/pmc/articles/PMC1497044
344. Bird S. Do not resuscitate: They're the fateful words meaning doctors won't try to save you if you collapse in hospital. But could they go on YOUR file without you being asked? *Mail Online*. 6 September 2011. www.dailymail.co.uk/health/article-2034160/Do-resuscitate-Theyre-fateful-words-meaning-doctors-wont-try-save-you-collapse-hospital.html
345. Do not resuscitate case studies. *The Telegraph*. 12 October 2011. www.telegraph.co.uk/health/healthnews/8821262/Do-not-resuscitate-case-studies.html
346. Ebrahim S. Do not resuscitate decisions: flogging dead horses or a dignified death? *BMJ* 2000;320:1155-1156. www.bmj.com/rapid-response/2011/10/28/do-not-resuscitate-orders-1
347. Unified Do Not Attempt Cardiopulmonary Resuscitation (DNACPR) Adult Policy. NHS South Central, March 2010. www.uhs.nhs.uk/Media/Controlleddocuments/Clinical/AdultDNACPRpolicy.pdf
348. Sayers GM, Schofield I, Aziz M. An analysis of CPR decision-making by elderly patients. *Journal of Medical Ethics* 1997;23(4):207-212. www.ncbi.nlm.nih.gov/pmc/articles/PMC1377268
349. White A. Guidelines have been misquoted [letter]. *BMJ* 2000;320:1155. www.bmj.com/rapid-response/2011/10/28/guidelines-have-been-misquoted
350. *National Care of the Dying Audit of Hospitals*, England. Royal College of Physicians, May 2014. https://www.rcplondon.ac.uk/resources/national-care-dying-audit-hospitals
351. Lorraine Bayless death: Inquiry after nurse refuses CPR. *BBC News US & Canada*. 5 March 2013. www.bbc.co.uk/news/world-us-canada-21664236
352. Newman MM. Glenwood Gardens case provides a teaching moment: cpr saves lives. *Huffington Post*. 4 May 2013. www.huffingtonpost.com/mary-m-newman/glenwood-gardens-case_b_2810495.html
353. Molloy M. Woman dies after nurse refuses CPR. *Metro*. 5 March 2013. metro.co.uk/2013/03/05/woman-dies-in-california-retirement-home-after-nurse-refuses-to-perform-cpr-3526267
354. Fantz A. To perform CPR or not? Woman's death raises questions. *CNN*. 6 March 2013. edition.cnn.com/2013/03/04/health/california-cpr-death
355. Ferguson C. Family OK with Glenwood Gardens; many still question CPR call. *BakersfieldNow.com*. www.bakersfieldnow.com/news/local/Statement-from-family-of-elderly-woman-denied-CPR-195476801.html
356. Marco CA, Bessman ES, Kelen GD. Ethical issues of cardiopulmonary resuscitation: comparison of emergency physician practices from 1995 to 2007. *Academic Emergency Medicine* 2009;16(3):270-273. onlinelibrary.wiley.com/doi/10.1111/j.1553-2712.2008.00348.x/abstract
357. Adams S. GPs could prescribe 1.6m fewer antibiotics. *The Telegraph*. 9 February 2012. www.telegraph.co.uk/health/healthnews/9071706/GPs-could-prescribe-1.6m-fewer-antibiotics.html
358. Devlin K. GPs 'should think twice about renewing sick notes'. *The Telegraph*. 25

March 2009. www.telegraph.co.uk/health/healthnews/5044479/GPs-should-think-twice-about-renewing-sick-notes.html

359. *Guide on the decision-making process regarding medical treatment in end-of-life situations.* Council of Europe, 2014. csc.ceceurope.org/fileadmin/filer/csc/Ethics_Biotechnology/CoE_FDV_Guide_Web_e.pdf
360. O'Neill O. A Question of Trust. The Reith Lectures 2002. www.bbc.co.uk/radio4/reith2002
361. Levy F, Kelen G. Resuscitation attempts in asystolic patients: The legal tail wagging the dog? *The Journal of Emergency Medicine* 2006;30(2):223–226. www.sciencedirect.com/science/article/pii/S0736467905004439
362. Guru V, Verbeek PR, Morrison LJ. Response of paramedics to terminally ill patients with cardiac arrest: an ethical dilemma. *CMAJ* 1999;161(10):1251-1254. www.cmaj.ca/content/161/10/1251
363. Hakim RB, Teno JM, Harrell FE et al. Factors associated with do-not-resuscitate orders: patients' preferences, prognoses, and physicians' judgments. SUPPORT Investigators. Study to Understand Prognoses and Preferences for Outcomes and Risks of Treatment. *Annals of Internal Medicine* 1996;125(4):284-293. www.ncbi.nlm.nih.gov/pubmed/8678391
364. Richter J, Eisemann MR. The compliance of doctors and nurses with do-not-resuscitate orders in Germany and Sweden. *Resuscitation*. Volume 42, Issue 3, 203-209, November 1999 www.resuscitationjournal.com/article/S0300-9572(99)00092-1/abstract
365. Adams RW. Daughter is suing LRMC and nursing home for disobeying "DNR" order. *TheLedger.com*. 11 April 2013. www.theledger.com/article/20130411/NEWS/304115037
366. Hallada vs. Lakeland Regional Medical Centre, Inc.In the circuit court of the tenth judicial circuit in and for Polk county, Florida. www.thaddeuspope.com/images/Hallada_Complaint_-_FINAL_3.5.13.pdf
367. Hospice Patients Alliance. New designation for allowing a natural death would eliminate confusion and suffering when patients are resuscitated against their wishes. www.hospicepatients.org/and.html
368. Peninsula Community Health. 2012. Allow Natural Death Policy and Guidance Framework for Adults. www.rcht.nhs.uk/DocumentsLibrary/PeninsulaCommunityHealth/OperationsAndServices/PalliativeCare/AllowNaturalDeathPolicy.pdf
369. CCF Implementation of the New Ohio 'DNR Comfort Care' rules and regulations. Department of Bioethics, Cleveland Clinic. www.clevelandclinic.org/bioethics/policies/ccfohdnr.html

Chapter 7: War truth and lies at the end of life

370. Reisfield GM, Wilson GR. Use of metaphor in the discourse on cancer. *Journal of Clinical Oncology* 2004;22(19):4024-4027. jco.ascopubs.org/content/22/19/4024
371. Facebook. Stephen's story. 13 January 2013.
372. Petticrew M, Bell R, Hunter D. Influence of psychological coping on survival and recurrence in people with cancer: systematic review. *BMJ* 2002;325:1066. www.bmj.com/content/325/7372/1066.1
373. Byrne A, Ellershaw J, Holcombe C, Salmon P. Patients' experience of cancer: evidence of the role of "fighting" in collusive clinical communication. *Patient Education and Counseling* 2002;48(1):15–21. www.ncbi.nlm.nih.gov/pubmed/12220746

374. Wolf JH, Wolf KS. The Lake Wobegon effect: are all cancer patients above average? *The Milbank Quarterly* 2013;91(4):690-728. www.oucom.ohiou.edu/hpf/pdf/bios%20april%202014/Volume91_Issue4_Are_All_Cancer_Patients_above_Average.pdf
375. Weeks JC, Catalano PJ, Cronin A et al. Patients' expectations about effects of chemotherapy for advanced cancer. *New England Journal of Medicine* 2012;367(17):1616-1625. www.nejm.org/doi/full/10.1056/NEJMoa1204410
376. Brucjber-Holt, C et al. Dying in hospital – is there an unmet palliative care need for patients who die within 48 hours of admission? . spcare.bmj.com/content/4/Suppl_1/A109.3.abstract
377. National audit of care of the dying in hospital. Royal College of Physicians, 2014. https://www.rcplondon.ac.uk/sites/default/files/ncdah_national_report.pdf
378. Murray K. Why doctors die differently. *The Wall Street Journal* 25 February 25 2012. online.wsj.com/news/articles/SB1000142405297020391830457724332124 2833962
379. Wittink MN, Morales KH, Meoni LA et al. Stability of preferences for end of life treatment after 3 years of follow-up: The Johns Hopkins Precursors Study. *Archives of Internal Medicine* 2008;168(19):2125-2130. www.ncbi.nlm.nih.gov/pmc/articles/PMC2596594
380. Gallo JJ et al. Life sustaining treatments: what do physicians want and do they express their wishes to others? *Journal of the American Geriatric Society* 2003;51(7):961-969. www.ncbi.nlm.nih.gov/pubmed/12834516
381. The Gerson Therapy. The Gerson Institute. 16 September 2011. gerson.org/gerpress/the-gerson-therapy
382. Summary of the evidence for Gerson Therapy. National Cancer Institute, 2012. www.cancer.gov/cancertopics/pdq/cam/gerson/healthprofessional/page7
383. Moore M. 'I feel empowered, in control of my body': four women on fighting cancer with alternative therapies. *The Telegraph*. 20 October 2013. www.telegraph.co.uk/health/10383724/I-feel-empowered-in-control-of-my-body-four-women-on-fighting-cancer-with-alternative-therapies.html
384. Stabo L. 8/7/14 Doctor accused of selling false hope to families. *USA Today*. 8 July 2014. www.usatoday.com/story/news/nation/2013/11/15/stanislaw-burzynski-cancer-controversy/2994561/
385. About the Burzynski Clinic. www.burzynskiclinic.com/burzynski-clinic.html
386. Bainbridge L. The worst year of my life: cancer has my family in its grip. *The Observer*. 20 November 2011. www.theguardian.com/theobserver/2011/nov/20/a-family-gripped-by-cancer
387. Lewis A. The Burzynski Clinic threatens my family. *The Quackometer*. 24 November 2011. www.quackometer.net/blog/2011/11/the-burzynski-clinic-threatens-my-family.html
388. Pritchard S. The readers' editor on… kind hearts and a cruel illness. *The Observer*. 4 December 2011. www.theguardian.com/theobserver/2011/dec/04/observer-readers-editor-cancer-treatment
389. Billie Bainbridge dies after battle with brain stem cancer. *BBC News England*. 5 June 2012. www.bbc.co.uk/news/uk-england-devon-18331017
390. Szabo L. Doctor accused of selling false hope to families. *USA Today*. 8 July 2014. www.usatoday.com/story/news/nation/2013/11/15/stanislaw-burzynski-cancer-controversy/2994561
391. Szabo L. Texas medical board charges controversial cancer doctor. *USA Today*. 25 July 2014. www.usatoday.com/story/news/nation/2014/07/24/new-charges-

for-burzynski/13111483

392. FDA warning letter to Stanislaw R Burzynski, MD 12/3/13. www.fda.gov/ICECI/EnforcementActions/WarningLetters/2013/ucm378237.htm
393. Harley Street practitioner claimed he could cure cancer and HIV with lifestyle changes and herbs, court hears. *The Telegraph*. 11 December 2013. www.telegraph.co.uk/news/uknews/law-and-order/10510345/Harley-Street-practitioner-claimed-he-could-cure-cancer-and-HIV-with-lifestyle-changes-and-herbs-court-hears.html
394. Thomason L. Who can I complain to about Errol Denton? *Josephine Jones blog*. 9 October 2012. josephinejones.wordpress.com/2012/10/09/who-can-i-complain-to-about-errol-denton
395. Maitland O. How do you tell someone with cancer that all hope has gone? *The Telegraph*. 17 January 2011. www.telegraph.co.uk/health/8257911/How-do-you-tell-someone-with-cancer-that-all-hope-has-gone.html
396. Le BHC, Mileshkin L, Doan K et al. Acceptability of early integration of palliative care in patients with incurable lung cancer. *Journal of Palliative Medicine* 2014;17(5):553-558. www.ncbi.nlm.nih.gov/pubmed/24588685
397. Barclay S, Momen N, Case-Upton S et al. End-of-life care conversations with heart failure patients: a systematic literature review and narrative synthesis. *British Journal of General Practice* 2011;(582):e49–62. www.ncbi.nlm.nih.gov/pubmed/21401993
398. Innes S, Payne S. Advanced cancer patients' prognostic information preferences: a review. *Palliative Medicine* 2009;23(1):29–39. pmj.sagepub.com/content/23/1/29.long
399. Hagerty RG, Butow PN, Ellis PM et al. Communicating with realism and hope: incurable cancer patients' views on the disclosure of prognosis. *Journal of Clinical Oncology* 2005;23(6):1278-1288. jco.ascopubs.org/content/23/6/1278
400. Buecken R, Galushko M, Golla H, Strupp J, Hahn M, Ernstmann N, et al. Patients feeling severely affected by multiple sclerosis: how do patients want to communicate about end-of-life issues? *Patient Education and Counseling* 2012;88(2):318-324. www.ncbi.nlm.nih.gov/pubmed/22480629
401. Barclay S, Momen N, Case-Upton S et al. End-of-life care conversations with heart failure patients: a systematic literature review and narrative synthesis. *British Journal of General Practice* 2011;61(582):e49–e62. www.ncbi.nlm.nih.gov/pmc/articles/PMC3020072
402. Innes S, Payne S. Advanced cancer patients' prognostic information preferences: a review. *Palliative Medicine* 2009;23(1):29–39. pmj.sagepub.com/content/23/1/29.long
403. Sokol DK. How the doctor's nose has shortened over time; a historical overview of the truth-telling debate in the doctor-patient relationship. JRSM Dec 2006 99(12) 632-636 www.ncbi.nlm.nih.gov/pmc/articles/PMC1676322/#!po=12.5000
404. Hagerty RG, Communicating with realism and hope: incurable cancer patients' views on the disclosure of prognosis Butow PN, Ellis PM et al.. *Journal of Clinical Oncology* 2005;23(6):1278–88. jco.ascopubs.org/content/23/6/1278
405. Clayton JM, Hancock K, Parker S et al. Sustaining hope when communicating with terminally ill patients and their families: a systematic review. *Psychooncology* 2008;17(7):641-659. www.ncbi.nlm.nih.gov/pubmed/18022831
406. Mack JW, Wolfe J, Cook EF et al. Hope and prognostic disclosure. Journal of Clinical Oncology 2007;25(35):5636-5642. www.ncbi.nlm.nih.gov/pubmed/18065734

407. Quill T, Norton S, Shah M et al. What is most important for you to achieve?: an analysis of patient responses when receiving palliative care consultation. *Journal of Palliative Medicine* 2006;9(2):382-388. www.ncbi.nlm.nih.gov/pubmed/16629568
408. Srivastava R. Speaking up – when doctors navigate medical hierarchy. *New England Journal of Medicine* 2013;368(4):302-305. www.nejm.org/doi/full/10.1056/NEJMp1212410
409. Rawlinson K. Dehydration and malnutrition led to 2,162 deaths in care since 2003. *The Guardian*. 2 December 2013. www.theguardian.com/society/2013/dec/02/dehydration-malnutrition-care-homes-hospitals
410. Riley-Smith B. More than a thousand care home residents die thirsty. *The Telegraph*. 1 December 2013. www.telegraph.co.uk/health/healthnews/10487305/More-than-a-thousand-care-home-residents-die-thirsty.html
411. McCann RM, Hall WJ, Groth-Juncker A. Comfort care for terminally iii patients: The appropriate use of nutrition and hydration. *Journal of the American Medical Association* 1994;272(16):1263-1266. jama.jamanetwork.com/article.aspx?articleid=381346
412. Ellershaw JE, Sutcliffe JM, Saunders CM. Dehydration and the dying patient. *Journal of Pain and Symptom Management* 1995;10(3):192-197. www.ncbi.nlm.nih.gov/pubmed/7629413
413. Meier DE, Ahronheim J, Morris J et al. High short term mortality in hospitalised patients with advanced dementia. *JAMA Internal Medicine* 2001;161(4):594-599. archinte.jamanetwork.com/article.aspx?articleid=647434
414. Mitchell SL, Kiely DK, Lipsitz LA. Does artificial enteral nutition prolong the survival of institutionalised elders with chewing and swallowing problems? *Journals of Gerontology Series A* 1998;53(3):M207-13., www.ncbi.nlm.nih.gov/pubmed/9597053
415. Social Care Institute for Excellence. End of life care in dementia.; Eating and Drinking. www.scie.org.uk/publications/dementia/understanding-dementia/end-of-life-care/eating-drinking.asp.
416. Gov. Lamm asserts elderly, if very ill, have 'duty to die'. *International New York Times*. 29 March 1984. www.nytimes.com/1984/03/29/us/gov-lamm-asserts-elderly-if-very-ill-have-duty-to-die.html
417. Kennedy EO. An octogenarian's view on prolonged life [letter]. I*nternational New York Times*. 18 April 1984. www.nytimes.com/1984/04/18/opinion/l-an-octogenarian-s-view-on-prolonged-life-129724.html
418. Art Buchwald: I just died [video]. *TimesVideo US. & Politics, New York Times*. 18 January 2007. www.nytimes.com/video/obituaries/1194817093353/i-just-died.html
419. Boodman SG. Kissing hospice goodbye. *The Washington Post*. 3 October 2006. www.washingtonpost.com/wp-dyn/content/article/2006/10/02/AR2006100200958.html
420. Pruthi R, Steenkamp R, Feest T. *UK Renal Registry 16th Annual Report: Chapter 8 Survival and Cause of Death of UK Adult Patients on Renal Replacement Therapy in 2012: National and Centre-specific Analyses*. UK Renal Registry, December 2013. www.renalreg.com/Reports/2013.html
421. Birmelé B, François M, Pengloan J et al. Death after withdrawal from dialysis: the most common cause of death in a French dialysis population. *Nephrology Dialysis Transplantation* 2004;19(3):686-691. ndt.oxfordjournals.org/content/19/3/686

422. *Planning, Initiating and Withdrawal of Renal Replacement Therapy*. The Renal Association, 17 December 2009. www.renal.org/guidelines/modules/planning-initiating-and-withdrawal-of-renal-replacement-therapy#F6
423. Russ AJ, Shim JK, Kaufman SR. The value of "life at any cost": Talk about stopping kidney dialysis. *Social Science and Medicine* 2007;64(11):2236-2247. www.ncbi.nlm.nih.gov/pmc/articles/PMC2196209
424. Hussain JA, Mooney A, Russon L. Comparison of survival analysis and palliative care involvement in patients aged over 70 years choosing conservative management or renal replacement therapy in advanced chronic kidney disease. *Palliative Medicine* 2013;27(9):829-839. www.ncbi.nlm.nih.gov/pubmed?term=23652841
425. Smith C, Da Silva-Gane M, Chandna S et al. Choosing not to dialyse: evaluation of planned non-dialytic management in a cohort of patients with end-stage renal failure. *Nephron Clinical Practice* 2003;95(2):c40–46. www.ncbi.nlm.nih.gov/pubmed/14610329
426. Munday Daniel F, Maher E Jane. Informed consent and palliative chemotherapy. *BMJ* 2008; 337:a868. www.bmj.com/content/337/bmj.a868
427. Wright AA, Zhang B, Keating NL et al. Associations between palliative chemotherapy and adult cancer patients' end of life care and place of death: prospective cohort study. *BMJ* 2014; 348:g1219 www.bmj.com/content/348/bmj.g1219
428. Terminally ill denied right to a good death. *MailOnline*. 22 July 2004. www.dailymail.co.uk/health/article-311170/Terminally-ill-denied-right-good-death.html
429. Boggan S. 'Many NHS nurses are still the finest in the world. But they let my poor father die in agony like a dog'. *MailOnline*. 28 August 2009. www.dailymail.co.uk/news/article-1209571/Many-NHS-nurses-finest-world-But-let-poor-father-die-agony-like-dog.html
430. Leith P. Prue Leith asks: Why did my brother die in agony? *The Telegraph*. 26 October 2012. www.telegraph.co.uk/health/healthnews/9633356/Prue-Leith-asks-Why-did-my-brother-die-in-agony.html
431. Bernat JL. *Ethical Issues in Neurology*. Lippincott Williams and Wilkins, 2004
432. Morita T, Tsunoda J, Inoue S, Chihara S. Effects of high dose opioids and sedatives on survival in terminally ill cancer patients. *Journal of Pain and Symptom Management* 2001;21(4):282-289. www.jpsmjournal.com/article/S0885-3924(01)00258-5/fulltext
433. Grond S, Zech D, Schug SA et al. Validation of World Health Organization guidelines for cancer pain relief during the last days and hours of life. *Journal of Pain and Symptom Management* 1991;6(7):411-422. www.sciencedirect.com/science/article/pii/0885392491900397
434. Walsh TD. Opiates and respiratory function in advanced cancer. *Recent Results in Cancer Research* 1984;89:115-117. https://my.clevelandclinic.org/Documents/Cancer/Opiates%20and%20Resp.pdf
435. Regnard C. Double effect is a myth leading a double life. *BMJ* 2007;334(7591):440. www.ncbi.nlm.nih.gov/pmc/articles/PMC1808133
436. Clarifying the data on double effect [editorial]. *Palliative Medicine* 2006;20:395-396. pmj.sagepub.com/content/20/4/395
437. Gao W, Gulliford M, Bennett MI et al. Managing cancer pain at the end of life with multiple strong opioids: a population-based retrospective cohort study in primary care. *PLoS ONE* 2014;9(1):e79266. dx.doi.org/10.1371/journal.pone.0079266

438. Harold Shipman: the killer doctor. *BBC News*. 13 January 2014. news.bbc.co.uk/1/hi/uk/3391897.stm
439. Gardiner C, Gott M, Ingleton C et al. Attitudes of health care professionals to opioid prescribing in end-of-life care: a qualitative focus group study. *Journal of Pain and Symptom Management* 2012;44(2):206-214. www.jpsmjournal.com/article/S0885-3924(12)00138-8/fulltext
440. Hadjiphilippou S1, Odogwu SE, Dand P. Doctors' attitudes towards prescribing opioids for refractory dyspnoea: a single-centred study. *BMJ Supportive and Palliative Care* 2014 Mar 6. doi: 10.1136/bmjspcare-2013-000565. [Epub ahead of print]. spcare.bmj.com/content/early/2014/03/06/bmjspcare-2013-000565.abstract
441. Reid CM, Gooberman-Hill R, Hanks GW. Opioid analgesics for cancer pain: symptom control for the living or comfort for the dying? A qualitative study to investigate the factors influencing the decision to accept morphine for pain caused by cancer. *Annals of Oncology* 2008;19(1):44-48. annonc.oxfordjournals.org/content/19/1/44
442. Campbell D. District Nurses will disappear by 2025, says Royal College of Nursing. *The Guardian*. 17 June 2014. www.theguardian.com/society/2014/jun/17/district-nurses-disappear-2025
443. *District nursing – harnessing the potential: the RCN's UK position on district nursing*. Royal College of Nursing, April 2013. www.rcn.org.uk/__data/assets/pdf_file/0009/511983/004366.pdf
444. Common questions about Macmillan nurses. Macmillan Cancer Support. www.macmillan.org.uk/HowWeCanHelp/Nurses/YourQuestions.aspx
445. More nurses per hospital bed: what's the catch?. Full Fact. 28 November 2012. https://fullfact.org/factchecks/hospital_beds_nurses-28628
446. Beds: hospital care. Information Services Division, NHS National Services Scotland, 2010. www.isdscotland.org/Health-Topics/Hospital-Care/Beds
447. *NHS Beds 2010-11*. SDR 191/2011. Knowledge and Analytical Services, Welsh Government, 25 October 2011. wales.gov.uk/docs/statistics/2011/111025sdr19 12011en.pdf
448. *Hospitals on the Edge: The Time for Action*. The Royal College of Physicians, September 2012. https://www.rcplondon.ac.uk/projects/hospitals-edge-time-action
449. *Trends in Consultation Rates in General Practice 1995/1996 to 2008/2009: Analysis of the QResearch® database*. Final Report to the NHS Information Centre and Department of Health. Qresearch and the Health and Social Care Information Centre, 2009. https://catalogue.ic.nhs.uk/publications/primary-care/general-practice/tren-cons-rate-gene-prac-95-09/tren-cons-rate-gene-prac-95-09-95-09-rep.pdf
450. GP workload survey results. Health and Social Care Information Centre. 31 July 2007. www.hscic.gov.uk/pubs/gpworkload
451. Funding for general practice set to plummet by fifth by 2017, while patient consultations to increase by 69m (press release). Royal College of General Practitioners. 2 April 2014. www.rcgp.org.uk/news/2014/april/funding-for-general-practice-set-to-plummet-by-fifth-by-2017.aspx
452. Steck N, Egger M, Maessen M, Reisch T, Zwahlen M. Euthanasia and assisted suicide in selected European countries and US states: systematic literature review. *Medical Care* 2013;51(10):938-944. www.ncbi.nlm.nih.gov/pubmed/23929402
453. Steck N, Egger M, Maessen M et al. Euthanasia and assisted suicide in

selected European countries and US states: systematic literature review. *Medical Care* 2013;51(10):938-944. journals.lww.com/lww-medicalcare/Abstract/2013/10000/Euthanasia_and_Assisted_Suicide_in_Selected.12.aspx

454. Rachels J. Active and Passive Euthanasia. *New England Journal of Medicine* 1975;292(2):78-80. www.nejm.org/doi/full/10.1056/NEJM197501092920206
455. Loggers ET, Starks H, Shannon-Dudley M et al. Implementing a death with dignity program at a comprehensive cancer center. *New England Journal of Medicine* 2013;368(15):1417-1424. www.nejm.org/doi/full/10.1056/NEJMsa1213398
456. UK Government. Abortion Act 1967. www.legislation.gov.uk/ukpga/1967/87/section/1
457. CQC today publishes 249 individual inspection reports into providers offering termination of pregnancy services (press release). Care Quality Commission, 12 July 2012. www.cqc.org.uk/content/findings-termination-pregnancy-inspections-published
458. Carter C. Illegal abortion doctors face no action. *The Telegraph*. 22 April 2012. www.telegraph.co.uk/health/healthnews/10778981/Illegal-abortion-doctors-face-no-action.html
459. Robert Burns, To a Mouse. en.wikipedia.org/wiki/To_a_Mouse

Index